LOW DOWN
THE STORY OF
WIRE

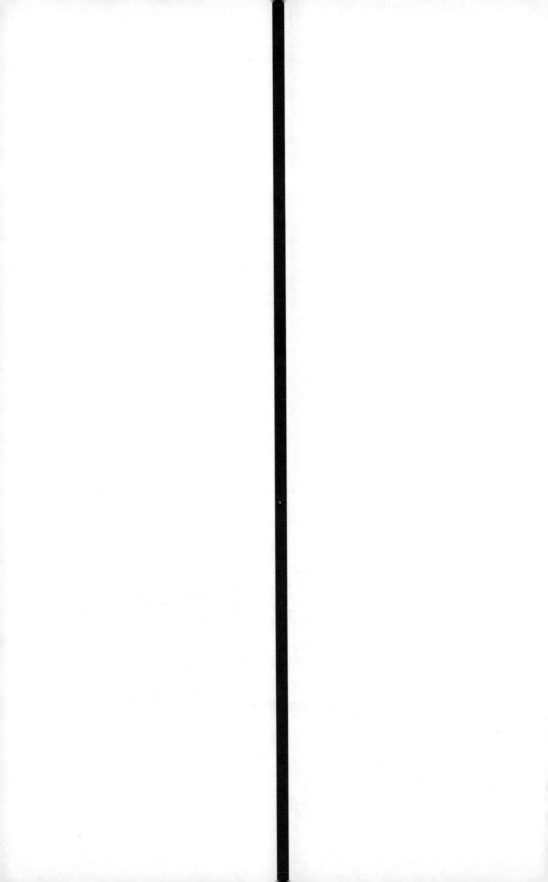

LOWDOWN

THE STORY OF

WIRE

PAUL LESTER

OMNIBUS PRESS

LONDON / NEW YORK / PARIS / SYDNEY /
COPENHAGEN / BERLIN / MADRID / TOKYO

Cover designed by Fresh Lemon
Picture research by Sarah Bacon

ISBN: 978.1.84772.710.7
Order No: OP52822

Exclusive Distributors
Music Sales Limited,
14/15 Berners Street,
London, W1T 3LJ.

Music Sales Corporation,
257 Park Avenue South,
New York, NY 10010, USA.

Macmillan Distribution Services,
56 Parkwest Drive
Derrimut, Vic 3030,
Australia.

Every effort has been made to trace the copyright holders of the photographs in this book but one or two were unreachable. We would be grateful if the photographers concerned would contact us.

Typeset by: Phoenix Photosetting, Chatham, Kent
Printed by Gutenberg Press Ltd, Malta

A catalogue record for this book is available from the British Library.

Visit Omnibus Press on the web at www.omnibuspress.com

Contents

Foreword

Why I Love Wire
By Johnny Marr

I first got into Wire when a lot of my mates bought the *Live At The Roxy* album. That was a really important and smart record and was an affordable picture and document of what was happening at the time. It was quite an unusual thing, to be able to get all of those bands on one, albeit badly recorded, album. I'd be playing truant and hanging out at my friends' houses, and it seemed as though nearly everyone had a copy of *Live At The Roxy*.

Some of my friends at that time were either in local Manchester punk band Slaughter & The Dogs or working for them. They were the local rock stars, even before punk came out, when they were Bowie copyists, and they were on *Live At The Roxy*. I didn't think they were particularly good on it, and actually I was quite disappointed with the record, but everybody had it; it was one of those records that you had to have. I liked very, very few of the British groups that were around at that time and that forced me to get into older music, which was quite unusual at that time, and quite unusual for someone of my age.

I was starting to get into playing the guitar really seriously by this point, and a lot of the groups designed for my age group in 1978/79, I considered pretty crappy. In '77 I was too young to get into a lot of the punk shows that were in the clubs because I would have been about 14.

There was the Damned album, of course, which I didn't take seriously at all. There was the Pistols record, eventually, and the Clash album, which all of my mates liked, and then there were various singles which I really liked such as 'Shot By Both Sides' by Magazine. I also liked Buzzcocks' 'Spiral Scratch'. I really liked 'Outdoor Miner' later on. But my first awareness of Wire had been the *Live At The Roxy* album and the track 'Lowdown'.

One thing with the *Roxy* album was that the cover was really great to a kid; it said what punk was supposed to be about and was intriguing. The actual recording was a bit of a letdown, and was a bit of a shouty affair, but I thought Wire really stood out. The impression I got at the time from some of the punk bands was that they weren't actually that modern; they were quite old-fashioned. Some of them sounded a little bit like the back-end of pub rock to me. To this day I still consider the punk movement, great as it was, to be the letter 'Z' in the old rock alphabet, rather than the 'A' in a new alphabet – I didn't think it was a new beginning. I thought it was like a very glorious and interesting end of something. Wire, though, seemed to be genuinely modern, whereas with a lot of punk you could hear Chuck Berry in it, and a lot of that kind of boogie and rhythm & blues. Even the Dolls have that aspect to them. But Wire really stood out because they weren't trying to be a sped-up old rock band; they didn't copy old rock riffs.

I don't agree that they had a non-image, and I don't believe they were like a Manchester band in that respect. Far from it. I do think Joy Division were influenced by a similar kind of aesthetic or ethos but Wire, like most great bands, sounded like the environment they came from. Kraftwerk, for example, really do sound like Germany, like Düsseldorf. The Beach Boys could only be from California and paint that sort of picture. The Kinks are so obviously London, ditto The Rolling Stones, and Wire always struck me as having that same thing about them. A lot of their placement I think is in Colin Newman's voice. It's in his speaking voice, and it's in his singing voice. Most punk bands, even some Manchester bands, were uber kind of Hope & Anchor Londoners with cockney affectations. But when you heard Wire, they didn't sound provincial at all. They sounded like a London group, but a quite arty one.

If you were a modern rock band at that time, then you were throwing a lot of things away from rock culture. You were throwing away distorted guitar sounds. You were throwing away bluesy guitar structures, even a power-chord kind of approach to guitar. All of those things had reigned for years. The key question people asked of bands at the time was: do they rock? And if you examine quite a lot of the bands that were supposed to be modern at that time, whether it's The Stranglers or The Lurkers or even The Ruts, then the old sound is dominant, whereas Wire and Joy Division seemed to be throwing away a lot of the old stuff. As Colin said of [debut album] *Pink Flag*, it was all about rejecting all the records the members of the band had heard up to that point. Wire seemed genuinely modern. The new groups that were really worth anything seemed to have that similar thing in the way they looked or presented themselves on stage: it seemed to be about rejecting the old, and I'd put Subway Sect in that same category.

This approach came out in the song-titles and the lyrics. A lot of bands were still writing about 'chicks' – in inverted commas, please – and drugs. It was all, "We're gonna rock!" and all of that. Wire were different. They intrigued me no end. Because what lyrics you could make out on the first Wire album were obviously different. I couldn't work out what the concepts were at that time, but I knew they *were* conceptual. It was like, if Bowie and Eno had made a punk album... In fact, I got into Eno's solo stuff through Wire. My mate and I used to swap records all the time, and he swapped me 'Outdoor Miner' for something, I can't remember what. The fact that it was on Harvest intrigued me even more, because a lot of punk records that I owned were either on Sire or Virgin, and I found that quite weird because I didn't really have a lot of Harvest records. Harvest artists seemed very classic and very English and just a little odd – you pick up things like this from records when you're young. That's one of the great things about pop culture, all these little clues... The only other singles that

I had on Harvest were by Be Bop Deluxe. Anyway, I remember someone saying that they thought 'Outdoor Miner' sounded like Brian Eno's solo stuff. So because of that I got into this labyrinth of other things like *Here Come The Warm Jets* and *Taking Tiger Mountain By Strategy*. It's funny how you go off on all these tangents just by hearing a little B-side or seeing a photograph or hearing a comment – my friends and I used to analyse the hell out of everything.

Wire were from the capital but they weren't typical punks singing about tower blocks, council estates and dole queues. Certain bands are more effective visually because of this idea of reduction: like Joy Division, when you saw pictures of them, they were unadorned, whereas a lot of groups at the time still wore scarves and had that Rolling Stones look; there was still a lot of long hair about. But the way Wire and Joy Division appeared with their some-might-say-now non-image was quite startling and definitely modern. People don't realise quite how shocking their stance was. It reminds me of the first ever time I saw Kraftwerk. It was scary, and it was gutsy as well. When you saw a picture of Wire in the music press, they definitely looked gutsy and with attitude. Even the Buzzcocks looked a little bit rock'n'roll in comparison.

Wire seemed somewhat about less-is-more. I think that with anything artistic, if you're working within a reductionist scheme, you come up with some pretty interesting and direct work. The reason I say this is because when The Smiths came out, people assume indie was around, and 'alt. rock' and all those kind of terms, when in fact we came out of post-punk. Punk rock was the generation before me, even though they were a lot of my older friends, so I was able to eavesdrop on a lot of it and be the beneficiary of a lot of the good stuff – like being turned on to The Stooges and the Dolls, but nevertheless it was a different generation. I was quite into fashion, and forming my own band was almost like striking a blow for the generation after punk. That was post-punk to me and my guitar sound came out of post-punk and that reductionist attitude. Wire were probably the first great band to make the post-punk sound and they were obviously ahead of their time. There was no adornment, there were no effects; there was no blues rock or distortion, no elongated self-expression, and certainly no improvising. It was very, very difficult to be 'rock' at the time. You could either be like A Certain Ratio or Orange Juice on one side and take on this sort of lexicon of funk sounds and appropriate black dance music, which is what most bands did in the early Eighties, or you were left with all the aspects of rock that were considered old and off-limits... Luckily for me, I had a way of playing that didn't use any of those elements but still could be regarded as rock: it may even be that it came from folk. God knows how, but I had all the attitude from post-punk, but didn't want to form a funk band.

Wire were doing what became known as post-punk a few years before anyone else. It's almost an anomaly that they happened within punk rock, because they weren't about force; they were about being weird in a much more effective way. They weren't a late-arriving punk band; they were an early-arriving post-punk band. It felt like they cut and chopped and edited everything down to the bare minimum, the bare essentials. You can hear that most obviously on their first two albums, and that was really startling because rock culture was set up to be sacred. They were irreverent in a way that was much more effective than just social rhetoric and gobbing on people or whatever. Colin said that his mission was to destroy rock'n'roll. I love that. But if you're going to stand there and say, "Everything is shit. Old music is garbage" and you actually look like you're in the Stones, then that is obviously nonsense. Wire managed to look different − weird − by dressing normally. It was really quite odd.

I was so into absorbing everything. Wire were just one of a load of bands that I was investigating through other people's record collections and through the music press, because I was still a schoolboy, so getting enough money to buy an album was a big deal. To buy Raw Power I had to go and get a Saturday job in the Co-Op, and it was a toss-up as to whether I was going to have some cigarettes and a bottle of cider, go out with my girlfriend or go for the album.

Weirdly, what really got me into liking Wire were Colin's solo records. I went back to *154* after getting into *A−Z*. To this day, *A−Z* is one of my favourite ever records. I played the hell out of it; I liked everything on it. This friend of mine owned a record shop, and he loaned it me, and I just loved it. And then I started to work at a new clothes shop in Manchester around 1981, and a guy I was working with had the live album *Document And Eyewitness*. And that then got me shelling out my cash for *154*. I see those albums as being connected, soundwise. I liked the song 'Map Reference' and 'A Touching Display' and '40 Versions'. I thought the guitar playing on *154* was the great because I couldn't put my finger on it. I like it when there's something that resonates with you and excites you but you actually can't quite put together where all the pieces of it come from, whether it was from Colin or Bruce Gilbert. That's always the best way in a two-guitar group, because it's all about the whole.

Wire certainly didn't sound like they were American, even though you could vaguely detect the influence of the Velvets. The singing was certainly a long way away from that notion of soulfully "expressing yourself". I wasn't old enough to realise that there were concepts of irony or even artiness at play on Wire's records, or even what the concept might be, but I knew there was some kind of concept. Colin was an anti-performer, and that was great. Because with a lot of the punk bands, you could see that they wanted to be famous when they performed, there was a lot of affectation, but with Wire you got the impression that there'd been a lot of deliberation, and an agenda, which was something of a no-no in some circles. Rock music was supposed to be from the heart and soul, and organic. There was this idea, particularly in guitar culture, that singing and playing were supposed to be from the heart and soul and born out of a certain kind of poetic anguish; born out of misfortune and soul-searching. It was meant to be anything but an intellectual exercise. It was supposed to be authentic, and that was another startling thing about Wire. Just by looking at their photographs, you could tell they were taking the piss. It's like the terse descriptions of the band on the back cover of *Pink Flag*: in hindsight, with all that clever-dickery, you can see what was going on there, but it was just so considered. It was pretty shocking because you weren't supposed to do that. You weren't supposed to take the piss – it was always supposed to be, you know, 'soulful'. It was supposed to be about things like 'the groove'. Wire used the word 'process' a lot with regard to making records, which was later appropriated by dance artists. And yet the records don't sound soulless, because Wire care, like Kraftwerk care. They're just not done with the old, corny ideas, and if you care, you can't hide it.

On *154* the band display the art of falling apart. But, for me, the enjoyment of the record was quite simple. It was interesting music, with an original approach particularly to guitars. I didn't want avant-garde music. I wanted a good, modern record from a good British group. So there were good little riffs in there, and some proper good, catchy ideas, but it was still really, really original, and un-American, too. And I like that they weren't so anti-guitar that there was no guitar on there but in fact two guitarists. They were making the guitars do really interesting things without being virtuoso players and it sounded as though everything had been treated in the studio. With The Smiths, because we took away the option of using the synthesizer but you wanted some unusual sounds here and there, we had to use the guitar, and the very limitations of the guitar mean that you will do things that are slightly more interesting than you would do these days with digital recording. If you're trying to make a guitar emulate what would normally be the job of a synthesizer or a violin, then you stretch those limitations and kind of get it wrong, which is actually a lot more interesting than if you were to just use a synth or a sampler or just a regular guitar sound; it's between two worlds. That's one of the things I liked about *154*, and Colin's solo stuff, too − it was the very fact that he was stretching guitars beyond their usual capacities that made for something new.

Wire are a shining example of how to mix up the experimental with the commercial. They're commercial because they've got a good knack with a tune. They were probably as much anti-commercial as they were anti-everything, but probably being anti-rock meant being pro-commercial. Because, as I've said, the 10 commandments of rock involve Authenticity and Rocking Out and Sounding Macho, and the notion that Commercialism Is A Bad Thing. Commercialism was part and parcel of what rock fans hated. Wire had a knack for sounding commercial, but what commercialism they may have had might well have been the result of bloody-minded perversity.

I'm not so sure that the world would have been a better place if

'Outdoor Miner' had been a hit. I think it did perfectly what it was meant to do, in exactly the right way, in the way that [Magazine's] 'Shot By Both Sides' did. The music was too clever to sit alongside The Boomtown Rats or The Stranglers. Besides, who cares? It was almost more alluring for it to have not been in the Top 15. Looking at it philosophically, they had enough ideological issues to be concerned with, without the messy business of having had a hit. No, it was perfectly placed. We all knew that it was one of those really great hit singles from a parallel universe. It was in my own personal Top 10, put it that way. It was on my radio, and it was commercial enough to be on my radio, and it would have been nice to have seen it weird-out the *Top Of The Pops* audience in the suburbs, but really I'm glad that I don't have memories of it being on there. I'm glad that it stayed in the ether. It's one of those twilight 45s that are truly great, that are neither out on the podium nor in the ghetto. Do you know why it's so great? Because we know it's a commercial track, a proper, great 45, but it wasn't soiled by the fact that it was actually commercial. So they really had their cake and ate it.

I don't think Wire could have been one of those 'entryist' groups like Heaven 17 or ABC who subverted the charts with pop ideas, because I think that as individuals they were part of a different generation. I don't know how old Wire are, but I think there was a certain inherent English melodic aspect to what they did that possibly came from the shadow cast by Sixties groups. My guess is that they grew up as teenagers in the Sixties, hearing the Pink Floyd singles and the Move singles and those kind of quirkily British 45s that were on the radio. I'm guessing that may have sparked those guys as youngsters and in Wire's more commercial mid-period music I can hear echoes of that kind of creepiness that you get from some of the Move singles and the Syd Barrett stuff. There's a remoteness there in the melodies – they seem somehow emotionally suspended. I always got a feeling of suspension from them, and suspense, as though nothing's been quite resolved, emotionally. It's psychedelic, even psychotic, slightly, subtly. And maybe they were able to reject rock's past because they'd spent their adolescence listening to that stuff, and yet somehow it still managed to seep through into their music.

For such a minimalist group, with such a pared-down sound, it's interesting how so many different types of groups took what Wire did and used it as a blueprint for their own careers. They influenced the goth contingent, the US early Eighties hardcore bands, and the Britpop generation. But all these bands were affected by them because they were more than just arch conceptualists with a bunch of great ideas. There are feelings in their music; it's just that they're not the usual feelings that you get on a rock record. Wire were not U2. They weren't about passion and intense emotion. But I don't think you could actually make music if you were as emotionally blank as some might imagine them to be. Wire were blank in the sense that each person could take what they wanted out of them. A lot of it is between the cracks, and there are a lot of cracks in England. There might be American bands with similar ideas, and there are ones that may have been influenced by Wire, but they don't have that sense of claustrophobia that one has growing up in the UK, and particularly the UK as it was in the Sixties and Seventies; there just isn't that kind of concrete decay, that sense of prevailing greyness. I think American bands were intrigued by that and wanted a part of it. There's a similar kind of contrariness in some of the weirder American bands, and similar deconstructionist ideas in a group like The Residents. But like I say, there are real people inside there; it takes more than concepts. You are what you play. Wire might have had this aura of being aloof, intellectual and detached, but that was just a mechanism to hide whatever was going on inside them. Their music isn't without humanity. It doesn't sound like a bunch of robots. You can hear that in their approach to textures on *154* because it definitely sounds like human beings experiencing something and expressing it.

I kept up with Wire in the Eighties, with *The Ideal Copy* and *A Bell Is A Cup... Until It's A Jar* – I liked that one. I liked 'Boiling Boy' and 'Kidney Bingos'. But the world had caught up with them by then. Bands like New Order and maybe even Depeche Mode were also doing what they were doing. That's always going to happen. But certain things that you have an affection for, and that impress you when you're young, are always worth keeping an eye on, I think. And that's the way I'll always be with Wire. I've always followed what they do. Yes, the world did catch up with them, but when each new record came out, I would play it a lot, very, very loud, and I was really happy to hear them do whatever it was that they were doing.

I only met Colin once, and we've exchanged a few emails, and it's our intention to try to get to know each other at some point in the future. Interestingly enough, when, in 1981, I met Matt Johnson for the first time – one of those very, very important times when you meet someone and you do feel like kindred spirits – he asked me to be in what he was then going to call his new band, which was The The. And he really made an impression on me because he'd made that album, *Burning Blue Soul*, which is an awesome record. If you're an 18-year-old kid, and you like Wire, this is the record for you – it was like an even more fucked-up version of *154*, in a way. Anyway, Graham [Lewis] and Bruce [Gilbert] were both involved in that album. So I had a tenuous connection with Wire through Matt.

I don't know if Wire were an influence on The Smiths. I did form the group out of that shop that I was working in in 1980-81, which is roughly when *154* and Colin's *A–Z* came out so there might have been some kind of influence. There might be a similarity in the approach to the guitar, in the economy and the precision and the rejection of rock'n'roll. Aesthetically, there is a connection there. The idea of no distortion, no solos; a clean sound. On The Smiths' early records, I started layering as soon as I could; but when we went out live, we were definitely the first band to be post-punk and rock at the same time, the first post-punk rock band. And in that sense I guess you could say that The Smiths were post-Wire.

Wire were cool. I'd say they were 20 years ahead of their time. They anticipated a lot of what came after. Maybe groups like Franz Ferdinand and Bloc Party – so make that 25 years ahead of their time. Wire are the only guitar band who, when describing them, I'd use the word 'European'. They're the only British guitar band that I like that make me feel European. Wire make British music seem as though it's part of Europe. I can think of no higher compliment.

December, 2008

Chapter 1

It's Beginning To...

"Whereas much of punk's revolt quickly became mired in clumsy politics (The Clash) and caricature (Generation X), it wouldn't be overstating the case to say that Wire were among the only real subversives. Their reconceptualisations of song structure and content and their expansion of the possibilities of performance pushed rock in directions that many of their contemporaries in the class of '76 would have been hard-pressed even to imagine." – US Rock Critic

IT'S hard, given the steely immaculacy of their sound and completeness of their concept, to imagine Wire as anything other than the intimidatingly aloof, supremely focused and fully-formed outfit that reached our eyes and ears in early 1977. But the four members did, indeed, have normal backgrounds, go to normal schools, and do all the normal things normal boys do – even ones who go on to form bands with such a coherent vision and such enormous sonic precision that they are still being talked about, in the grandest possible terms, more than 30 years later.

That they didn't know each other, any of them, were different ages and came from four quite different backgrounds, but were able to function so perfectly together as a unit for so long, with such a similar spirit of adventure and audacity, not to mention seeming unity of purpose, is also quite difficult to fathom.

Colin Newman, Wire's singer and guitarist, was the last to be born of the band's four members, on September 16, 1954, in Salisbury, Wiltshire. He spent the first six or seven years of his life in a large village called Durrington, near Bulford Camp, a military installation on the Salisbury Plain. Newman's family had been in the area for a while, and his uncle ended up running the camp.

His father, Roy, was an electrical power engineer who worked for the Southern Electricity Board, his job eventually taking him to Newbury in Berkshire, where Colin went to St Bartholomew's, then a grammar (he was the first in his family to attend such a school), now a secondary school.

"My dad's great because he really isn't at all interested," he says of his father's bemusement at his career choice. "It's a generational thing. He doesn't come from a generation that understands rock music of any kind."

Roy Newman did actually achieve some notoriety in the contemporary music arena, appearing in a 2008 feature in the *Guardian* newspaper about rock musicians and their parents. In it, he reminisces about his son's early musical predilections.

"Colin always had a vivid imagination," he told journalist Dave Simpson. "When he was about five he used to lag behind us with his hand held up making a clicking noise. He told us he was taking his pet horse for a walk. He was always very driven. We once took him and his younger sister Janice to Woolworths so he could buy the latest Beatles record. Fifteen minutes later Janice was crying – no sign of Colin. We found him two hours later: he'd run home, climbed in through the bathroom window and was in his room, blaring out the record."

He did love The Beatles, although the first record to really excite the young Newman was 'Telstar' by The Tornados. Why? "Because I heard somebody say on the radio it was the sound of the future, and I just thought that was the most exciting thing you could imagine.

'The sound of the future': how exciting is that?" As for The Beatles, what attracted him to them weren't their lyrics so much as their music, and what he calls "their harmonic world", which proved a sonically complex, polychromatic delight after the primitive, mono-chrome din of Fifties rock'n'roll. "The Fifties were always very much black and white, and I absolutely hated that. My emotions around music were so strong that I could feel physically sick from something I didn't like, such as Fifties rock'n'roll. I absolutely hated Elvis Presley when I was a kid."

He was, he says, a bohemian teenager of sorts. "I tried to be," he says. "We weren't allowed to have long hair, which was a bit of a drawback, so that was the first thing I did when I left school – grow my hair."

He describes himself as "extremely rebellious", a condition exacer-bated by his parents' divorce when he was 15. "That didn't really help my temperament. I was very angry. It was tough." He lived with his mother, with whom he had a sometimes fractious relationship, but still kept in touch with his father. "I really didn't have any idea of how my parents' relationship worked, so it was more like, 'How dare they do this [i.e. get divorced] when my life is starting?' It was a selfish reaction."

Newman's anger manifested itself as surliness towards adults in general, both at home and at school. "I tended to regard most adults as idiots. They were quite critical of me because I had my own ideas about what I wanted to do, and I thought all their stuff about, 'Oh, you need to get yourself an apprenticeship' and all that was just bullshit.

"I was the first one to go to grammar school," he continues. "I was supposed to be the clever one, the achiever, but I didn't think I was that clever. I remember going to a school careers officer who asked what I wanted to be. I said I wanted to be an artist. He said, 'Have you consid-ered landscape gardening?'"

Newman had other ideas. "I had this theory that the future was going to be all about leisure, and what you needed to do was be working in an industry which caters to people's leisure, because that's how you'll make money. You weren't going to make money working in a factory, so I wasn't at all sure how I planned to do anything about it, but I was also quite arrogant. I was full of myself. It was a typically British mixture of arrogance, laid on top of being completely petrified of absolutely everything."

At school, he was ostracised by the cool kids known as "the Aces", a group to which he eventually gained membership towards the end of his time at St Bart's. "That was quite a big achievement because I'd been a gawky kid. I had spots, and I wasn't regarded as being that cool, but I got in by virtue of the fact that I knew all of the good music, even though I was never going to be the one to get off with the coolest girls."

It was at St Bart's that Newman met up with Desmond Simmons, with whom he would later end up working on Wire as well as some of Colin's solo projects. The pair formed a band at school called CNDs, their musical direction changing weekly, depending on whom or what they'd read about in *NME*, of which they were avid readers.

"I started subscribing to the *NME* from the age of about eight and read it from cover to cover every week – I even did the crossword," he says. "Me and Desmond knew absolutely everything in it, and whatever they were into, we were into. We were complete and utter fashion victims, before anyone had even invented that term. We were stuck in a small town so, for us, that was our culture. We took it incredibly seriously."

From the age of 12, Colin would lay in bed and dream of jamming on stage "with an endless parade of stars – it was a world I wanted to be part of".

Newman and Simmons made their own modest, DIY bid to attain rock'n'roll glory by recording a set of self-penned material in preparation for that great day when they would be a legitimate performing and recording unit. "There was no doubt," says Newman, "that that was what we were going to do with our lives." At this point, however, it was all make-believe. "We never played outside Desmond's front room. In our heads we were a band, and there was a great deal of discussion about how we'd show them all down at the folk club. We never got that far, actually playing in front of other people. But we'd record everything to practise for the time when we would be a band in a studio. For us it was life and death. It was absolutely the most important thing in our lives. I can't overstress how important music was. There was really nothing else."

It was after leaving St Barts (where he managed 7 'O' levels and 'A' levels in art, history and geography), when he arrived at the Winchester School of Art, to do his Foundation course, that Newman found the right cosmopolitan environment for his obsession with rock.

"They didn't have a Paul McCartney School of Rock or anything like that in those days," he says. "It would probably have been really bad for me if I'd gone to a place like that anyway. It seemed obvious to me that I should go to art school – here was a place and a culture where it was all taken seriously. As far as my dad was concerned, music was all light entertainment. That was the world of my parents."

His intention was to become a graphic designer "because that was all about doing album sleeves", even though he would eventually be steered towards fine art before a career in rock became an option. He had no idea that he would be able to pursue his penchant for rock music beyond the level of private obsession until he arrived at art college. "At Winchester, I ran up against a culture I'd never come across before. I had never been exposed to serious culture as opposed to, you know, pop culture. But on the first day of college, my tutor played us Steve Reich's 'Piano Phase' on an old tape recorder, and I was just transfixed. It blew my mind. I just thought, 'Fucking hell, this is unbelievable.'"

Meanwhile, Newman was devouring every bit of music, experimental or otherwise, that he could lay his hands on, satisfying his seriously eclectic tastes with everything from reggae and Motown to David Bowie, Crosby Stills Nash & Young, Spirit, The Velvet Underground and, especially, Todd Rundgren.

"*A Wizard, A True Star* is one of my favourite all-time records," he says of Rundgren's 1973 "stream-of-consciousness" opus. "I'm a big, big, Todd Rundgren fan. I also like *Something/Anything* [1972] and *Todd* [1974]. I loved everything about him. All these people would be going on about Eric Clapton and Jimmy Page and I'd be like, yeah, but I'm into Todd Rundgren – he could play the guitar like a fucking bastard. He's a genius. What can you say about Todd, you know? Todd is god."

5

Newman was beginning to venture out to see bands live at the Corn Exchange in Newbury, including Genesis around the time of their first album in 1969 ("Complete rubbish") and Van Der Graaf Generator. "They really impressed me because they were so fucking loud. I'd never heard anything so loud. It was full-frequency as well, with [frontman] Peter Hammill screaming over the top. You knew they were really serious."

However, Newman's most significant close encounter with a rock musician came after he'd left Winchester to study illustration at Watford College of Art in the early Seventies ("I was the world's worst student," he says. "I mean, I can't draw, which was a bit of a drawback"). Brian Eno used to lecture there and Colin would get to share a car with the Roxy Music synth whiz as well as artist Peter Schmidt, another lecturer at Watford, on journeys along the A41 from north London to the college in Hertfordshire.

"I'd get a lift every day," he recalls, "which was fantastic because they didn't treat me as some bloke or a student, but as a fellow artist. I could come up with my crazy ideas, and they'd all laugh, but they wouldn't laugh *at* me, as though I was some stupid student. It was the first time in my life that I felt like, 'I am an artist' instead of, 'I'm aspiring to be an artist' or, 'I would like to be an artist when I've done this.' I suddenly thought, 'No, I am an artist.' And that was really liberating. In fact, it was the best thing that happened to me at art school."

NEWMAN had other significant encounters either at or around Watford when he met for the first time the young men who would later comprise Wire. The first whose acquaintance he made would have been Bruce Gilbert, the audio-visual technician in charge of a small studio at the college. The oldest member of the band, Gilbert was born on May 18, 1946, in Garston, near Watford, and was brought up in the centre of town, in the area currently occupied by the giant Harlequin shopping precinct. He attended the Francis Combe School in Garston, quite a rough place these days, but back then a formal establishment with pretensions towards grammar status where the headmaster wore a mortarboard and gown.

His mother was very musical, with, he says, "a very good jazz voice – she could have gone professional but I think she was frightened of leaving Watford." Gilbert himself, by the age of 10, was experimenting with tape machines and found sounds, recording comedy shows at friends' houses. Inventive even then, after wondering how to extend parts of his recordings, the young Gilbert discovered a way to make tape loops.

"I just got very interested in making noises, really," he says. "It was quite silly stuff, but it amused us."

As for rock'n'roll, his favourite song around this time was Duane Eddy's twang-fest 'Peter Gunn', because "it was very repetitive and very simple. I didn't like songs, really; I liked instrumentals." The first record Gilbert bought was 'Take Five' by Dave Brubeck, and he soon discovered the blues, he and a friend regularly walking into Watford town centre to buy blues EPs from a specialist R&B store.

Gilbert left school when he was 16, having hardly excelled at his exams. "I was awful," he admits, "absolutely hopeless." He found a series of "really quite ridiculously boring jobs" before deciding he wanted to go to art school, which meant, insufficiently qualified as he was, going back to college in Watford to get a couple more 'O' levels. Eventually, he acquired a place at the nearby St Albans School of Art, where he took a two-year preparatory course, before studying graphics at Leicester Art College. There, he says, he spent little time in the graphics studios, opting instead to hang out either in the photography department or the painting studio.

It was while he was at Leicester, in summer 1967, that The Beatles released *Sgt Pepper*, which apparently "caused great interest and a lot of excitement" at the college. However, Gilbert considered The Beatles' *meisterwerk* "rather old-fashioned" in its vaudevillian ostentation and excessively florid, with "too many notes", preferring instead the artful minimalism and avant-drones of The Velvet Underground & Nico. He was hardly able to immerse himself in the counter-culture anyway, being already married by this point with a child. "I was a bit of an outsider, really," he says. "I never really was part of anything. I was always at home, as it were."

After graduating from Leicester, Gilbert was forced to endure "various horrible jobs to keep bread on the table" before accepting a post as a pottery technician at an art college in Hemel Hempstead, followed by a position as slide librarian and visual-aid technician at the Watford College of Art. Apart from doing his job, he would while away his time in the studio, as he puts it, "making strange noises", influenced by the early Seventies German school of experimental rock'n'roll known as "krautrock" and the avant-garde classical music he heard on Radio 3. He hadn't yet begun playing guitar properly, although he had started experimenting with one.

"I fiddled around and used one as a noise source, and briefly I taught myself how to play a bit of blues on a Woolworths guitar," he recalls. "And for a couple of months I accompanied one of the lecturers who always had two blues songs in his repertoire, and I just put a bit of slide guitar on and waited patiently until his blues songs came up. I was pretty awful, because I played the same thing each time."

By 1974-5 and the early stirrings of the pub-rock scene that presaged punk, Gilbert started noticing two students at Watford: Colin Newman and his belligerent northern flatmate, George Gill – "the wild man poet troubadour in college", according to Newman.

"There were occasional gatherings after the pub around Colin and George's flat, and I think that it was probably Colin who was starting to be much more aware of that [i.e. pub rock and punk] than I was. I'd obviously heard bits in passing, but Colin actually bought records and played them when I went around to his flat. Patti Smith's *Horses* was the first thing I heard at Colin's."

Before long, Gill and Newman had persuaded Gilbert out of his studio, to join them in an ad hoc band they'd formed just in time for an end-of-term party. By all accounts, the show was a shambles, but Gilbert was sufficiently intrigued by the minimalist droning Velvets-ish rock being produced by the group to continue with practice sessions in the house shared by Newman, Gill and Slim Smith (now the designer for *Art Rocker* magazine, then on the same course as Newman), on Leavesden Road in Watford, where they would bash away at songs that Gill had written.

"It was intense," Newman told *MOJO* magazine's Keith Cameron. "George's songs weren't exciting, but it was an exciting noise and that was what kept me there, apart from the fact that it was going on in my bedroom."

The fledgling band, then known as Overload, featured a rhythm section comprising one Robert Gotobed on drums and a bassist called Graham Lewis, a fashion design graduate from Hornsey Art College whom Gilbert had met through his then-girlfriend, Angela Conway (later a recording artiste herself under the name of AC Marias, for the Mute label).

"He [Lewis] looked like the living embodiment of the New York Dolls," Gilbert told Cameron. "I saw him in a pub in New Barnet where they sold the strongest beer. He was playing darts and beating everyone, playing crib and beating everyone. Very competitive. But he looked like this girlie. He said he could play bass. He clearly couldn't."

The eldest of three children, Graham Lewis (born February 22, 1953, in Grantham, Lincolnshire) had spent his childhood moving around Europe's RAF bases, where his father "worked on fighter squadrons" as an electrician. When he was aged 18 months, the Lewis family went to live in Germany for two-and-a-half years, then to Holland for six months, before moving back to the UK when he was about four-and-a-half. They spent two years in Norfolk, then relocated back to Lincolnshire, where they spent another couple of years, followed by a sojourn in Newcastle, where Lewis lived between the ages of 10 and 11 and discovered pop music, in arcades and on the radio.

The first record to make an impression on the pre-teen Lewis was Helen Shapiro's number one hit from 1961, 'Walkin' Back To Happiness'. The following year, The Beatles' debut single, 'Love Me Do', had an even bigger impact. He felt a glow of pride at the burgeoning success of local rock'n'roll boys made good, The Animals.

Lewis recognised in himself some artistic proclivities from a young age, encouraged by a realisation that he had "a half-decent voice" and by his junior school teacher, Miss Mason, who brought out his artistic bent. It was one Christmas, while the Lewis family was living in Suffolk, not far from Stowmarket, on an RAF base called Wattisham, that he was given his first transistor radio, on which he heard for the first time the wild new sounds of Jimi Hendrix, The Electric Prunes, The Move, Cream, The Rolling Stones and The Young Rascals.

This, Lewis soon decided, was all the education he was going to need. Although he attended grammar school, he found the study of such ancient texts as *Tess Of The D'Urbervilles* "absolute torture". "That," says Wire's future lyricist, "was my introduction to the English language and academia. I didn't do very well. I had verbal skills, but I didn't really start seriously reading until I was 19." Like many of his generation who wound up changing the face of British music in punk and post-punk bands, he experienced negativity, even outright hostility, from teachers and careers advisers and the so-called arbiters of "proper culture" who refused to believe he would amount to very much.

"People like John Lydon and me – we all share some similarities in the sense of the way these bastards would tell us we wouldn't be any good. And it was, like, 'Well, fuck you and your pretentious crap.' The guy who took great pleasure in explaining to us simpletons what 'azure' means. I will never forget, but I'd like to stick it right up his ass, you know?"

Two other signal events that occurred around Lewis' 15th birthday were the appearance of an entire collection of classic soul singles sold to the local youth club by a young West Indian guy in the Air Force called Mick, and the 1968 *NME* Poll Winners' Concert that took place at the Newcastle City Hall. This featured, as well as the de rigueur Cliff Richard & The Shadows, Amen Corner, Love Affair, with a 40-piece orchestra, and Dave Dee, Dozy, Beaky, Mick & Tich, the incendiary likes of Scott Walker "being jeered and booed by about 15,000 people", The Move, who were the loudest band of the night and climaxed their set by trashing their equipment, and surprise guests The Rolling Stones, playing 'Jumping Jack Flash' and '(I Can't Get No) Satisfaction', which Lewis remembers as being "absolutely astonishing".

Lewis doesn't, however, remember the counter-culture making many inroads up in Newcastle. "Although people grew their hair and things, it wasn't very hippie up there, you know?" he says. "There were quite a lot of drugs around, though. More people that I knew died of drugs during my two years in Newcastle than at any other time in my life." Was he particularly rebellious himself? "I don't know about revolution or being rebellious. I think up there people were drinking and surviving, basically. It was a very, very tough environment."

When he was 16, Lewis was put on a path to rock'n'roll glory when a local coffin-maker – and former Teddy boy – called Jimmy Moore gave him a bass guitar he'd made himself based on an article he'd seen in a magazine. Early heroes of the aspiring bassist were Jack Bruce of Cream, whom he liked because he sang as well, and Andy Fraser of Free, whose playing Lewis particularly enjoyed, influenced as it was by Motown and with those seemingly vast spaces between the notes.

Lewis' enthusiasm for rock music reached fever pitch in 1971, when, having received the necessary 'A' levels, he began a foundation course at Lanchester Polytechnic in Coventry. There, during something called music appreciation on Wednesday mornings, he was introduced to the German "motorik" of Neu!, acts from the "Canterbury scene" such as Gong, Soft Machine and Kevin Ayers, the space-rock of Hawkwind and avant-classical composers like Stockhausen. He was also rather taken with a new British group called Roxy Music and the way they allied strange noises to a glamorous image, mixing and matching sounds and ideas from different eras in a way that would later be termed "postmodern". "I had," he decides, "been infected by postmodernism." He even caught Roxy live during their first tour in 1972, at the Belfry Country Club in Sutton Coalfield.

In his second year at Lanchester, because "they had the best arts festival in Britain at that time", he "had the great honour" of DJ-ing and working with the entertainment production crew, playing records between sets by acts as varied as mime artist Marcel Marceau and American jazz multi-instrumentalist Roland Kirk. "It was," he marvels, "a pretty fantastic time."

At Lanchester, Lewis was inspired by "some really good teachers", including John Mockett, who later designed sets for Pink Floyd as well as motorbikes for Lord Hesketh. He was also encouraged to destroy all the ideas about art that he'd thus far acquired in his young life and try a bit of everything, from screen printing to textiles, before being, as he puts it, "shovelled off to the fashion department because they liked the look of me, whatever that meant".

It was the fashion department that suggested to Lewis that he apply to study for his BA Honours degree in fashion at Hornsey Art College in London, where he pitched up in 1973. There, he also served as social secretary for two years, booking bands such as Dr Feelgood "for 60 quid" and Kilburn & The High Roads, starring Ian Dury.

At this time, Lewis did indeed look like the living embodiment of the New York Dolls, all Biba-style glam finery, severe cheekbones and seven-inch stack heels. He was every inch the fashionista and, after completing his degree, he managed to sell some work from his degree show, which eventually became manufactured and shown in a variety of style magazines, including *Honey* and *19*. "It was," he says, "tremendously exciting." Even more exciting was the call he got from Lynne Franks, the legendary PR woman on whom Jennifer Saunders based her character Edina Monsoon for her sitcom *Absolutely Fabulous*. She offered Lewis a job designing garments for high-street fashion outlets; he agreed, his only stipulation being that he should have his name in the items, plus a royalty. She agreed, paying Lewis "five grand a year plus royalties to produce drawings". He designed a collection that appeared in Harrods, Top Shop and other emporia, and he takes the credit for the invention of the big, baggy T-shirt as fashion must-have, the sort that Katherine Hamnett would later use to emblazon giant slogans across, paving the way for the 'Frankie Say' T-shirts of the Eighties.

And then, just as his career in fashion was taking off, Lewis met Bruce Gilbert at a punk gig by several former Hornsey alumni going by the name of The Vibrators, in a pub called The Nelson on London's Holloway Road. Mutual fans of Captain Beefheart, the Velvets and Free, Gilbert invited Lewis to a rehearsal in Watford with Colin Newman and George Gill. Only it wasn't quite as benign as that sounds.

"Graham turned up," recounts Newman, "to be interviewed for the part of being the bass player, and Bruce, typically, told us, 'I know this bloke, he's a cunt, you know, you won't like him.' And so George got drunk and shouted at him, and everyone else was fairly unfriendly. Graham was completely gobsmacked, but he got offered the job."

"I think George decided to find out if I was bully-able," Lewis told *Mojo* in 2006. "From my accent he could tell I was from up north like he was – my family were shipbuilding people from Jarrow – yet there I was designing fashion, and successfully, too. George was really oikish about this and Colin was like his pet dog, so they really had a go at me. It ended with a general stand-off."

There was some slagging-off going on during the gig at the end-of-term party at Watford College, albeit of the quiet variety – there were, according to Newman, "only about four and a half people there". Colin had never sung in public before. "But I was cocky," he adds, "and I had this theory that, if I wanted to make it with girls, I'd have to join a band." Trouble was, they weren't, at this point, very good. "They were all George's songs, and they were, frankly, rubbish."

It was around this time that Lewis pointed out, quite reasonably, that the band, still called Overload, would need a regular drummer. As though by chance, at a garden party in Stockwell in September 1976, a tall, thin young man walked through the throng of revellers busy tucking into their cucumber sandwiches. He was wearing Levi jeans, black Doc Martens, a leather jacket... and a huge sunflower in his lapel. "And," recalls Newman, "I just went, 'Wow, that guy looks amazing!' It was Rob."

"ROB" was Robert Gotobed. Born Robert Grey on April 21, 1951, in Marefield, Leicester, he had no musical background of which to speak. "The people at school who played a musical instrument, I always thought, well, they're from a musical family, and I'm not, so I won't be able to do it," he says. "I didn't start playing until I was 25 – I was a very late developer." He might not have been able to play music, but he enjoyed listening to it. "Cream were the first group who I thought were, you know, fabulous. I didn't particularly like The Beatles. Cream were heavier, and that got through to me."

After briefly undertaking a humanities course, and following a brief stint doing house removals for a living, Grey moved to London, where he found a squat and immersed himself in the capital's alternative culture. The only member of Wire to have any previous experience in rock bands, he had been singer with The Snakes, a pub-rock outfit featuring Nick Garvey and Richard Wernham, who later formed The Motors (of "Airport", a Top 5 hit in 1978, semi-fame).

He began to use the surname Gotobed when he was 21, advancing the idea of a new identity as practised by Johnny Rotten (formerly

Lydon), Sid Vicious (John Beverly), all four Ramones and many others in the front wave of British and US punk.

"Part of my youthful rebellion was to adopt a different name," he explains, "and it happened that my family name before it was changed to Grey had been Gotobed, and so I thought, well, this is perfect. I will re-adopt the old name because it sounds more interesting than Grey. But my grandfather had originally changed it because he thought people didn't take him seriously in business because he had a funny name, and that's true, but then when punk happened, there was this outbreak of funny names, and so me being called Gotobed sort of fitted in." It also helped for keeping the social services at bay. "Yeah, it had quite a lot to do with signing on – you obviously didn't want the DHSS to know your real name, did you? But 'Rotten' and 'Vicious' were stage names. That was pantomime."

South London's squat-land suited Gotobed, because he lived in a whole house, the basement of which provided a perfect drumming room – he would bash away on a kit supplied by Wernham to his heart's content. "It worked out well that I had no money for rent," laughs Grey, "because if I'd been renting somewhere there's no way I could have made as much noise practising drums as I did."

It was during a Snakes gig that Graham Lewis saw Grey/Gotobed in action, and proposed to Colin Newman and the others that he should be their formative band's permanent drummer, although Robert, feeling anxious about his lack of ability, originally put forward Snakes sticksman Wernham instead. Newman immediately dismissed this out of hand, apparently on the grounds that Wernham had acne! Eventually, they all managed to persuade Gotobed to make the journey out to Hertfordshire for a rehearsal underneath a furniture store on the St Albans Road in Watford.

"Colin could be very persuasive," he says. "We just made lots of noise in this basement. I haven't got a clue what I played because I find, if you're in a state of some worry or distress, or in unfamiliar surroundings, it's difficult to remember things. I just felt that, if somebody wants me to play with them badly enough, even though I can't play well, I'll give it a go."

He recalls playing such Gill classics of sophisticated songwriting as

'Mary Is A Dyke' – "these aggressive blues-based ideas", which the band were forced to perform through gritted teeth because "he was the dominant person in the early days; it was his group. We'd go along with his ideas, and he wanted a backing for his songs and his guitar solos". There would also have been souped-up renditions of live standbys like JJ Cale's 'After Midnight' and the 1964 Dave Clark 5 chart-topper 'Glad All Over', which, says Gotobed, "we'd play at 100 miles an hour to amuse ourselves".

Gilbert, Newman, Lewis and Gotobed were at that rehearsal, but George Gill, the nominal leader of Overload, wasn't, due to the fact that he had broken his leg and was laid up in hospital, an event that would prove Gill's undoing and momentous for the development of Wire. With Gill absent, and Gotobed behind the drum kit, Newman, Lewis and Gilbert discovered that they played better, faster, harder, the songs sounding more fluid, focused and succinct, without Gill's extraneous guitar solos and general lyrical and instrumental excess.

They also didn't have to put up with his lairy behaviour and brutish demeanour – at their first gig proper, for example, supporting a band called The Derelicts at the Nashville Rooms in West Kensington on December 5, 1976, a drunken Gill began hurling abuse at someone in the crowd who had the audacity to stare as he changed a guitar string. According to Bruce Gilbert, Gill proceeded to storm off the stage after this incident and, only halfway through the set, refused to come back, a par-for-the-course demonstration of his erratic temperament.

"George used to do a lot of shouting and extend everything with guitar solos and just generally make a mess," says Newman. "And then he broke his leg. It was pretty much common practice in those days to go and see other bands and rubbish them. So George went to see this band in Kilburn, and he was drunk, and he decided that they were so rubbish he could steal their amplifier, you know, because they were crap. And he was making his way down this set of stairs with the amplifier and fell down and broke his leg and got hospitalised – he was in hospital for quite a long time.

"So we started rehearsing without him, and it was like a veil had been lifted. Suddenly, we didn't have the guitar solos so the songs became short pieces, and we realised we could actually play them quite well. From this messy, meandering, screamy, untogether bollocks that was the band with George, we very quickly progressed towards this tight, shortened song approach. We discovered that, when we played one of George's songs without the guitar solos or anything else, they only lasted a minute and a half. It felt pretty efficient and, you know, good. I was saying to Bruce and George, 'You've got to listen to this,' and playing them records by Patti Smith, Jonathan Richman and the Ramones."

As Gilbert puts it, without Gill and his fussy overmatter, it soon became apparent that a pared-down sound was not just achievable, but the only sensible way forward. "That was quite instructive, and seemed to be a much more interesting possibility."

"It was then," claims Newman, "that we realised we were going to have to get rid of George. A friend of mine, Paul Lowe from my foundation course at Watford, turned to me and Graham during a Damned gig at the Roxy and said, 'You've got to get rid of George, he's rubbish; he's the weak link and he's pulling you back.' And Graham and I were like, 'Yeah, that's kind of what we were thinking.'"

Now all they had to do was tell Gill he was being sacked from his own band. They just couldn't decide who was going to be the one to do it.

"We all came up to the pub, one of those ones on the St Albans Road, with a jukebox, and we were supposed to announce to George that we'd outgrown him or something like that," recalls Newman. "But by the time we arrived, Bruce had already told him. We were sitting there, looking really embarrassed, wondering when the news was going to be broken, when suddenly George turned to us and said, 'It's all right, he's told me. You're a bunch of cunts. You can all fuck off.'"

Gilbert remembers it well. "We arranged to meet George at this pub, and we were all going to be there to tell him, but I got there half an hour early so I told him myself. So I said to him, 'Don't let on that I've told you and let's watch 'em squirm.'"

Bruce hasn't seen Gill since, nor have any of the others, although Colin has heard that he became a seascape artist on the south coast, which would fit the George they knew. "He was visually aware. He could certainly paint. But he doesn't want anything to do with us. George remained in the band for a while, nominally if nothing else, but then he started to become very marginal to it, and in the end we just threw him out. To put it in brutal, *Sun* headline terms, we stole his band."

Chapter 2

Roxy And Elsewhere

"I sat in my bedroom in north Watford in 1977 and had this notion that rock music needed destroying, and the way to destroy rock'n'roll was to take the 'and roll' bit out and make it into this monophonic thing. Arrogant as I was at 22, I considered I was reinventing rock music" – Colin Newman

Having wrested control of the band from hospitalised founder member George Gill, the four members of Overload snapped into action as 1977, one of the most important years in rock history, came into view. First, they changed their name to Wire, which they chose, as Graham Lewis told Simon Reynolds, author of *Rip It Up And Start Again: Postpunk 1978-1984*, as much for "its graphic quality" as for the sense it gave of the metallic, thin and, well, wiry, as well as of electrical power lines. Plus, as Lewis told Reynolds, "It was short and stark and would look big on a poster even if we were low on the bill!"

It was a suitably simple, no-nonsense, stripped-down name for a band whose natural penchant, give or take the occasional sunflower or red carnation in the lapel, mirrored shades (Bruce Gilbert) or beret (Lewis), was for stark, unadorned, monochrome black, white and grey clothes (jeans, shirts, Doc Martens). In terms of action and image, Wire were quite at odds with the safety pins, bondage trousers and generally outrageous peacock finery of the punk brigade. Even Roy Newman, Colin's dad, has noted Wire's almost ascetic lack of frills with regard to their appearance, telling the *Guardian* newspaper in 2008, "In his schooldays Colin took every opportunity to look dishevelled, but Wire's image then – and now – is soberly dressed young men. When I first saw them play they wore black and didn't say much, a complete contrast to all the other groups."

But then, Wire were quite clear about not being part of the new wave of punk bands, or indeed of any other movement prior to their emergence. As they told notorious journalist Jane Suck, the Julie Burchill of *Sounds* (who, says Newman, "really knew her stuff" and, despite being "a junkie, a bit barmy and gay", tried to get off with him one night):"We've got no heroes." More than 30 years later, interviewed for this book, they're still adamant about their distance from the spiky-haired throng and their separateness from the scene, any scene. They inhabited a world of their own creation: Wireworld.

"We didn't really want to be thrown in with the punk thing at all," says Bruce Gilbert, who at the time of Wire's formation was an audio-visual technician at Watford Art College and an abstract painter. "We kept ourselves very much to ourselves. We were self-motivated."

Graham Lewis was entirely unimpressed by most punk music, considering it merely a speeded-up version of pub rock. "It sounded like rather sad and very badly played folk music to me, quite honestly," he contends. "It was R&B, just jumped up a bit. That's not what we were interested in. We had our rock'n'roll and R&B detectors on at all times. You could detect that in the Sex Pistols, and in The Clash. We'd all seen Joe Strummer in The 101ers; we knew where these people came from. You could see what The Jam really were, with their working-men's-club greatest hits and Tamla Motown covers. We saw through all of that stuff."

Wire weren't mired in Sixties garage rock or sweaty R&B. If anything, at this point they would have more likely been listening to the artful "punk" of the American "CBGBs" bands such as Television, the Patti Smith Group, Richard Hell & The Voidoids and Ramones, even Velvet Underground acolytes Jonathan Richman & The Modern Lovers, whose records Colin Newman had been playing to the other three as soon as the idea of the band had been mooted.

The other area of music proving inspirational to Wire at this time was the experimental rock that had been coming out of Germany since the early-Seventies known as "krautrock". "Our vision," says Lewis, "came from Germany, from the likes of Can, Neu! and Kraftwerk, as well as the American bands – music that came out of art and 'the beats'; out of a cultured scene – that I had an affinity with. If people want to call it 'art punk', fine. But we didn't give a fuck about punk. We weren't a punk band. We told everybody we weren't a punk band. They just kept telling us we were. Really, we were interested in art. That's where I came from. I'm an artist."

Wire had the drainpipes and the intimidating presence – actually, they were more glacially aloof than mere scowling misanthropes – of the punks, but that was about it. That, plus a similar short, sharp, minimalist approach to songwriting; what Simon Reynolds calls their "reductionist disdain for extraneous decoration". With Robert Gotobed already 25 years old and Bruce Gilbert 31, positively ancient for the punk era, and with Lewis and Newman's art-school background, Wire were able to keep a safe distance from the comings and goings of the Class of '77 while using it as a way of kick-starting their career. They were punk sub-versives, observing the action from afar and occasionally dropping in to smile disdainfully at the gobbing hordes, a baleful, glowering presence, with a keen sense of the absurd.

"I thought bands were embarrassing, because they all looked the same and they all did the same things, and while I'm not averse to enjoying myself, there are different ways of enjoying oneself," says Bruce Gilbert, whose look of droll bemusement was very Wire.

"Without humour we couldn't do it," agrees Robert Gotobed. "There are so many funny things that happened that I probably laughed more with Wire than in any other circumstance in my life. The absurdity of it all – I think that's been there since the beginning, and thankfully it is still there, and maybe that's one of the things that holds it together. How can you not go through that process without seeing how ridiculous it is? It is serious, but it's funny as well. You need both."

For Wire, acknowledging the absurdity of what they were doing was essential. And in a way, it was very punk, even though, as Newman insists, "I wasn't a punk in any real terms." But in one way he was: he was an iconoclast, only one more concerned with tearing up the plans completely than adhering, as per The Clash et al, to tried/tired and tested rock'n'roll modes of expression. Wire were about as far removed from the punk-age notion of rebel-rock as it was possible to get.

Newman had, he admits, "been incredibly excited by punk, at first", rushing down to see the Sex Pistols at Middlesex Poly where he saw a divided audience: half "pissed-up rugby types who hated them" and "the rest of us who thought they were fantastic, funny and culturally defining". It wasn't long, however, before the punk revolutionaries got mired in the same old routines and rituals.

"Everything started to sound the same and doing something new seemed like a good idea," he says. "I wanted to reinvent rock'n'roll because I thought it should be new, not old. Bruce wanted to bring in fine-art connotations, to deliberately not talk about us in a punk way. We weren't talking about living in council flats and being on the dole, we were into Marcel Duchamp. Our generation was the first to bring the 'criticality' that you find in fine art to music. With Wire, there was a cultural savvy."

As he told *Mojo* in 2006, "I liked the idea of rock music that didn't rock, taking out those things people thought they had to have. No middle-eights. No guitar solos. No key changes. What makes old music sound old? Clichés. It's all about playing with the format."

In keeping with punk's Year Zero dictum, Newman wanted to rip things up and start again. "I absolutely hated rock'n'roll," he says. "That was one of the big things that was wrong with Brit-punk: it was very old-fashioned. I hated all those bands like The 101ers. It was all so retro.

"I grew up in the Sixties, so for me the best music was psychedelic – Fifties rock'n'roll sounded quite naive and tedious," he furthers. "So while George was in hospital, I was sitting in my bedroom in north Watford reinventing rock music, basically. I had this notion that rock music needed destroying, and the way to destroy rock'n'roll was to take the 'and roll' bit out and make it into this kind of monophonic sound with just one chord. It sounds fearfully arrogant, but that's what you're like when you're in your early 20s. I was the youngest one in the band,

I was fairly cocky, and I thought, basically, here's a chance to do it. I could see that exciting things were going on at the time, but I definitely didn't want to be doing the same as everybody else. Like Patti Smith, Jonathan Richman and the Ramones, we were dealing body blows to the concept of Fifties rock'n'roll. I just thought rock'n'roll was rubbish. It had too many chords."

It had too many of many things. Wire wanted to pare things down, they wanted every aspect of their music and art to have the bare minimum but to have the maximum impact. Not that it was as planned-out as that sounds; there was less theory and strategy than one might imagine. Things happened organically, a natural corollary of the chemistry between the four members.

"Reviewers have always said that Wire had this genius idea of combining punk with minimalism," laughs Robert Gotobed. "What? None of us said, 'Oh, we should combine punk with minimalism, what a great idea.' It's the chemistry of the people that you're involved with. The input of each person gives shape to what you're doing, and everybody contributes their ideas of how they would like things to be. But there was no grand plan, not that I was aware of."

A certain disdain for the absurd art of rock performance, and a discomfort at appearing on a stage before a crowd, inevitably led to frontman and singer Colin Newman adopting – again, naturally – a uniquely minimalist, less is more approach to stage craft. Not for him the lecherous cavorting or prancing narcissism of a Jagger or Stewart, or even the pantomime surliness of a Rotten or rebel posturing of a Strummer. As harsh white lights caught Wire's players in their glare, he would barely move, staring straight ahead, and if you weren't sufficiently entranced, you knew where the door was.

"There was a deeply deconstructive element to everything we did from the beginning," he says. "If you look at the Sixties generation, they were all a bit showbiz and Las Vegas. The so-called punk generation were sufficiently distanced from the original rockers to be able to take a critical look at everything they did. I remember at the very beginning, going onstage, one thing that I was completely aware of was I didn't want to do any sort of rock posing, and I used Rod Stewart as an example of what not to do. Because Rod Stewart did every single sort of rock pose that you could imagine. It was all about making it look as though he was really enjoying himself. So I would just stand completely still, because I was refusing to look like I was trying to make the music more interesting. You either got it or you didn't. It was about the content. It wasn't about how I performed it."

When Newman did have a change of heart and start to move onstage, that, too, happened organically. It was, as he explains, a necessary procedure rather than a display of look-at-me! egomania and self-importance.

"I started to get bored and bring some gestures into it. I would have to move eventually because as the person writing the tunes, and in the early days not playing the guitar onstage, the only way anyone would know when to change between the verse and the chorus with absolute certainly, because memory isn't always brilliant in any member of Wire, would be when I would put my hand up. So I evolved a series of subtle gestures that would indicate to members of the band, 'This is when you change; this is where you go to the next bit', or whatever. That became a sort of choreography – I began moving in a slightly jerky way based on signals I was giving to the band. Then they could feel confident, especially considering how short the songs were – they required everyone to stop abruptly. In a way I was conducting the band."

Musically, Wire made a virtue out of their lack of technical ability, prioritising economy and precision over virtuosic displays because they couldn't play solos and wanted to avoid fussy excess at all costs. As Newman says, "I was always the one who was supposed to be the musician but I'm not a great guitarist. In fact, I'm crap."

Or as Lewis put it to Keith Cameron in *Mojo*: "Suddenly we could rely on our inadequacies rather than George's rock'n'roll virtuosity."

Wire's lyrics were equally sparse, featuring just enough words to say what they wanted to say. And just as Wire tried to avoid clichés sonically and in terms of presentation, so, too, did the words to their songs bypass the usual hackneyed notions of rock revolution and angry energy. Newman shared lyrical duties with Lewis, the pair penning their first song, 'Lowdown', together soon after the dismissal of George Gill – Newman describes their first collaboration as "grinding, slowed-down funk music; sort of deconstructed funk". He admits that rage was a feature of their songs, but it was expressed in oblique, abstract ways.

"I always hated all those punk groups singing about, you know, 'I'm living in a flat on the dole.'"

Adds Lewis, "I didn't want to be repetitious and do what other people were doing – that would have been daft. My first essay at art college in 1972 was about being in the queue at the dole office! And I got an extremely good grade for it. I just didn't feel the need to do it any more. I mean, in 1975 I was in a dole office in Finsbury Park where I used to sign on and this strange carrot-haired bloke called John Lydon came in… So it wasn't something I felt I needed to report on any more. 'Lowdown' takes that subject and carries it a lot further; it says a lot more about what to do when that feeling of despair or hopelessness sets in. You've got to have dreams, project them and follow them. It stands up perfectly today, 32 years on, as things appear not to be getting easier, socially or economically, again."

WIRE drew a line in the sand between All Other Rock Bands and themselves in another way: they maintained a literally healthy distance from degeneracy, mistrusting excessive behaviour as much as they did musical excess.

"We've never been very rock'n'roll," admits Graham Lewis. "It's all over, really; it's all been done. We went for art and culture. Besides, we led a far more degenerate life before getting involved with the job of being in a band. After that, there was just too much work to get done, you know?" Lewis reserved particularly harsh judgement for the truly excessively debauched jet-setting superstars of the pre-punk era who, as he saw it, betrayed their talent in favour of drugs and women. "It was pure jealousy!" he laughs. "I liked The Small Faces, and I saw The Faces four times, but Rod Stewart broke my heart when he started hanging out with Brit Ekland and became a prat."

Punk was notoriously amphetamine-fuelled, but Wire didn't do pills or much else on the psychoactive or pharmacological front.

"We found that amphetamines and trying to do a very efficient, sharp gig didn't go together, strangely enough," says Bruce Gilbert. So were Wire the high-minded, abstemious, conceptual rockers offstage as well as on? They were, according to Robert Gotobed. "We didn't get involved in drugs, drink and women, but then we didn't have the sort of success that would put us in that area. Besides, I liked the work. I liked the playing. I liked the practising. I liked learning to improve my playing on my instrument. The rock'n'roll lifestyle just wasn't me. It still doesn't appeal. Illicit intoxicants? I don't use them. I'm very boring. People would say, 'Do you really want to feel the same for the whole day?' Well, I don't mind feeling the same for the whole day. I did try drinking and drumming, and it just made it, well, not impossible, but it didn't help at all. In fact, it was a disaster."

Colin Newman did inhale, at least once or twice, before and during Wire. "I remember somebody gave me something and I smoked it and I lay in my bed because I thought I was going to die. I thought, 'This is absolute crap, and I'm not going to do it any more.' That was his last experiment with drugs, except for the time he sampled some mushrooms, which "kind of helped my creative juices" but which he found "super-weak". And he tried speed on one occasion but he didn't, he says, "get on with it at all. I'm just not speedy enough."

As for more exotic substances, there was no way he was going to go there. "I was absolutely petrified of everything else," he admits. "I wasn't going to touch pills, coke or smack or any of that stuff. I did coke once in my life and it got rid of my headache; I thought that was quite expensive for a headache cure! And I hate people who do coke. I find it's had a terrible effect on virtually every London scene. Once the coke gets in, people turn into bullshitters – it's the maximum bullshit drug. As for the dangerous stuff, I mean, I was just a boy from Newbury, and I've never been into the lifestyle. That's not the reason for being in a band. It's all about doing the music; the art. It's not about, 'I want to get fucked and have sex with groupies' or whatever you're supposed to do, throwing chairs out of hotel room windows. I've never done any of those things. I find that aspect of it somewhat distasteful. Why would you need to? It's just tragic. Billy Idol made a living out of it. It's like, fuck off."

Not surprisingly, with Wire's fondness for all things brutal and minimalist, and their refusal to kowtow to the punks' demand for fast and furious anthems of hate and revenge, they soon found themselves facing hostile audiences, whose macho bonehead contingent considered them cerebral, aloof and pretentious. This was music for the brain, not the groin, or so they assumed.

"The punks hated us right from the beginning," says Newman. "For me it was summed up by somebody in Plymouth who said, 'You can't get a decent pogo going to that – it's too short! Write some fast songs!'" When the band played their first significant date as a four-piece, at the famous Roxy club in London's Covent Garden on April 1, 1977, people thought they were a joke – literally, an April fool. "They thought we were weirdos. We didn't adhere to any of the punk conventions, and they just didn't really like us very much. In the very early days, audiences would stand quite a long way away from us. They wouldn't come to the front. They would stand back in the room. No one would dare come close to the stage. I think they found us quite intimidating, because we made a big noise and I did a lot of shouting. They were trying to work out what they'd done wrong – like, 'Why is that band shouting at me?'"

Lewis has similar memories of alienating audiences with their different kind of tension. He puts it down to the usual fear of The New, of radical ideas and mistrust of convention. "People thought it was incredibly pretentious, and I think that reflects more on the rock media at the time, and of society and its attitudes towards intelligence in this country. At certain times I suffered significant amounts of abuse for it. It was like, for fuck's sake, what is it you want – something obvious? Well, don't come here! It's not that we were doing anything obscure; we just weren't doing anything simple and stupid. Or there again, if we did 'do' simple and moronic, we were really good at it, you know?"

In a way, considers Newman, Wire could do sophisticated and stupid, complicated and moronic: they used simple chord structures and "punk" melodies to convey complex ideas. "Both those things are present in Wire," he says. "There is a combination of the highest sophistication and the completely moronic. As a performer, I'm a complete idiot. I can't really play the guitar and I can't really sing. But maybe that's part of what's so attractive about what we do."

"They described us as 'the death throes of cock-rock'," adds Lewis. "At least we were trying to do something that nobody else was doing. We didn't want to make a noise like anybody else, and I didn't really have six years to throw away so that I could play bass like 'whoever'."

Gilbert and Lewis would later make explicit their disdain for what they called "the classic rock'n'roll machinery" by embarking on a project called Dome, which involved making music described by one source as "lurching mechanical noises infrequently keeping a vague beat". But even at this early stage there was a feeling in the band that the rock business, and the business of making rock music, was somehow absurd and unpleasant.

"There was certainly a desire to expose it for what it was, especially some of the more superficial areas of rock'n'roll," says Gilbert, who admits that the most "rock'n'roll" thing he ever did was get drunk once before a performance and completely forget all the songs. "We knew what we didn't like, and we didn't like rock'n'roll."

"It always seemed to me," adds Lewis, "that punk quickly became a movement or fashion or whatever, and a lot of the impetus for change, the ideas of anarchy in terms of creativity, sort of got lost. But the people, like us, who were around in the beginning understood that, and were not consumed by the fashion."

Because they were different, Wire attracted a different type of punk fan, according to Bruce Gilbert. "There was a small band of people who used to come to hear us and quite enjoyed it, but to be honest, I think we alienated at least 80 per cent of the audience. And even they nearly always seemed quite confused. We attracted serious loners."

They did, however, get their fair share of archetypal pogoing, gobbing punks, as Robert Gotobed recalls. "There was this disgusting flow of spittle coming out of the audience onto the stage. I was at the back, so it didn't reach me, but it certainly reached Colin, the vocalist being the most exposed person there. That was something of a test of our resolve. I don't think Colin caught anything unpleasant, but it was quite degrading. It was horrible, but it was normal. It was expected behaviour."

"The punks didn't like us," confirms Newman. "We were the wrong colour, you know? They thought we were pretentious. We wanted to be art, and 'art-rock' was just a synonym for wanking as far as the majority of the record-buying public was concerned at that point. It was like, 'Stop talking about art.' It was just not considered the right thing at all. We were not loved. In the very early days we would stand onstage and there would be a semi-circle of people pinned up against the back of the wall, and they would just be staring at us. They didn't know what to do.

They didn't know what to make of us. They certainly didn't really like us that much."

Unlike The Clash and their ilk, there was no sense of Wire as one of those quasi-mythical Last Gangs In Town, a bunch of desperados running around creating havoc and/or righting society's wrongs. They were simply four individuals with a similar artistic bent and novel ideas about how to create modern music within the four-piece rock band context.

"I'd been round to Colin and George's flat after the pub for a coffee or whatever, and I kind of half-knew Graham because at that time I was living in Barnet, and I'd seen him walking down the street, and my girl-friend at the time, who was at Hornsey, kind of knew him, and I saw him a couple of times at my local," recalls Bruce Gilbert. "But we weren't really mates. Colin and I basically recruited Graham, and Colin knew this bloke who wanted to play drums, which was Rob, but it wasn't really a social band at all. The only time we ever met was at rehearsals."

"We weren't a gang," agrees Newman. "We were never a gang."

WIRE may not have spent the first few months of 1977 marauding through London, battling imaginary evil authority figures and threatening to destabilise the monarchy, but they were furiously busy, either rehearsing, writing songs or performing live. Sometimes, the members of Wire, despite their strict work ethic, even found time to socialise as London became a hive of cultural activity.

Not that they were right at the punk centre of things – "we were," as Colin Newman states, "very much outsiders." So they didn't hang out with the Bromley Contingent, nor did they join forces with the punks from Watford who would follow the Sex Pistols and The Clash from gig to gig. Nevertheless, they were, as Lewis says, "having an absolutely marvellous time. I mean, I loathed the people in London, and as far as I was concerned, that whole rock-star thing had already finished. That was just dumb. It wasn't a very dignified thing to be involved with. But we were having a great time, watching football, listening to music, going to gigs, going to see films, drinking, going to see reggae bands, going to see fashion shows, going to see art shows, hanging out with people whom we'd gone to art college with: just what we'd always been doing."

It was on one of Lewis' nights out that he found himself invited by rock-writing eminence grise Nick Kent and Nick Cash of punk also-rans 999 to form a band, an offer he politely declined because at this point Wire were making great strides, artistically if not instrumentally.

"We were evolving fast," says Colin Newman. "By the time we appeared at the Roxy the second time [in April '77], our set comprised half of [debut album] *Pink Flag* already."

Their first rehearsals as a four-piece took place in the South London squat occupied by drummer Robert Gotobed, which was "a total shell" but had a waterproof, lockable cellar and was sufficiently soundproofed that they could make a racket, albeit a tightly focused, rigorously methodical racket. Those rehearsals were apparently "terrible" but discipline was eventually applied and the players' limited musical talents were focused towards the creation of pithy song-bursts. It was an artful din that led one journalist at the time to ask, if they couldn't play very well, why the members didn't channel their energies into another field of art than rock?

"It's like any artistic endeavour," replied Lewis. "You can't do it to start off with, and you know that the only way that you're going to be capable of mastering the skills – which enable you to continue even in a small way to start doing something creative – is by hard work. None of us is a stranger to that ethic. Why music? Well, it's the cheapest thing to get into."

Added Newman, "As well as that, music tends to be the most publicised art form at the moment. It is easier for more people to hear music than to see paintings. Plus, there is a certain high you get from playing music – just standing in a room making a noise with an electric guitar is perfectly satisfying."

And so, with the high of performance in mind, the band cracked on, knocking out new songs at an incredible rate. "I had to figure out," recalls Newman, "how to write a lot of songs pretty quick, and it seemed to me that you wouldn't want to be writing the same song over and over again. And you didn't want to be writing songs that sounded like other people's."

Songwriting duties immediately fell to Newman and Lewis (and later to Bruce Gilbert, and even occasionally Robert Gotobed, by the time work began on *Pink Flag*). The former sat in his bedroom in north Watford mainly in charge of melodically concise song construction, while Lewis, stuck in his west Kensington bedsit, attempted to match the melodies to some highly unusual subject matter (for pop music, anyway) and strange idea-fragments – together, Lewis and Newman's collaboration produced songs "as exquisitely etched as a finely honed haiku", as Simon Reynolds describes them in *Rip It Up*. And so was born the Lennon & McCartney of angular post-punk pop.

And yet despite their unorthodox methods, and resistance to the conventions of pop songcraft, the usual reliance on verses, choruses, bridges and refrains, caused some consternation within the band. Newman particularly would drive Lewis mad by cutting and editing the lyrics to suit his melody.

"That's one of the things I've been somewhat reprimanded about," he admits. "Graham used to absolutely hate it because I would put arbitrary divisions in a song, and suddenly a bit was a chorus that hadn't been the chorus, or a line didn't get repeated."

Newman's "singing" style proved an acquired taste, too, barking and declaiming in a blank mockney style that was quite punk, but often overloading words into a song until they were fit to burst.

"We were described as being like a new-wave band fronted by a banker or an accountant, or a lawyer, because the songs were so wordy," he says. "I understood the absurdity of it. But there was also the notion of rage, which we expressed in quite an abstract way. Some of the lyrics are very, very funny; others are dark but still funny. Some were a series of dream images, so the punks would be wondering, 'Why is this man shouting?'"

In a way, agrees Newman, Wire songs were a rejection of all the records he and the band had ever listened to. "I think there was also a rejection of the cod-working-class thing which has always been big in British culture," he explains. "Actually, I am a working-class boy, but as soon as I went to art school, I could not continue to be a working-class boy because I'd entered into a middle-class structure. At that point you become classless in a peculiar kind of way." Wire's ascension towards a kind of elevated state of rootless classlessness became apparent in the other members' contributions, too.

"Graham has a certain amount of personal pomposity which plays very well into the way he expresses himself. And Bruce is kind of a minimalist poet who will come out with a set of words which are on one level quite funny, on another level quite disturbing. As for my lyrical contributions, they were slightly more mundane. I wrote the words to 'Three Girl Rhumba', which really was about three girls.

"In 1976, every band wanted to be the Sex Pistols," he continues. "By 1977, that was really not where anyone needed to be going, and if they were, they were going in the wrong direction. David Bowie [on his 'Berlin trilogy'] was particularly influential, but it was just really about wanting to do something that had more meaning. 'Anarchy In The UK', The Damned's 'New Rose' and Buzzcocks' 'Spiral Scratch' were fantastic records, but most of the rest of the punks' output sounded very similar and wasn't very good. I was never a fan of The Clash. There was nothing about them that really turned me on – it was everything I hated about music: some mouthy bloke going on about stuff that's really obvious."

And so Wire developed the sound and accrued the material for their debut album, not through the usual on-the-road slogging from venue to dingy venue beloved of rock authenticists and purists – they only played 15 gigs between George Gill's departure and September '77, when they began work on *Pink Flag* – but through the process of developing the material for Wire's debut album. And yet when they did play live, they were events of some importance, with a considerable effect on the band's future direction.

The first time they played at the prestigious punk hangout the Roxy, it was January '77 and George Gill was still in the band. That night, by most accounts, they were dreadful, so bad, in fact, that the punk entrepreneur who ran the club, Andy Czezowski, told them not to come back until they had learnt to play, a knock-back that forced the band to re-evaluate what they were doing and come up with the new game plan that led to the expulsion of Gill.

"I was very nervous that night," remembers Robert Gotobed. "As a drummer, just overcoming the physical stress and having no experience… I thought it was necessary to hit everything as hard as possible, and if you try to do that from the beginning of the performance, then your hands just run out of energy; they become useless, and it took a couple of gigs for me to realise that you have to pace yourself."

He also remembers the audience being "boisterous – they didn't just stand there and watch you; they would be shouting out 'boring!' and 'faster!' and 'get off!' and 'rubbish, you're too old!' It wasn't a respectful audience. But I don't think it was malicious."

Newman doesn't remember being nervous, mainly because, as he says, "there were only about three-and-a-half people there for us. How could we be nervous? We'd been in the Roxy before, and we'd seen it full, but not for us. Nobody was very interested."

Graham Lewis has vivid memories of violence breaking out at early Wire gigs, of bottles and glasses flying around and smashing, especially in the provinces. But, despite being unafraid of confrontation, he rarely entered the fray, opting instead for the odd withering one-liner. As he says, "I prefer a good put-down myself."

And yet, despite that debacle of a Roxy debut, Wire were invited back to the West End club on April 1 and 2, 1977, by the club's owner, Barry Jones, after he heard a tape of the new, improved four-piece, just in time for the now-legendary punk festival. Over two nights, and alongside such punk luminaries as Buzzcocks, X-Ray Spex, The Adverts, Eater and Slaughter & The Dogs, Wire performed a set of almost entirely new material, only three songs (the dubious and decidedly un-PC 'Mary Is A Dyke', 'TV' and a frenetic cover of JJ Cale's 'After Midnight') remaining from their first Roxy foray.

On the first night, Wire were bottom of the bill, but by the Saturday night they'd been promoted all the way up the ranks to third-from-bottom! Afterwards, they were £50 richer, and they'd successfully road-tested about 50 per cent of the material, amassed over the previous three or four months, that would comprise their debut album, *Pink Flag*, including the single '12XU' (they climaxed both nights with their version of 'Glad All Over'). There weren't too many people to witness Wire in all their early angular, clipped, dissonant, precise glory – you can just make out a smattering of applause on the live document *The Roxy, London WC2 (Jan-Apr 77)* – but those that did turn up were sufficiently impressed by what they saw and heard to affect Wire's future.

One of those early Wire supporters was journalist Jon Savage, who went to the Roxy to review the gig for *Sounds*. "They short-circuit the audience totally," he wrote, "playing about 20 numbers, most around one minute long. The audience doesn't know when one has finished and another is beginning. I like the band for that... good theatre. Image-wise they look convincingly bug-eyed, flash speed automatons caught in a '64 mod time-warp." Savage warmed to Wire's cold, brutal, short, sharp, shocking anti-punk punk songs such as 'Three Girl Rhumba' and '12XU', describing the latter as "the best of the set". He concluded: "There were glimpses of genuine originality", also noting that "the bassist blew his stack" at a heckler.

Another significant member of the audience at the Roxy on those two era-defining nights was Mike Thorne, who was there to produce the two nights' sets for the live album. Thorne has, in his 30-plus-year career, produced Soft Machine, The Shirts, John Cale, Soft Cell, Nina Hagen, Bronski Beat, Roger Daltrey, Communards, Laurie Anderson, China Crisis, Peter Murphy and Blur, among many others, and in 1977 alone he produced five albums, probably the most significant of them being Wire's own debut, *Pink Flag*. Thorne was also working at EMI Records as an A&R man – included among his charges were the Sex Pistols and Kate Bush.

Thorne was, recalls Bruce Gilbert, "the first proper record industry person that we met. I think he saw something in us. Because we were fairly serious and possibly dour, and we weren't a 'lifestyle' group, I think he thought we might be good for the label. He heard something in the music as well. He knew that we were quite efficient, considering we couldn't play. Well, I couldn't play guitar properly. But he saw something that he could work with."

As soon as he saw Wire at the Roxy, Thorne knew he had to sign them to EMI. He liked their attitude, the fact that they weren't, as Gilbert says, "swearing, gobbing, arrogant teenagers – well, we were certainly arrogant, but pretty self-contained and quiet. We were there to do a job." Like Thorne, Wire looked as though they could hold their own in conversations about things other than rock'n'roll, although his experience behind a studio console would prove useful for Wire. And Thorne could see that Wire, despite their shortcomings, had potential.

"They had the best sound of all the punk bands," he says. "It was very different, much more controlled, slower, even though they did have some fast songs. Buzzcocks had also got their sound together but they had a more frantic, poppy style." Thorne was equally impressed by Wire's anti-image, their wry detachment from the punk hurly-burly. "They liked to stand back and watch the carnage." He made a conscious effort to see the band play live as often as he could. "Throughout my career as a producer I've always made a point of see-ing bands live as much as possible. Wire were good live. They were exciting. You didn't always know what would happen. There was an element of danger as there should be with any performance. They were hanging on for dear life in many ways. But their message came through, and people could jump onstage even if they weren't suavely equipped with musical chops. In 1976, we had been swamped by very capable musicians with good musical technique but not much to say. Wire had things to say even if they did so in an oblique manner. Hostility from crowds was par for the course."

Thorne would discover this to his cost first-hand later on, when he would, as Wire's producer and de facto fifth member, join them onstage as keyboardist. "I played with them onstage for 15 gigs, one time at the Rock Garden in Middlesbrough. It was a flat-out punk crowd, and they were a bit bemused, so the gob was flying. I was at the side of the stage, and my hands kept slipping because my keyboard was covered in spit and beer. Colin came to the mic and said, 'We don't like being spat at' and the crowd stopped spitting, in this rough part of Middlesbrough. He had a commanding presence in the face of adversity. Mind you, when we decided not to do an encore, beer glasses started smashing against the dressing-room door. I think we disappeared to the pub, sharpish."

Thorne remembers the distinct personalities in the band that led to their fruitful, if sometimes tense, sessions and rehearsals, where ideas were exchanged and debates often raged, but it was often hard to work out who was responsible for what in Wire's music.

"They were good and harmonious meetings, such that you often couldn't remember who contributed what," he reveals. "Bruce was older and calmer. Graham and Colin were more volatile, especially Graham. But he and Colin were natural front people. Bruce was the centre half, the calm centre of things. There were furious arguments, about everything. They were very contentious. Fights, too. Robert threw his drum sticks at Graham a couple of times during rehearsals and in the studio. Robert got very good at throwing drum sticks, either from being annoyed at someone else or at himself for not managing to make the right 90mph drum-fill.

"They weren't friends so much as four individuals who came together to create Wire," he adds, "although things certainly became more relaxed once we got down the pub. Thing was, everybody cared about what was going on, and when something's at stake, there are often arguments."

The producer/A&R man could see how much was at stake, and he was able to recognise the rewards they were capable of achieving, so after the Roxy show he immediately approached his boss at EMI, Nick Mobbs (who had signed Pink Floyd and the Sex Pistols and perhaps realised that he had a strange sort of cross between the two with Wire), and suggested the label sign them. Thorne knew the record company would be keen to regain some credibility after the fiasco that was the signing, and subsequent dropping, of the Sex Pistols earlier that year. So the band presented versions of their Roxy recordings, cleaned up at EMI's Manchester Square HQ, to Mobbs as demos. Able to hear beyond the band's musical limitations and visualise their promise, Mobbs agreed to sign them in June '77 to EMI subsidiary Harvest, which had a reputation for being the label's "progressive" offshoot.

"I wanted to sign Siouxsie & The Banshees and Johnny Thunders [formerly of the New York Dolls] but Nick didn't go for either of those," says Thorne. "But he went for Wire."

Newman, for one, was surprised to have elicited such a positive response from such a high-ranking official at rock's premier multinational conglomerate. "When, after the Roxy gig, Mike said, 'You guys are really good,' we went, 'What?!'" But then, in a way, Wire never really seriously considered "going professional".

"I still think of us as willing amateurs as opposed to professional musicians," Newman said at the time. "As long as we retain the idea that we're doing it because we actually enjoy it without any ridiculous motive, we'll keep progressing."

They were becoming professionals in a sense, though: Wire would use their EMI advance to pay themselves a weekly wage – every Friday, they'd meet at the White Lion in Covent Garden and their manager, Mike Collins, would give them £40 each. But they almost didn't sign the deal with EMI because, initially, the company offered Wire a singles deal, which they rejected out of hand because they were only interested in one thing: making unified statements in album form, comprising their own highly varied material (prior to this, Dave Fudger, a journalist and early Wire supporter from *Sounds*, offered to put the money up for a single, which they also turned down).

"EMI asked us if we'd like to make a couple of singles, and we turned that down," says Graham Lewis. "We said no – the idea of putting all your chips on one tune didn't seem like a terribly good idea to us. We didn't want to give a false impression."

Another thing Wire wanted to make absolutely clear from the outset, before they inked the deal with EMI, was that the band would have total control over their output, from music to artwork to marketing. "We don't need Hipgnosis and we don't need nude tarts to sell records," Colin Newman said at the time. "We're not selling sex and drugs."

What they were selling, however, was clear: new music for a new era.

"There were bits of newness around," Newman wrote in *The Independent* newspaper in 2006. "The first Buzzcocks EP, 'Spiral Scratch', was way ahead of anything else. It was stark and minimalist, very hard to understand or decode. When Howard Devoto left the Buzzcocks, I thought, 'We've got the field to ourselves.' The Pistols were just a rock band, in the end. By 1977, it was time to go on to the next thing. People were excited by the energy of punk, but wanted to do something original with it, and in that way, Wire were a post-punk band.

"When we played our first two gigs, at the Roxy in 1977, we were picked up by EMI almost immediately," he continued, hardly surprised three decades on. He knew why: "We sounded like we came from the moon."

Chapter 3

From Punk To Pink

"They called us Cold Wave, New Musik, even Power Pop. But for us, we were just unclassifiable." – Colin Newman

WHEN Wire entered Advision Studios in London's West End in September 1977, barely 12 months after first picking up their instruments, most of punk and new wave's key albums, British and American, had been released, or were about to be. Earlier in the year, The Clash had issued their incendiary, eponymous debut, Elvis Costello released *My Aim Is True,* as did fellow Stiff artist Ian Dury with his band The Blockheads' *New Boots And Panties!!* The Stranglers put out their *Rattus Norvegicus.* The Damned – who had unleashed arguably the first punk single back in October 1976 with 'New Rose' – released their *Damned Damned Damned,* the Sex Pistols' epochal *Never Mind The Bollocks* was but a month away, and The Jam had issued their first LP, while their second, also from 1977, was imminent. Then there was the spate of classic albums from New York's "CBGBs" bands: Television's *Marquee Moon,* Richard Hell & The Voidoids' *Blank Generation,* the Ramones' *Rocket To Russia* and *Leave Home,* Blondie's *Plastic Letters* and Talking Heads' *Talking Heads 77.*

Pre-punk art-rock heroes Brian Eno, David Bowie and Iggy Pop were furiously active throughout 1977: there were Bowie's Eno-enhanced *Low* and *'Heroes'*, Iggy's Bowie-produced *The Idiot* and *Lust For Life* (all four albums recorded at Hansa Studios by the Wall in Berlin), as well as Eno's own *Before And After Science*. There were, in addition, great albums from the world of proto-electronica and synthetic and/or symphonic dance: the genre-defining synthpop of Suicide's eponymous debut; Kraftwerk's staggeringly influential *Trans-Europe Express*, Chic's self-titled debut; Earth Wind & Fire's *All 'n All*; the sequenced throb of Donna Summer's double-LP *Once Upon A Time;* and Summer collaborator Giorgio Moroder's solo album *From Here To Eternity*.

It was a good year, too, for reggae (Bob Marley's *Exodus*, Burning Spear's *Live!*, Junior Murvin's *Police & Thieves*, Culture's *Two Sevens Clash*, The Congos' *Heart Of The Congos*) and funk (Parliament's *Funkentelechy Vs The Placebo Syndrome*, Bootsy Collins' *Ahh… The Name Is Bootsy, Baby!*). It was even, despite the pioneering noisy and experimental work being undertaken elsewhere/everywhere, a great year for MOR, power pop, progressive pop, West Coast neo-psychedelia and mainstream US metal, jazz-rock and pop-rock: Peter Gabriel's *Peter Gabriel*, Blue Öyster Cult's *Spectres*, Steely Dan's *Aja,* Weather Report's *Heavy Weather*, Fleetwood Mac's *Rumours*, Randy Newman's *Little Criminals*, Todd Rundgren and Utopia's *Ra* and *Oops! Wrong Planet*, Shoes' quietly seminal *Black Vinyl Shoes*, Dwight Twilley's *Twilley Don't Mind*, Cheap Trick's eponymous debut and *In Color*, and Spirit's absurdly underrated sci-fi sample-fest *Future Games*… Terrific albums all, and they all came out in 1977.

Wire were oblivious to all of this, even if they would admit that they had been affected by punk as a galvanising force and used it as a catalyst to get started. But when they entered Advision with producer and unofficial "fifth member" Mike Thorne at the controls (aided by engineer Paul Hardiman and assistant engineer Ken Thomas), they weren't particularly, or even remotely, aware of the latest developments in rock, dance, dub or soul (although they were fans of all these types of music), nor were they concerned with the competition or intent on outstripping their peers. They just wanted to make the best album they could, in their own unique way, using the ideas and songs they had been steadily accruing over the previous six months.

In a way, their approach and attitude recalled those of one of their favourite bands from the pre-punk era: 10cc, a four-piece from Manchester who lacked a discernible marketable image and relished their blank anonymity, who rarely gigged (remember, Wire played live precisely 15 times between *Live At The Roxy WC2* and the Advision sessions), and who seemed to put all their energy into, and focus all their talent on, the recording process. The hermetically sealed environs of the studio suited this thoughtful quartet. As one early reviewer noted, "Wire are the first new wave studio band."

Wire had for a while envisaged an album, not a series of singles, as their first major statement of intent. And so singer/guitarist Colin Newman began concocting melodies on an acoustic guitar in his room in north Watford, while bassist Graham Lewis, the other principal songwriter in the band, worked on lyrics at his place in west Kensington. Then the pair would meet up and pass ideas back and forth before the four of them would get together at rehearsals and work the sketches and fragments into songs.

Bruce Gilbert, who played guitar and brought a key sense of the absurd to the table, as well as Wire's all-important minimalist aesthetic, also contributed melodic and lyrical ideas. Drummer Robert Gotobed, too, no stranger to sardonic humour himself, received compositional credit on the sleeve of their debut album, keen as the band were to preserve a sense of democracy, to add to the idea of the band as a unit, but also to retain an aura of mystery with regard to the genesis of the songs. As Mike Thorne says, "The sign of a good group is that it is hard to work out who exactly does what, and it was definitely that way with Wire."

"The majority of the songs were written by Colin and Graham," admits Gilbert, who also points to the band's use of the "oblique strategies" employed by Bowie and Eno in Berlin during writing. "Graham would give Colin lyrics and Colin would come to the next rehearsal with a song sketched out. I did a couple of things on my own, sort of random chord progressions. It was like throwing dice, and from time to time we'd do quite a lot of lyric experiments and writing with Graham, passing a notebook backwards and forwards, alternating the lines."

Gotobed doesn't believe Wire were actually ready to make anything as daunting as a whole long-playing record by autumn 1977, although he puts this down more than anything to a lack of confidence on his own part.

"I didn't think I knew enough of what I was doing to actually record our set," he admits. "I thought we ought to wait until we were better. But we started meeting Mike Thorne, and we did demos, and that gave us a doorway into recording with a record company. But for me, personally, it just seemed like it was happening too quickly. I mean, the group had only been going for a year, and we were still learning to play, and now somebody wanted us to record an album! But I don't think anybody else in the group was saying, 'No, let's practise longer until we can play.' Maybe they had a higher opinion of my playing than I did."

The sight of the "expensive, purpose-built studio" that was Advision did little to allay Gotobed's fears. "It was my first time in a serious studio; we'd only done the demos before. I didn't know what we were doing, and I hoped it was all going to work out all right in the end. We weren't established in any way." It wasn't as though Wire had a solid cult following at this early stage in their development. "You'd expect to have the support of an audience before you make your first album, but the number of Wire fans that we had was, well, small at this point. We weren't established.

"For me there was a lot of anxiety," he continues. "I think there was anxiety within the group as well."

Because of their limited technical and instrumental abilities, the band were free to explore new musical territories without fear of being hidebound by convention or tied to traditional song structures. The absence of prior technical ability in Wire produced a "ground level" on which to build together. This was opposed to, say, three or four musicians forming a band and trying to reach a compromise of styles. They already knew how they wanted to proceed. But it also meant the album took longer to record than they imagined: six weeks in all, a month and a half of painstaking recording and re-recording.

"In the first couple of days we played that set about 20 times," Gilbert said in *Mojo* magazine in 2006. "And I hesitate to say I may have been chemically altered, but I was completely convinced we'd finished the album. I said, 'That's as good as it's ever going to get – you must have it now?!'"

"And," added Newman, with a laugh, "they're still sorting out the bass drum sound!"

Wire, says Gilbert, made considerable leaps during that period. "We learnt a lot in those six weeks. Playing the songs over and over again in quick succession was quite a learning curve." He explains the recording process thus: "Basically the strategy was to get down a good basic drum track and a good rhythm track – something to build on, you know. That was the strategy. Then we'd add a guide vocal and build on that."

The guitarist doesn't remember the songs changing much in the studio. "We nailed the intros fairly early on, and of course we'd multi-track the guitars to make them sound chunkier [what Newman refers to as 'textural thickening' in his sleeve notes to the 2006 CD reissue of *Pink Flag*]. And the backing vocals were developed and became more sophisticated. But [the songs] were more or less there. I'm amazed we didn't actually write any new songs in the studio. It felt a bit odd playing the same thing over and over again instead of actually writing new ones at some point." Overall, he was impressed by what they were capable of achieving, having been little more than amateurs when it came to playing their respective instruments. "When the mixing process started and we started hearing how things were locking together, I suppose I might have felt, 'Oh my God, we've got away with this one.'"

Gilbert recalls the sessions being both light-hearted and intense. "There were times when people got a bit anxious. But I think it was mostly light-hearted, and of course very interesting as well." Thorne recalls the period as being "all very sociable", with lots of trips to the pub, although he concedes that "things only got tense when we thought there was something at stake". He remembers trying to lighten the atmosphere, alleviate nerves and generally get the band going on day one in the studio via a jam-jar full of weed. As he recollected in a 2000 essay for his website, The Stereo Society: "The first day was thrown away in the interests of settling in comfortably and getting the sound. Assisted over the day by a prodigious amount of home-grown, Wire played all 21 tracks, and felt at home. It [the marijuana] floated nicely through the day, and all their studio fright was gone."

"I seem to remember there were some substances, yes," agrees Gilbert. "Liquid and otherwise…" Not that Advision had anything resembling a party vibe. "I think there was an occasional visit from a record-company type, but I don't think there was much of a social scene going on." Nor did the studio become a drop-in centre for EMI employees eager to see how their new charges were getting on. "They gave the impression that they wanted a pet punk group to scrape back some credibility [after dropping the Sex Pistols], but they didn't come to see us."

Wire were never going to be a conventional punk group. They were even less likely to fit the mould of a pop group, as Gilbert explains. "We stated our intentions at a very early stage because the very first thing they offered us was a three-singles deal, which we turned down flat. There was absolutely no way on earth. We were there to do an album. We weren't going to be a pop group. This was a group that wanted to make, you know, Big Things."

But that didn't necessarily mean Big Songs with big solos and big, stadium-friendly arrangements. "Brevity and severity," wrote Simon Reynolds in *Rip It Up And Start Again*, "became Wire's hallmarks, as heard on *Pink Flag*, which crams 21 compressed bursts of abstract fury into just 35 minutes." Reynolds praises the harsh, forbidding beauty of Wire's music: the "brutal elegance" of their power chords and riffs, and the way you could "practically visualise" the music as "clean lines, deliberate spacings and blocs of texture". Excuses for extemporisation and extrapolation were just not taken, a decision based on aesthetic principles as much as technical restrictions. "There's no way on earth I could have played a solo in the classic form," says Gilbert. "I think there were a couple of non-solo solos. The trouble was, we knew what we didn't like, and we didn't like solos because they tended to dissipate the tension and the strength of the song."

Many of Wire's songs clocked in at the one or two-minute mark: brevity was a guiding principle, an aesthetic decision. Songs ended when the band ran out of steam, or felt they had fulfilled what they wanted to achieve on that particular track. "A coverall statement is that an idea is only worth as much as it is worth, which in part explains why something is only a certain length," Newman said at the time, citing the 28-second 'Field Day For The Sundays' as an example. "It's almost just a thought, a very sort of monochrome thing. It's just about one thing. It would be pointless to dwell on certain things, once you've made a statement about something. That also applies to the writing of the songs, to not duplicate.

"There are guitar solos on the album, which accentuate a certain point so they're necessary to that degree," he continued. "You have got to be able to see the idea because the song is about the idea." They eschewed formula at every turn. "What seems to be usual with rock-'n'roll is that there are certain things that get written about in terms of words and then in terms of tunes. It seems to be that those themes require certain types of tunes. If it's a song about being on the road and getting drunk it has a certain Rock Beat. It's just like formula. I'm certainly not interested in that sort of area. I try and remain as open as possible."

"The songs are short because they're not long," Lewis added, appropriately succinctly.

Fortunately, Mike Thorne was on their side every step of the way. Newman appreciates Thorne's contribution. "He was a wacky guy who fancied himself as a bit of a George Martin, but we didn't know how to make a record and he allowed us to learn."

Gilbert's memories of Thorne's input on *Pink Flag* are of the producer as useful foil for their ideas. He also had a lucky box of tricks – gadgets and gizmos to enhance Wire's music. "He was very, very helpful and very sympathetic, and he had toys as well, which was very good. My first distortion box was something I made myself using a tobacco tin, so seeing these shiny American sound-boxes and stuff was very exciting. And of course I had a real guitar for the first time – actually playing a real guitar not from Woolworths was quite exciting.

"It was mostly distortion boxes," he adds, remembering some of the devices brought to bear on the band's sound. "I can't remember whether Graham might have used a flanger on *Pink Flag* or on [second album] *Chairs Missing*. But we were really getting into effects, pedals and stuff by the end of the *Pink Flag* recordings. I think there was quite a lot of purchasing of stuff. Because we'd heard what was possible in a studio with studio effects, and we all felt that we could have some fun and really extend our tonal range and textures."

As Thorne details on www.stereosociety.com, "to help the group's sound, I augmented my collection of guitars and amps, so that the sessions had a most non-punk Les Paul Pro guitar and a Music Man combo amp. The group had replaced their collapsing Roxy equipment, and Colin had bought himself a new Ovation electric guitar in white, which we all agreed looked very nice on him. Also for me was a Yamaha electronic piano tuner, £500 for something that is £50 now. Contrary to what you might expect of the staple punk sound, those big, distorted guitar sounds have to have an in-tune instrument, otherwise the power is gone."

Rupturing the sense of splendid isolation and self-containment during the *Pink Flag* sessions was the occasional extra musician brought in to add a dash of colour, much like the solitary dash of pink on the otherwise monochrome album sleeve. There was someone called Dave Oberlé on backing vocals on 'Mannequin', and Kate Lukas, who added experimental alto flute textures to 'Strange', a track later covered by Wire acolytes R.E.M. It was Thorne's idea to invite Lukas, "a virtuoso and performer of tough contemporary art music in London at the time", to play on the song, but presumably it was Thorne himself who chose to multi-track the instrument several (actually, 10) times, making each a semitone apart, to achieve the disconcerting effect – an odd warbling sound like seagulls in distress; or, as Thorne puts it, "a completely uncategorisable noise". The producer, unconcerned that a flute might have repelled punk hardliners, regrets not placing the studio-mutated sound further upfront in the mix. "As with many of the tracks, I wish we had been more aggressive and blatant in the mixing, so that events like this were more in your face, or changed the contour of the recording more assertively." Vocals, he points out, were kept similarly low in the mix, "in deference to the chainsaw guitar sound and the punk style of the time".

Thorne recalls the sessions in some detail on The Stereo Society. "Unlike the normal, clinically regulated sessions typical of the time, Robert's drums were placed in the middle of the large studio, to hear real ambience. Colin was isolated in the booth where the drums might have been. The group could hear each other and converse, not a possibility on contemporary super-sessions where the musicians were isolated, cut off from each other in the interests of the sound itself.

"Some of the songs stretched them to their technical limit. '12XU', remade after its appearance on the Roxy album, took several takes to get, hanging on by the fingertips, and it shows wonderfully. Both Colin's introduction and his vocal are live. Lou Piñada, the owner of the café near their Thorne Road rehearsal space and dedicatee of the song, would have been proud. Singing songs with that intensity, going for a live take every time [all vocals are the live original except for 'Strange' and parts of 'Lowdown'], is a real testament to their latent competence. Colin applied himself heroically, taking a sip of water before every take after he had found out that it brightens up your voice timbre. There were lots of visits to the toilet. Southern Comfort was also applied medicinally, and he would emerge with bloodshot eyes to scare us at the end of a particularly intense day [Gotobed also remembers Newman becoming, via this method, 'increasingly pissed'].

"My best contribution to 'Strange'," Thorne continued, "is the clattering you hear taking the track out. Late in the session, it seemed that some banging would complement the wind-down, so I took Robert's drum sticks and did a soundcheck on the fire escape door at the back of the studio. I still remember clearly where I hit the door, the shape of it, and the lighting at the time. Three tracks of manic banging and the cut was finished. The group in the control room thought I'd gone crazy, and I thanked them for the compliment when they told me later."

Thorne considers the *Pink Flag* sessions to have been "not technically great – they were aspiring musicians", but believes some of the performances, such as the one for '12XU', to have been "immaculate". Then again, despite having previously worked with the likes of Deep Purple and Fleetwood Mac, he was never overly concerned with virtuoso prowess. "I never think about musicianship," he says, "just the music. And my function in the studio was to get that down on tape, and to work round the obstacles." The obstacles on *Pink Flag*, he says, included the fact that this was, when all's said and done, "a brand new sound". He credits engineer Hardiman for the quality of the sound on *Pink Flag* and its two successors, *Chairs Missing* (1978) and *154* (1979). But he baulks at the notion of giving that sound an appropriate new name, such as prog-punk, or krautrock-thrash. "If someone had come up with a stylistic appellation like that they'd have been thrown out. For me, the job of a creative producer is simply to get the clues the band have to offer and to conjure a sound out of that. My job was to refine, not define, their sound, and get good performances out of them."

This, he says, is in direct contrast to producers who bring their own sound to bear on a job. An auteur he is not. "I always looked at the band," he insists. "It's their ideas. The producer provides the support system. You just want to enhance and exaggerate what they do." His favourite moments from the sessions were, he says, "always the most intense ones", like 'Strange' and the title track, which was so heavy they all had to take a break and go out for dinner before Gotobed felt able to deal with the pressure. And the fire-escape incident remains uppermost in his mind when asked to recall Great Moments. "It was just a completely intuitive gesture."

It wasn't all japes and adventures in stereo recording *Pink Flag*, however. "Tempers were often frayed," wrote Colin Newman in the CD reissue sleeve notes, "as a take had to be re-taken because of a mistake by one or other member."

Today, Newman sums up the atmosphere in the studio at the time in one word: "Difficult."

"It was difficult," he explains, "because we hadn't played a lot of gigs. This was not a band that had been on the road for five years. We got our record deal then we went into the studio. Some of the material had only been written the week before, you know? Rob was not confident and nervous. You always had this situation where Graham would decide that Robert had made a mistake and would stop playing, and then Robert would get really pissed off because he didn't think he had made a mistake, and it was up to Mike to say if a mistake had been made. It was old-school recording: basically, you needed to get the bass and the drums recorded; the guitars were really just there for vibe, and you could always replace them later; the same goes for the vocals. But you can't replace the bass and the drums: they had to be solid and the right speed all the way through. It was absolutely miserable. I hated it. It was bad-tempered and fractious, and very, very hard work to get it down. It certainly wasn't very relaxed. We weren't good enough at playing to relax into it. It was about the songs and the ideas.

"Mike had this old-school approach. He'd be like, 'Right, if we're going to do 'Strange' we need the right kind of mood', and we'd go out and have a curry. I don't know if anybody makes records like that any more. It was our exposure to the big stage. We had to be serious. We had to get it right."

According to Newman, there were occasions during recording when things got so fraught that drum sticks would start being hurled around the studio. "It was always going to happen. Mike and Paul Hardiman, the engineer, used to get underneath the mixing board, even though it had glass in between, and the sticks used to go flying across the room." Because they provided that all-important rhythmic base for the songs, the biggest source of tension was the musical relationship between Lewis and Gotobed. "They had to get it right," stresses Newman. "And remember with Rob, the first thing he did when we formed was to tell us he had access to a drum kit, but he never claimed to be a drummer. So it was hard for him. He felt like he wasn't up to it, and there are still bits on *Pink Flag* that make him wince, that he feels he didn't play right, and it doesn't really matter what anybody else thinks."

Gotobed does indeed wince at the memory of those *Pink Flag* sessions and the six weeks at Advision. "Anxiety would come out in the form of disagreement," he says, recalling the almost forensic scrutiny afforded every performance on every track. "You'd go into the control room and everything that you'd played would be put under a microscope; every instrument would be separated out and listened to over headphones. We had never done that before.

"Recording studios were for people who were experienced in those surroundings, and they know how to work under those conditions," he says. "If you've got people in the studio who have only played live and have next to no recording experience, and little experience on their instrument either, it's sort of asking a lot, really. But somehow it worked."

INDEED it did. Eventually, the band overcame all the difficulties they'd faced, made a virtue out of their limitations, and produced the last classic album of 1977 (it was released in December that year).

The front cover of *Pink Flag*, its bold, simple design credited to BC Gilbert and Graham Lewis, featured a pink flag atop a white pole in the ground, against a pale wash of blue. The band spotted it in the west of England on their way to a gig, a parade ground with a flagless pole and a suggestively curving ground that seemed to fall away to nothing. A photo of the pole and a slap of paint led to the creation of a bold, powerfully simple yet enduring image – the sleeve has not dated one jot.

It reflected the contents of the album. *Pink Flag* featured one short, sharp shock of melodic noise after another. It might not have been a concept album as such, but it felt like one. Its 21 tracks, ranging from the 28-second 'Field Day For The Sundays' to the near four-minute long 'Strange', lasted a total of 35 minutes, giving it a compressed, highly charged air, and making it seem like a statement of artful concision as well as a declaration of the importance of economy and an implicit criticism of over-indulgence.

Mike Thorne denies that the album was a theoretical exercise, but concedes that, musically and lyrically, it was an oblique affair. "The words and music," he says, "were both crucial. You can't separate them."

"Anything is possible," Colin Newman said at the time, "just expect anything. Ideas are always occurring to all of us."

The album showed that the group did not have too much trouble adapting to the recording studio. The dense, deft production ensured maximum impact, right from the first moments of opening track 'Reuters', where tolled-bell guitar chimes buckled under an oppressive sheet of doomy guitar.

Wire were progressive while at the same time pushing minimalism to new heights. *Pink Flag* was complex but offered the simple pleasures of volume and power. Each of its 21 tracks was self-contained and distinct, and yet, although all but one of them had lyrics, they were more like idea-fragments than fully-formed songs – capsule visions spoken or shouted or sung over a combination of guitar, bass, drums and keyboards. Despite their length, each track required many plays before you could remember their tune. There were no easy structures or rhythms here. Each track challenged the listener. It was far from easy listening, but neither was it a joyride for punks: you'd start a pogo, only to be forced to abruptly stop when the track came juddering to a halt after a matter of seconds.

Pink Flag was many things, but perhaps above all it was a triumph of

Wire, photographed on December 10, 1978. Clockwise from bottom left:
Colin Newman, Robert Gotobed, Graham Lewis and Bruce Gilbert. (JILL FURMANOVSKY)

Overload, featuring members of Wire, June 1976, (l-r): Angela Conway, Petra, Bruce Gilbert, Ron West, Colin Newman and George Gill. **(COURTESY OF BRUCE GILBERT)**

Wire, with George Gill in the stripy jacket, February 1977. **(COURTESY OF BRUCE GILBERT)**

The fab four at London's Nashville, December 5, 1977. (PAUL SLATTERY)

Wire, the New Romantic Years, 1977. (COURTESY OF COLIN NEWMAN)

Wire, live at CBGB's, New York, July 1978. (EUGENE MERINOV)

Wire celebrate being in New York, 1978. (EBET ROBERTS/REDFERNS)

Live in Brussels, Belgium. February 4, 1979.
(PHILIPPE CARLY/NEWWAVEPHOTOS.COM)

Live at the Jeanetta Cochrane Theatre, London, 1979.
(ANNETTE GREEN)

Colin backstage in Brussels, February 4, 1979. (PHILIPPE CARLY/NEWWAVEPHOTOS.COM)

Wire circa 1979. **(ANNETTE GREEN)**

Live at the Electric Ballroom, London, February 1980. **(STEVEN RICHARDS/RETNA)**

Colin circa *Provisionally Entitled The Singing Fish*, 1982. (ANNETTE GREEN)

Colin auditions for a power pop combo in Amsterdam, Holland, December 18, 1985. (LEX VAN ROSSEN/REDFERNS)

Wire surrogates The Ex Lion Tamers, opening for Wire at the old Ritz in the East Village, New York, 1976; l-r: Jim DeRogatis, Mick Hale, John Tanzer and Pete Pedulla. (JIM DEROGATIS)

critical thinking over musicianship, and a masterpiece of editing, as Colin Newman acknowledges.

"It was all about what you don't do," he says. "Editing is a very strong thing in art. It's one thing that I've discovered over the years. You can do anything you like, really. But it's what you choose not to do that is what counts the most. It's what you take out."

The album realised Newman and Lewis' dream of combining the moronic with the intelligent, and much as they mistrust the term "cerebral", the 21 bursts of noise were simultaneously brainy and boneheaded. It had the impact of the most brutal punk, but it felt like an intellectual exercise, as though at any given moment they could break away and head off in an avant-classical or free-jazz direction.

Pink Flag was seriously stoopid. And yet it was a level above the conceptually dumb antics of New York's favourite scuzzy sons. It has been said that Wire were "simultaneously raw and detached with a rock'n'roll irony grimmer and more frightening than Ramones". In a way, Wire's first album was the obverse of Da Brudders' cartoon dementia and bubblegum nihilism, even if it did have a similar unified feel to that band's landmark 1976 debut. Only instead of songs about sniffing glue, beating up brats and girls called Sheena – really just punk-age variants on escapist thrills, teen violence and adolescent heartbreak – on *Pink Flag* Wire were offering a new way of looking at the world, through songs that suggested a new type of intelligence at work, and a whole new range of subject matter, or at least new formulas for established ideas.

Sometimes conventional lyrical ideas were subverted due to the musical context; other times, a three-chord drone suddenly sounded alien and strange because of the unusual words, unexpected juxtapositions or odd images that accompanied it. Overall, standard punk thrash rage was abstracted to the point where a sense of intellectual distance was achieved, as well as a sort of thematic unity.

Here were songs about suspicion of the media ('Reuters', 'Field Day For The Sundays'), terror of sex ('Lowdown') and loathing of conformity ('Mr Suit'). 'Surgeon's Girl', a comment on media illusions of beauty, highlighted the difference between the glossy version of female pulchritude presented in magazines and the real thing. Even when they sang about love ('Feeling Called Love'), because it appeared in an environment as chilling and forbidding as *Pink Flag*, not to mention the grinding 'Louie Louie'/'Wild Thing' chords, it felt like a savage critique of romance. 'It's So Obvious' was almost their statement of intent in reverse – they avoided the obvious at every musical and lyrical turn.

The band talked about the musical and lyrical content of *Pink Flag* at the time in an interview with Kris Needs of *Zigzag* magazine. 'Feeling Called Love', they explained, had a riff you've heard many times before, deliberately so for this subversion of romance. The menacing album opener, 'Reuters' ("This is your correspondent, running out of tape, gunfire's increasing, looting, burning, rape"), was about, explained Lewis, a war correspondent witnessing "the degeneration" that occurs during conflict. 'Field Day For The Sundays' concerned the red-tops' love of scandal. The album's explosive final track, '12XU' ("Saw you in a mag, kissing a man"), was about "cottaging" and, explained Bruce Gilbert, "sexual exertion" in general. "If you see your boyfriend kissing a man, if you see your girlfriend kissing a man... It could be a woman or a boy. That was my line." Newman said of the song's title: "It was a joke about censoring. Lots of people were putting out records with 'fuck' on them and immediately getting banned."

The music on Pink Flag felt like rock reduced to its bare essentials, even if there was actually more layering, overdubbing and multi-track-ing than initially met the ear (but no rocking out, and no key changes – none of those rock'n'roll clichés and excuses for excess). "Of course, if you listen to it now, there's loads of ornamentation on it," says Newman, "but it was, at the time, as minimal and stark as you could get." Many of the individual tracks on *Pink Flag* kick-started whole new pop and rock movements, from early Eighties US hardcore punk to mid-Nineties Britpop. Despite its poor commercial showing, it had a tremendous impact on serious music fans. 'Ex Lion Tamer' would later inspire an American band to form and call themselves The Ex Lion Tamers with the express intention of playing nothing but *Pink Flag* in its entirety every night. And 'Three Girl Rhumba' so appealed to Britpop band Elastica that they "borrowed" the melody for their 1994 hit, 'Connection'. Even if Wire didn't chart themselves with *Pink Flag*, they could perhaps derive some solace from the fact that they were providing other musicians with the opportunity to have successful careers themselves.

Pink Flag was stripped-down and simple yet rich in detail, such as the handclaps and bubbling bass on 'Champs'. It was also a feat of "deceit". Many of the tracks could, heard fleetingly, pass as standard-issue upbeat punk-pop. 'The Commercial', opening side two, was a breezy instrumental that, even lacking lyrics as it did, had about it a sense of the band critiquing, as did many of their punk peers, our increasingly consumerist culture. The lyric to 'Mr Suit' was barked out at warp speed, like a parody of punk disdain and aggression. 'Mannequin' was another deceptively lightweight would-be pop single (it actually was issued as a 45) with a "la-la-la" chorus and benign harmonies that belied the lyrical barbs within ("You're a waste of space"). Newman described the lyric as "a deliberate ploy" to contrast music and lyric, form and content. "Before you realised what the words were you could hum the tune," he said, adding that he intended to sing it (in his customary sardonic mock-cockney) "with half a smile", but only sometimes. "Other times I want to sing it straight. It is ambiguous. Someone wrote about the 'ridiculous surfing harmonies' – they're supposed to be ridiculous. They're apt."

Finally, the title track was, they said, "incredibly nebulous" despite Newman's blank drone of "how many dead or alive?". It was, with its single chord and insistent beat, the musical equivalent of "banging your head against a brick wall". It was designed as an experiment to see whether you could rewrite 'Johnny B Goode' based solely on one chord. "We can play E for hours," they joked.

Looking back at *Pink Flag*, Wire are happy to pick the album apart, still fascinated by the processes that led to its successful creation. "Process" is a very Wire word; they use it a lot. There is a sense of exacting methodology throughout *Pink Flag*, as though they were, under strict scientific conditions, producing something spontaneous, raw and wild. "There were conscious principles behind all of the album's songs," as Newman wrote in *The Independent* in 2006. In fact, one of the tracks, '106 Beats That', was the result of a failed attempt by Lewis to write a lyric containing only 100 syllables – it actually contains 106 but, as Lewis has said, "That doesn't matter, because you've created a process." According to Simon Reynolds in *Rip It Up And Start Again*, Lewis and Bruce Gilbert "would play absurdist games with sense and nonsense, narrative and fragmentation" – 'Ex Lion Tamer' started out as being about a lion tamer before Lewis got bored of the lyric and removed all the bits he didn't like, hence the title. He and Gilbert used words as "material to be manipulated"; they were "dismembering sequential narrative" to encourage "kaleidoscopic perceptions", thereby mirroring "the fractured way in which we experience reality".

"There was something very, very contrived about punk, and it was something that needed to be passed beyond, so we had the idea of having lyrical content that was not really specific, that was more evocative than anything," explains Newman today. "Take *Pink Flag* and the lyric about, 'How many dead or alive in 1955?' Apart from being the year after I was born, it's not a meaningful year. I wasn't singing 'my girlfriend left me' or 'let's smash the system' or any of the popular topics for young men to write songs about. The meaning was more open. I really liked that notion. The meanings weren't obvious. And the way I delivered them would further obscure the meaning."

This obfuscation, this blurring of meaning, was the opposite of the music and its panoply of riffs and drones, which sounded like rock as a series of quadratic equations or mathematic principles, or a clean, clear diagram of rock'n'roll. 'Lowdown', for example, was like a brainiac notion of funk – funk deconstructed, reduced to arithmetic and formula.

"If you speed it up," suggests Newman, "it's like [late-Seventies disco group Heatwave's] 'Boogie Nights' or something like that. It's getting into disco territory. It was supposed to take the funk out of funk – to slow down classic funk till it was a dirge, the unfunkiest thing you can have. It was quite deliberate. We always had this concept of the distorting mirror: 'Let's just take this and turn it by 73 degrees or something, so it's really not recognisable any more, but its roots can be seen by anyone who can understand it.'

"That," he says, attempting to explain Wire's appeal to other bands, "is probably why musicians like us, because they can see those things, and people who aren't musicians can't so easily see them because they don't deconstruct it in the same way."

After the album was completed, all that remained was to come up with an appropriate running order. Again, while many bands might just place the potential hit singles at the top and allow the other songs to fall into place behind them, there was a greater sense of scheme and strategy behind the running order of *Pink Flag*.

"We gathered at my flat in Stockwell opposite the Thorne Road rehearsal space and hashed out a running order, thrashed it out, depending on context," recalls Mike Thorne. "This wasn't a standard album where you record 12 songs, drop the two weakest and then rearrange the survivors into the most effective running order. The songs needed context, so we sat for an afternoon in my basement and emerged with the two sides' running order. We gave each song a clear sense of where it belonged."

There was, as per the custom of the day, a lunchtime playback for the album at Advision, to which were invited some 50 or so EMI employees. Newman vividly recalls the sound of the album pouring out of the giant speakers. "It just sounded massive. Absolutely fucking massive. I just went, 'Fucking hell.' It pinned them to the back wall. There was this sheer visceral roar of noise coming out of the speakers. It was very, very exciting."

Thorne doesn't remember everyone at EMI being supportive, especially of the singlemindedly dense, heavy production. "One comment from an engineer at Abbey Road, provoked by mastering engineer Chris Blair's playing him this 'interesting new thing', was that it was 'the worst sound' he had 'ever heard'. Oh well, You can't please everybody, as they say."

On the contrary: *Pink Flag* pleased almost everybody who reviewed it for the all-important music press. "Wire are a challenge," wrote *Trouser Press*. "Just like Roxy Music were a challenge. Just like King Crimson were a challenge. Just like the Pistols are a challenge. Just like The Clash are a challenge." "The album has a scale and feel of its own," concluded *Sounds'* Dave Fudger at the end of a five-star review. "It is totally unique. I can't recommend it enough. It's not like anything you've heard and it'll leave its mark for a long time." *Melody Maker* considered it "brilliant, compelling and ambitious, often weird, occasionally bewildering, and obscure as the band are." The *NME* reviewer offered veiled praise: "Wire are disciplined and controlled pseudo-intellectuals, a heartless, contemptuous symptom of the times." Of all the weekly music papers, only *Record Mirror* wasn't impressed, complaining that the album was "a staccato wasteland with stereotypical lyrics".

Colin Newman remembers the album getting mixed reviews and journalists being confused by *Pink Flag*'s contents. "For us, we were just unclassified at that point," he says. "I think they called us the Cold Wave. Everyone said it sounded cold and hard, but we just thought it sounded like the songs. Some reviews said, 'This record is going to be important for a very long time.' Others didn't get it at all. I don't think *Pink Flag* is the best Wire record. But it was a breakthrough for the medium. And it was a breakthrough for us." And yet he could see its impact from the moment the album was finished. "We could see its influence, even in 1977 – not in London, but in the North," he says. "Joy Division were very influenced by us. Live, I had a dance that was very jerky, the furthest I could get from Rod Stewart. Ian Curtis developed those mannerisms. And [Sheffield's] Cabaret Voltaire told us, 'You're the only band in Britain that means anything.' They liked the fact that an experimental attitude was being taken. It was a signal that they could move on from punk. And, of course, by 1978, punk's leading lights were going into the same area we were, such as Public Image Ltd. If John Lydon hadn't heard any Wire records, I'd be very surprised."

Mike Thorne acknowledges the ambivalent reception for the album, but sees *Pink Flag* as not just the first step towards a new future for rock – post-punk – but as the record that opened up new vistas for Wire. "You never seem to know that you're doing something enduring at the time," he says. "The review polarity between five-star accolades and rabid put-downs showed we'd at least got under someone's skin, but you never know how long the rash might persist.

"The album captures Wire at the point of metamorphosing from assimilated punks – with the sound and stance that gave them birth and life – to the experimentalists who emerge from the chrysalis on their second album, *Chairs Missing*."

Chapter 4

Practice Makes Perfect

"EMI saw us as the next Pink Floyd, a band with a left-field attitude who could be successful without hit singles. But it didn't happen, did it?" – Robert Gotobed

PINK Flag didn't just get rave reviews in the British press, who hailed it as a punk-age masterpiece, one that, in fact, suggested new ways out of the trad-punk mire as 1978 loomed. It also, slowly but surely, began to seep its way into the American rock underground's consciousness. If anything, Wire's reputation in the US today outstrips even their one back home.

Meanwhile, back in December 1977, the band were given their first prestigious *NME* front cover, bearing the headline, "No pun(k)s please, we're Wire". In the feature, under another bold heading, this one, "We Are Not Showroom Dummies!", journalist Phil McNeill examined the band's reputation for cold dispassion on a par with the original men-machines, Kraftwerk: "Phil McNeill," ran the wry, humorous standfirst, "discovers that Wire are not just three robots and a mannequin, but actual human beings with Bodily Functions and Emotions and that."

In the article itself, McNeill emphasised the band's apartness from the throng, describing them as having "no concern for stock punk themes like politics, for quintessential rock'n'roll and the pop sensibility and all that stuff.

"Wire," he claimed, "are unique among the major bands to emerge in 1977 because they have 'made it' on their music alone. Unlike any other new 'stars', they've got absolutely nothing going for them except their music. No image, no charisma, no mystique, no following, no gimmicks, and virtually no press.

"Wire," he concluded, "are different."

It was Wire's very artful blankness that set them apart and saw them transcend the times from which they sprang, untied to fashion or music dictates. In the process, they have become one of those once-in-a-generation bands who endure and exert an influence that far exceeds their commercial impact and the numbers of records they sell. *Sounds* writer Jon Savage may have called them "the jokers in the pack" and meant it as a compliment, but really, it is their seriousness of intent and enigmatic aloofness, with a twin sense of the dislocating nature of modern life and absurdity of existence, not to mention their somehow minimalist yet layered and textured noise, that has seen them tagged "the Velvet Underground of the late-Seventies".

Now, the same claim has been made of Gang Of Four, and it's no coincidence that, of all the bands to emerge from punk, it is Wire and the Leeds' funk-rock radicals who have earned the highest renown in alt.rock circles, especially in the States. They both eschewed image and "attitude" to focus on the creation of a startlingly original sound that has seen legions of copyists trailing in their wake. Indeed, in the *Alternative Record Guide* put out by America's *Spin* magazine in 1995, the two highest-ranking records in their Top 100 by British acts were *Pink Flag* at number 12 and Gang Of Four's *Entertainment!* at number 15, ahead of seminal albums by Buzzcocks, The Clash, The Sex Pistols, PiL, X-Ray Spex, Elvis Costello, Joy Division, New Order, U2, even David Bowie and Roxy Music.

"The Velvet Underground of the Seventies, Wire has sometimes been called," wrote *Spin*'s Eric Weisbard in the *Alternative Record Guide*, "for those 'What Goes On' fans who finally worship punk most for the dynamic capacities of its outwardly ugly, secretly beautiful sound. English punk produced no finer document than the band's debut, *Pink Flag*. Art schoolers to the bone, the quartet turned punk rage into one of the fine arts – even garage purists would have a hard time denying their melodies and AC/DC-calibre power chords, played at a Ramones tempo with an Eno/Roxy Music coating over the guitars. Singer Colin Newman is able to be achingly tuneful and still convey Johnny Rotten contempt. Crazed but clean, DIY with nothing out of place, Wire were an aesthete's dream of the incendiary."

Meanwhile, *The Trouser Press Guide To '90s Rock* parroted the oft-repeated line, originally courtesy Brian Eno, about the Velvets not selling many records but everyone who did buy them went out and formed a band, and applied it to Wire, going on to place them in that superior class of experimental avant-rock extremists alongside Captain Beefheart, Roxy Music, Can, Eno and, yes, the Velvets.

Graham Lewis is nonchalant about Wire's position in the scheme of things, but appreciates the effort made to seriously rank them.

"The best discussion on this subject I think I've ever had was when someone from the Royal College of Art said that, in terms of art and the use of art and being conscious of it in their music, there were The Beatles, then The Velvet Underground, then us. That's very flattering," he says. "All three groups in their respective eras, he said, shone light on aspects of the culture. Lou Reed's writing, particularly, revealed much to those of us who knew nothing about other American writers. Lennon was always extremely good at that, and people always took the piss out of him for being a pretentious bastard, but he didn't give a fuck, did he? And he always tended to be right. His taste was pretty good, you know?"

The other significant thing about Wire (and The Beatles and the Velvets) is that they provided a blank canvas onto which bands were able to project their own ideas, their own versions/visions of how rock should sound, should be. And bands in America and bands in Britain responded quite differently to them, as Wire themselves have noted. In his 2006 sleeve notes to the CD reissue of *Pink Flag*, Colin Newman assessed Wire's impact on the US underground. He explained that, as a "new wave" band signed to a major label, they were one of the very few contemporary British acts to see national US release (distributed as they were through Capitol). And so their debut began a process of seeping into US alternative culture by dint of its national availability and a sound that was new to US ears compared with Wire's UK contemporaries.

By the early-Eighties Wire's minimalist aesthetic had been absorbed by the US hardcore scene in LA, Washington DC and Chicago. "It seemed," Newman wrote, "that the innately oppositional nature of Wire's rock deconstruction was more profoundly subversive [in] a nation of Rock Orthodoxy. Whereas the Ramones on their debut album had joyously reduced rock history to a kind of three-chord bubblegum speedcore, with the aim of celebrating and reinforcing rock's history and orthodoxies, *Pink Flag* had less charitable designs on the body of rock and the hardcore guys innately knew it. A wave of influence spread through the US Eighties indie scene starting with Black Flag and Mission of Burma and spreading through Big Black and on out to the likes of R.E.M. and the Pixies."

"People were thinking, 'Hmm, that's quite interesting,'" says Newman today of Wire's deceptively simple sound and what he earlier in this book identified as their moronic/intelligent duality. "They thought, 'That must be really, really easy to do because it's very naked, yet at the same time it sounds clever.' And that's quite attractive, I think, to a lot of musicians, especially if they're just starting out, so that was why Wire influenced the early-Eighties generation of US hardcore punk bands."

True enough, Wire fans among that generation included Ian MacKaye of Minor Threat (and later of Fugazi), who covered '12XU' for the Dischord Records compilation *Flex Your Head*, and Henry Rollins of Black Flag who, as Henrietta Collins & The WifeBeating Childhaters, covered 'Ex Lion Tamer' on the EP *Drive-By Shooting*. American music writer Michael Azerrad also reports, in *Our Band Could Be Your Life*, that at Minor Threat's second gig, each of the seven bands on the roster performed their version of a Wire song. The harder than hardcore Big Black covered Wire's 'Heartbeat'. The Minutemen, Sonic Youth, Nirvana and R.E.M. (who covered Wire's 'Strange' on their 1987 album, *Document*) acknowledged their love of the group. And Guided By Voices' Robert Pollard claimed that not only were Wire his favourite band, but that GBV's albums featured so many songs because Wire's albums did, too.

This took what Newman terms "*Pink Flag*'s iconic afterlife" well into the late-Eighties and beyond, not just in the States (where 21st-century art-electro duo Fischerspooner covered 'The 15th' from Wire's *154* on their 2001 LP titled *#1*), but in Britain as well. While the Americans regarded *Pink Flag* as rock reconstructed, wave after wave of Eighties, Nineties and 21st century groups evinced their fascination for Wire's rock deconstruction and their attempts to turn it inside out and outside in, from Manic Street Preachers to My Bloody Valentine (whose last recorded song of note was a cover of 'Map Ref 41°N 93°W', from *154*, for a Wire tribute album entitled *Whore*). Robert Smith was purported to have said circa 1982, after their 1980 split, "If Wire reform then I'll disband The Cure because there will be no point in us being here," while The Cure's road manager apparently concurred, declaring after one Wire gig, "Ah, now I know where Robert Smith got his ideas from!"

In the last decade and a half, 'Britpop'-era bands like Blur (whom Mike Thorne produced in the Nineties) and Menswe@r and post-punk revivalists with a keen ear for the "angular" and "arty" such as Bloc Party, Futureheads and Franz Ferdinand owe Wire a considerable debt. It was Britpop boy-girl band Elastica who took their Wirelove furthest, their appropriation of the melody to Wire's 'Three Girl Rhumba' for their 1995 hit 'Connection' resulting in an out-of-court settlement for plagiarism (they had actually, prior to this, approached Thorne to produce them). Back in America, one eager bunch of Wire devotees, The Ex Lion Tamers, formed with the sole intention of playing *Pink Flag* in its entirety every night, and once even toured as support to Wire, for whom conceptual art playfulness comes as second nature.

As Michael Bracewell concluded in *Art Review* in May 2005, "Wire are a direct expression of the determinedly enquiring art school sensibility in England," going on to describe them as "the Art World's favourite band". Or, as Garry Mulholland wrote in his excellent *Fear Of Music: The 261 Greatest Albums Since Punk And Disco*, "*Pink Flag* is an act of generosity that will live on for as long as art-rock does, and I dare say that will be forever."

"Art-punk is the drug of choice of a whole generation," says Graham Lewis of today's keenest Wire-ists, up to and including the highly touted likes of Liars and LCD Soundsystem. "I've got to know the Brooklyn punk-funk scene, and Wire is part of their fabric. It's ingrained in pop's DNA."

Wire's debut album won converts in all manner of unlikely places even at the time of its release. Yes, it sent shockwaves reverberating through the ensuing decades, but that doesn't mean it was ignored at the time. Far from it. As word began to spread about this brilliant new band who made a fiercely concise, furiously intense racket and allied it to a new critical way of thinking about rock'n'roll, certain members of rock's aristocracy who liked to consider themselves au fait with everything au courant on the contemporary music scene began to prick up their ears. People with names like Bowie (who had been seen turning up at Wire gigs), Lennon, even Dylan.

"I remember a lot of people quoting their shock," says Lewis, recalling the reaction to *Pink Flag*'s awesome terse communiqués and coded messages about the modern world, among rock's prime movers, "including such luminaries as Mr. Paul Weller, David Byrne from Talking Heads and David Bowie – I don't think much ever went past Bowie in those days. He was always extremely sharp when it came to spotting new things and important developments. I think even John Lennon made a point of investigating us. All these people went, 'Fuck, what's that? Have you heard what they're doing? That's kind of weird, isn't it? It's like the song stops when the words run out!' All of those things, you know. Basically, for the older rock star, we were the name you needed to drop if you wanted to 'be down' with the kids. People like that were usually fairly cautious about dropping names but they did it to make themselves look more credible. And also, of course, these were people who were truly interested in music, so obviously if you're doing something interesting, it would come up on their radar, wouldn't it?"

When news reached EMI HQ that even the godlike Robert Zimmerman had expressed an interest in Wire's compelling new rock sound, employees immediately snapped into action and prepared "As Recommended By Bob Dylan" flashes for Wire adverts. But the band wouldn't have it and put their collective foot down. They didn't, as Colin Newman once so memorably and colourfully put it, need "nude tarts" to sell their records; nor did they need rock heroes from another time, another place.

AND yet, for all that, for all *Pink Flag*'s greatness, influence and longevity, if anything, the album they made next was greater, more influential, and more enduring in terms of 21st-century relevance and impact. That album was *Chairs Missing*, one of the greatest guitar-rock albums of the period – any period – one that opened up whole new vistas for those from the Class of '76 keen to explore different territory after punk had thoroughly exhausted the three-chord garageland model.

Make that "guitar-rock enhanced by keyboards", because it was Wire before anybody else from their era who had the idea of incorporating more and more keyboard-derived sounds into their modus operandi, at a time when the keyboard was anathema to the guitar-slinging rebel-rockers of punk, who considered it an instrument of fussy ornamentation. In fact, one of Wire's most useful discoveries around this time was that, by heavily treating their guitars, they could sound just like synths, and vice versa – synths and keyboards could be put through various distorting gadgetry to achieve a sound comparable to that made by the electric guitar! On *Chairs Missing*, the originating instrument is often difficult to figure out, removing the potential for displays of solo heroics.

It started to make more and more sense, as time went on, that Wire had been signed to Harvest by Nick Mobbs, the man previously responsible for enticing Pink Floyd to EMI's psychedelic/progressive/art-rock imprint. Because if any band assumed the mantle of the Floyd (and their psych/art/prog ilk) in the late-Seventies, it was Wire. But not the Floyd at their most lumbering and windy, self-indulgent and bombastic; no, the questing, exploratory Floyd who retained their anonymity behind an enormous wall of atmospheric, sometimes menacing sound and often disturbing, mysterious lyrics.

"EMI thought Wire were going to be part of a new psychedelia, the next Pink Floyd," Colin Newman told Simon Reynolds for his post-punk treatise, *Rip It Up And Start Again*. "They saw us as the progressive element coming out of punk, with longevity and a more artistic approach – slower pieces, more depth and space in the sound, different noises that weren't just thrash thrash thrash."

Newman remembers other new sub-genres ascribed to Wire by journalists when they heard their latest music, by a generation of writers "hungry for the next thing in late '77": first there was new wave, then cold wave, used to describe the new wave of chilly European-influenced bands that emerged after punk, then new musick for the groups increasingly in thrall to the latest electronic sounds, and post-punk. They even found themselves co-opted into the skinny-tie power-pop movement at one point. "We were various things," he says, bemused. "But Wire remained unclassifiable. We didn't quite fit anywhere." (Graham Lewis also recalls an attempt to co-opt Wire into something called "The Ice Warriors Who Are To Come In '78"!)

Newman does, however, acknowledge that the Pink Floyd comparisons made some sort of sense, what with their longer, slower songs, use of electronics, and unsettling atmospheres. Wire had no truck with punk's Year Zero, scorched-earth loathing of any music made before 1976. How could they? They'd been listening to virtually every note of music made since the advent of rock in the early-Sixties and were fans of much of it.

"Obviously there are some elements of Pink Floyd, among other things, in there. Basically, we realised fairly early on that the punk philosophy of 'everything before 1976 is all bollocks and they're all a bunch of fucking hippies' was not going to get you very far, really. I always had an interest in classic music from other generations, and the idea of bringing elements of those exists already in *Pink Flag*." Nor was he fazed by the Syd Barrett comparisons when it came to that school of dream-logic lyric-writing. "Syd Barrett is a very, very intuitive songwriter. He just knew where to go with something, and I expect I have something of that. It's almost naive and childlike, and I would like to feel that, because of that, he and I have something in common there."

"On the release of their second album, Wire were dubbed 'the Pink Floyd of the New Wave'," confirms producer Mike Thorne, who also recalls the shorter, pithier new name ascribed to them: Punk Floyd. "They were called that because *Chairs Missing* was deemed to be 'progressive'," he says. "We weren't sure whether to laugh or cry because of Floyd's reputation as Boring Old Farts." Thorne did concede, in an essay for his website The Stereo Society, that it "might have been an ultimately flattering phrase" despite Floyd being perceived by the punks as the ultimate rock dinosaurs, because "the two groups had much in common": a focus on albums not singles, an impression given by those albums not of disposability but of durability, and an experimental mindset.

One thing Wire didn't have in common with Pink Floyd was a furious work rate. A mere four or five months after the release of *Pink Flag* (and its attendant three-track single, 'Mannequin'/'Feeling Called Love'/'12 XU'), the band re-entered Advision Studios to record the follow-up, *Chairs Missing*, with the other members of what had become the Wire ensemble: producer Mike Thorne, engineer Paul Hardiman, and assistant engineer Ken Thomas (who would go on to work with Queen, David Bowie, Cocteau Twins and Icelandic ambient-rockers Sigur Ros). They were fast amassing new material, much of it honed while on the road during the intervening months, and they were keen to get it recorded. They had just one stipulation: it had to be different from before.

"The group always wanted to do something different," confirms Thorne. "Doing the same thing twice runs against the grain for them. Once a band breaks out with a successful style, as Wire did with *Pink Flag*, it's tempting to repeat it, but those characters would never have done that. Everyone in the band was on board with that, and I as the producer followed. I was always looking for trouble, musically. All the way up to when I quit production in 1994, I was always looking for something to stretch the brain. I never wanted to mine the same seam."

Thorne's role as the unofficial fifth member of Wire became more apparent during the recording of *Chairs Missing*, when the demand for a more expansive sound would require his input and experience with keyboards.

"I had played keyboards on a few tracks on *Pink Flag*, but didn't think that my contribution warranted disturbing the rock-solid coherence of the group's sound," he wrote in The Stereo Society, explaining that the "keyboards" in question comprised such state-of-the-art equipment as a "cranky old RMI Electrapiano whose pedal would often fall off onstage and require a short, discreet technical session with sticky tape". "There is piano under 'Reuters' [from *Pink Flag*] as basic colouring [for Bruce's and Colin's guitars], and more forward noises in 'Options R'," he went on to explain, adding that he was uneasy about his own abilities, at which point the band made him an offer he couldn't refuse: "Wire said I should play synthesizers on the next album. I said, as ever, 'I can't move my fingers fast enough.' They said, 'If you don't do it, we'll get that Brian Eno in.' I said, 'OK.'"

The former Roxy Music whiz, who had apparently expressed an interest in producing Wire and approached the band after seeing them play live, is a suitable reference point for Thorne. His ability to push Wire towards uncharted territories was comparable to that of Eno circa Bowie's triptych of albums recorded in Berlin, or the trio of ground-breaking albums he worked on with Talking Heads. On *Chairs Missing*, the producer-musician added an Eno-esque layer of atmospherics to Wire's stark, stripped-down, monochrome-minimalist sound while the band, far better musicians now than they had been during *Pink Flag*, also became involved in pursuing new sonic textures and coaxing interesting noises from their instruments. Meanwhile, the tempos were slower, the arrangements more detailed and FX-laden, as the band stretched out and prepared to push their new instrumental prowess to the limit.

One of the reasons for Wire's musical evolution on *Chairs Missing*, apart from their superior musicianship this time round and their loathing of doing the same thing twice, was the arrival during this period of new technology.

"During 1977-8 there was an explosion of electronics," explains Thorne. "There were suddenly all sorts of creatively grungy pedals, which provided the basis for the guitar sounds you hear on *Chairs Missing*, as well as flanges and effects like tape delay. There were these completely fresh sound-effects units making it to market. You could buy relatively cheap – $100 or so – effects pedals, typically from MXR and Electroharmonix, both of which eventually went bust. I brought a huge amount of effects into the studio outside the control room, so many pedals... It was a golden age of electronic development, especially for guitars. Bruce would take a couple of pedals away for 'homework' and he'd come back into the next session and play a funny riff with a funny sound, very individual and distinctive. My job would then be to incor-porate or enhance that sound, so I twiddled the knobs and they did, too – I welcomed their input as we were all growing almost in parallel.

"These sounds promised a whole new world for us, so off we went. We found the Promised Land, at least for then. A gesture could come from a simple chord, non-virtuoso playing, and an inspired setting of some incomprehensibly named knobs. For me, too, that was liberation, since I can't move my keyboard fingers fast enough to impress, so a few keys and more knob-twiddles could do more for the music. There are, as there were on *Pink Flag*, some flutes, but overall, yes, *Chairs Missing* was a move towards a more electronic sound.

"*Chairs Missing* has persisted as my personal favourite of the three Wire albums that I was involved with," Thorne admits. "It doesn't have the rough clarity of *Pink Flag*, or the polish and arrangement coherence of *154*, which is a highly accomplished piece of record-making, but there's a spirit of newness and discovery about every moment and track that takes you on a journey relating to the one we made at the time. It's a transitional album, exploratory, but there's also something about it that is quite wild."

"We wanted keyboards on this album, and he [Thorne] was the obvious choice," Lewis explained at the time in *Melody Maker*, "because it would be very difficult for us to actually graft somebody on. Mike's been involved from the start, so in that way it was easy for him, because he understands what we want, generally."

"Also, he's not the most experienced keyboard player in the world," Gilbert pointed out, "so there's a certain amount of sympathy."

"The problem is, if we wanted a keyboard player, what we'd want would be somebody who's not an organ or piano player," added Lewis. "There are very few people who are willing to come in and just make a noise."

As for the extra production effects on *Chairs Missing*, the bassist explained that they were courtesy of the producer. "This time around, that's where the difference is, because obviously we'd learnt a lot from the year we'd been playing since the first album, and he was there, growing at the same time. So his productions were so much more creative."

Looking back in 2008, Thorne recalls the mood in the studio being one of excitement due to the new technology that had suddenly become available, and the "much more expansive" approach to songwriting. All of the ideas for their new direction came, he says, from the band. It wasn't as though there was a pop faction in the group and a more experimental faction, both vying for supremacy, as there would be later on. "I was just the facilitator," says the producer, who describes the atmosphere in the studio as "relaxed and confident" compared with the *Pink Flag* sessions. "We cared about what we were doing so we got down to it. It was work, not grind. When I cleaned toilets for a living, that was a grind. This wasn't. It was a marvellous project, involving people with something to say sonically and lyrically, who were guided not by style but by intensity. I always wanted intense music."

The *Chairs Missing* sessions were intense, recalls Thorne, because the execution of the ideas was so difficult, but he doesn't remember them being as creatively fraught as the *Pink Flag* sessions. Prior to recording band and producer demoed songs, which were then presented to EMI, just as Thorne, in his capacity as A&R man at the label, had done with everyone from Kate Bush to the Sex Pistols. "Constructive politics" is his term for such a procedure. When the powers-that-be heard the demos, they were very positive.

Then they entered the studio. *Chairs Missing* would cost a bit more than the £16,000 it took to produce *Pink Flag*, and it would take longer to record than the six weeks Wire spent on that debut – it would later become a habit of Thorne's to produce an album in two months, including a short break. He immediately recognised the quantum leap in terms of the members' instrumental ability, and their greater control of the studio environment. "*Pink Flag* was recorded live, including most of the vocals – only 'Strange' was an overdubbed vocal. The technique was to get everybody wired up and go for it in one mad rush and it worked well. With *Chairs Missing*, the aim was to broaden the way the studio and the sound booth were used."

"The sound is the most startling thing for me," he wrote for The Stereo Society, detailing some of the processes and effects that gave the individual songs on *Chairs Missing* their distinctive sound. "On *Chairs Missing* there were fewer songs [only 15 compared to the 21 on *Pink Flag*], and they were mostly much longer. There were no vignettes. 'Another The Letter' [the shortest track, at one minute and seven seconds] was based on a sequenced synth loop done on an old Oberheim analogue synthesizer. Robert [Gotobed] attempted it first on his drums, but he struggled to get it right, so someone had the bright idea to do it on a sequencer. I programmed it and it worked so we spent the rest of the day readjusting and developing it. It was all recorded in one day. I was absolutely flattened. Robert was OK about it – in fact, he really enjoyed hearing his drums thrown into a totally strange space."

In terms of length, the four-minute opener, 'Practice Makes Perfect', was a statement of intent, while the treated guitars, staccato rhythm and ominous electronic sounds, creepily enhanced by manic laughter towards the end, served notice to the effect that *Pink Flag* (Slight Return) this was not. 'Too Late', the final track, echoed the punk thrash that had informed, and allowed the band to use as a point of departure from, *Pink Flag*; its crackling guitars, Thorne explained, were "boosted by a sound from an RMI Electrapiano through a distortion pedal or over-driven amp". He noted the voice loops, temple blocks, flutes, and tubular bells processed through a ring modulator in 'Marooned' after Bruce Gilbert had objected that bell-tolling was too corny.

'Sand In My Joints' was another track that could have been a standard punk attack, were it not for the various treatments of the instruments, coatings and general sonic interference – the guitar solo is played by Newman and Gilbert through the ring modulator on the classic Synthi AKS. At almost six minutes, 'Mercy' was the longest track, and it gave Wire the space to really test their ability to create tense, compelling music over the distance. 'I Am the Fly', recorded for a single ahead of the album, was a synth-pop ditty two years ahead of schedule that served as a manifesto about the band's determination to act as an irritant – its lyric was a distant cousin to 'Anarchy In The UK''s "I am an anarchist". It could have been a huge novelty hit, while 'Outdoor Miner', a perfect compromise between Velvets drone and Byrds harmony, almost was a hit (see Chapter 5); both songs evinced a natural pop sensibility.

Although there were different shades and variations in tone on *Pink Flag*, *Chairs Missing* was a more diverse affair, a function of the group's low boredom threshold. Once, after a traditional pub lunch, Newman announced that "the whole album had to be recorded again" – meaning the removal of any traces of the familiar, which perhaps explains the penultimate, oddly pretty 'Used To', which Thorne considers the clearest sign of things to come on *154*.

"It became almost a dogmatic requirement in my production mind to have at least one thing completely fresh and striking about a track, something you hadn't heard before," he says. Hence the clean, clear, glass-like guitars on 'I Am The Fly', or the "vitreous shimmer", as Simon Reynolds describes it, of 'French Film (Blurred)'. But what gives *Chairs Missing* its unique quality of spontaneous methodology was that the songs were performed, complete, then treated afterwards.

"There are some extremely non-purist moments," says Thorne, "but it was still important to play the songs, to get the mood and the feeling down on tape before drawing on that performance as bottled energy, when we replaced crashing guitars with something stranger or more mysterious."

"Strange" and "mysterious" are good words to describe an album that takes its title from a slang term for mild mental disturbance (as in, "He has a few chairs missing in his front room"). There is even a track called 'I Feel Mysterious Today' that seems to mock the idea of the alienated young poet-musician. If *Pink Flag* used punk rage for a series of abstract rants, *Chairs Missing* delved deeper into the psyche, with its undercurrents of isolation and madness and images of cold, drowning, pain, and suicide – more reasons for those Pink Floyd comparisons: the Floyd circa Syd Barrett and their *Dark Side Of The Moon/Wish You Were Here* mid-Seventies pomp. But Wire never looked back, only to the future. They used icy-sounding synth/guitar textures to explore the art of darkness, making it a crucial landmark in the evolution of punk into post-punk and goth. It was Wire at the top of their game.

"I'd felt, when writing *Pink Flag* in Watford, that I was on it," says Colin Newman. "By the time I got to *Chairs Missing*, knowing there was a vehicle for anything I wrote was like I was in a feedback loop with my own culture. You're doing something that matters, and people care.

"When I wrote 'Practice Makes Perfect', I had shivers running up my spine. What makes it different from anything on *Pink Flag* is that it's... angular! It amuses me that people who cite Wire as an influence on each generation of angular young British contenders always cite *Pink Flag*, but *Chairs Missing* is the angular one. It's minimal, and it put the rhythm first.

"People said, in the early-Eighties, that those two records sounded like Eighties records, not Seventies ones, because of that. But the real difference between them is that the atmosphere had changed. And Wire were a bunch of fashion victims. We embraced whatever innovations were around."

According to Graham Lewis, EMI was pleasantly surprised by *Pink Flag*, so by the time they began *Chairs Missing* expectations were high. "I think they started to get a bit more excited when we came up with *Chairs Missing*," he says. Having three songwriters in the band gave them "fantastic access to change". And the change, he says, "was really, really fast and creatively brutal", to the extent that they probably discarded enough material for a further set because the ante had been seriously upped by 'Practice Makes Perfect'.

"Everybody went, 'That's it.' Anything that didn't compare or stand up to that went straight in the bin. That was the kind of warfare we were into." He recalls there being a good, creative atmosphere in the studio. "You got frustrated a few times, and there were disagreements and arguments, of course, but *Chairs Missing* was really quite a happy record to make. It seemed to come really quite naturally, which was rather different from *Pink Flag* where it was a case of deconstruction and constructing, sonically, the pieces individually. Whereas *Chairs Missing* had a more adventurous feel because everybody was that much more confident and actually understood some aspects of the process." Were EMI concerned that you were so quick with a follow-up album? "No, I think they were pretty delighted with the direction things were going in. They obviously felt that things like 'I Am The Fly', 'Dot Dash' [a June 1978 single not included on the album] and 'Outdoor Miner' could be the ones that were going to break the band."

Lewis believes the band's evolution between *Pink Flag* and *Chairs Missing* was "very organic. We were more confident and we understood a bit more about how the studio process worked. And we were more accomplished musicians: you can hear that there's a lot more ambition in the playing. It's very strong ensemble playing.

"*Chairs Missing* is full of atmospheres," he adds, "and an incredible number of songs that have water metaphors [they even had a song called 'Underwater Experiences' that didn't make the final cut], which is very English, isn't it? 'Practice Makes Perfect' is the first track because it set a benchmark; after that, we raised our game.

"I would say it's a self-contained piece of work, which is aware of what is going on in the world," he continues. He cites 'I Am The Fly' as an example of a track that exists on its own terms as a sonically intriguing piece of work but that acts as a critique of punk homogeneity. It also implicated such New York lowlife as Johnny Thunders, who had just arrived in Britain, in the contamination of the capital with junkie squalor, the antithesis of Wire's hygienic disregard for rock decadence. Theirs was a critical, baleful presence, glowering from the fringes at the scene.

Overall, Lewis considers, *Chairs Missing* is "more expansive in every way" than its predecessor, with "wider horizons". Also, he says, "the viciousness is more vicious, the beauty is more beautiful, and the weirdness is weirder – we were getting better at what we were doing, basically." He believes Wire encouraged other bands, by their example, to pursue a more experimental direction: "By doing it you say, 'This is possible. You can do it.' So that's what one tends to do: rather than talking about it, you try and put it into practice."

Lewis acknowledges the spirit of healthy competition, as groups arrived at similar points of departure during 1978, groups like Magazine, PiL, Siouxsie & The Banshees and Joy Division who would soon be subsumed under the rubric "post-punk", the logical next step on from punk. In a way, Wire was the first of all the post-punk bands: anti-image, stark, dark, intelligent, rigorous, informed by literature and obscure art. Sometimes Wire's superficially "doomy" rock was taken literally. "Tracks like 'Too Late' were a big influence on what would become the goth scene," he says, "and groups like Alien Sex Fiend. I don't know about Joy Division. Peter Hook once said to me, 'God, we stole tons from you.' But he was pissed at the time."

For Wire, Buzzcocks, when Howard Devoto was still in the band, were always the ones to watch and worry about. "Buzzcocks were probably the band that we felt in England we had most in common with. We even did a residency with them at the Marquee for a month in '77 every Monday. They had about 900 people in there. It was insanity. Colin always used to say it was the best thing that ever happened to Wire, Howard leaving Buzzcocks, because after he left they just became a sort of pop band. He was smart, intelligent, but not pretentious; or at least, it was pretentious in a good way. It was trying to advance good ideas."

Bruce Gilbert, comparing the sessions for Wire's first two albums, remembers the latter being "more experimental" after the "baptism of fire" that were the debut album sessions. Because of the demand for greater flexibility and variety with regard to the sound, Colin Newman was forced to play a lot more guitar, a situation made more pressing because Gilbert found himself unable to play some of the trickier chords.

He says they were all, however, responsible for the darker atmosphere and often morbid imagery this time round. "That was something we all found a bit more interesting than some of the subject matter that we'd previously been exploring. There's a slightly gloomy atmosphere about the material we were doing, and it seemed to suit us." The guitarist, also Wire's resident absurdist, feels *Chairs Missing* works not as a statement about the times in which it was made nor even really as a reflection of the way the individual members were feeling, but as an expression, somehow, of the absurdity and meaninglessness of existence. "Life is rather meaningless, and we were exploring in text how to express that, I suppose." Rants against the authorities, prevalent at the time, were few and far between on Wire's second album. "There were still a lot of people directing the blame at political targets. You look to yourself or you look to society. The government's an easy target."

Wire weren't angry so much as in agony – existential agony, which found its perfect expression in the icy arrangements and chilling textures of *Chairs Missing*. Did people have doubts about the sanity of the members of Wire? "I seem to remember one or two articles or reviews in which journalists assumed that because the sound was like that we were like that," says Gilbert. "They honestly thought we were very disturbed individuals. Very few of them ever got the absurd side." One of Wire's favourite absurdist tricks, he says, was to disrupt things whenever the chords, say, got "too pretty or poppy" by putting in "something horrible or funny" either sonically or lyrically.

Unlike *Pink Flag*, where all four members were co-credited for the compositions, *Chairs Missing* had individual credits; Gilbert was named as co-writer of 'Practice Makes Perfect', 'Another The Letter', 'Marooned' and 'Used To' and received a solo credit for 'Too Late'. He considers his lyrics to have been "definitely bleaker" than Lewis'. "Bleak absurdism was definitely something I was interested in. I think it's a combination of things I was reading and me feeling a bit disappointed in myself, or disappointed in the human race to be more accurate."

For Robert Gotobed, *Chairs Missing* signalled an increase in anxiety, especially when the band had to let go of the songs from *Pink Flag*, with which they'd all become very familiar. "We had the feeling of starting from scratch again." Then again, this being their second time at Advision, they had established an identity for themselves, and they did at least have some experience of recording, so in that respect it was less stressful. Plus, Mike Thorne was on board once more, and the drummer found his presence reassuring, particularly when it came to sequencing, using keyboards and generally getting more involved in the studio process than on *Pink Flag*, which was, he says, "just a recording of the live set with an added bit of overdubbing". He describes Thorne as "a great enthusiast" who "showed us how the studio worked and solved problems for us, talking us through the mechanics of it all". If the producer sensed anyone struggling, he would "come out of the control room and do this very exaggerated conducting" to point the way. "His involvement," says Gotobed, "was essential, to have somebody who could connect your group with the studio, because it's all such a complicated process. Was he our fifth member? He came very close." As with Eno and Talking Heads, Thorne's job was to transcribe Wire's ideas and put them into practice.

Wire's second album had "stronger themes and ideas" and marked the moment where music saw "more of the influence of Wire rather than Wire being influenced by the outside". The band was as much of a self-contained unit as before, socialising more with each other than with other bands. "I don't think we really fit in with musicians," says Gotobed. "I think we fitted more with our art ideas than our musical ideas. I think Graham was probably better at getting to know other people in groups. But for me it just didn't happen. I don't know why. It was never like I was socially inadequate. Do other drummers get together and have a sort of instant rapport? I don't know." He isn't sure, either, of the impact, if any, of his precise, metronomic approach to rhythm, although it was sure to have registered with Joy Division's Stephen Morris.

He can't recall a change in the sorts of people coming to see Wire in 1978 than in 1977 (although the others in the band noted increasingly serious, furrowed-brow types venturing to Wire gigs after *Chairs Missing*), but he does remember, over at EMI, a feeling of impending commercial breakthrough for Wire as 1978 progressed.

"I think they did regard us at one time as being the next Pink Floyd – a band with a left-field attitude who could be successful and become famous without hit singles, without anybody really understanding why," he says. "But it didn't happen, did it?"

Chapter 5

Two People In A Room

"There's a dichotomy in Wire between, 'Is this an artistic enterprise or is this a commercial enterprise?' Those two sides were always in conflict" – Robert Gotobed

WHEN Wire began making *Chairs Missing* so quickly after *Pink Flag*, the band weren't exhausted by the demands of their touring and recording schedule; instead, Graham Lewis remembers, they felt a "tremendous sense of relief" that they'd survived "the first part of the process, and here we were, with another chance. It was a good period."

On its release, in September 1978, little surprise was expressed in the press that it followed so swiftly on the heels of the band's debut. It came in a similar washed-out, mainly monochrome sleeve to *Pink Flag*. Its design was credited once more to BC (Bruce Clifford) Gilbert and Graham Lewis; the dash of colour this time was provided by the green and purple flowers (Lewis' idea) placed on a table (Gilbert's idea, as was the album title) in the centre of the sleeve as per the pink flag in the middle of the front cover of their debut.

The mainly five-star, rave reviews, meanwhile, supported the idea that

Wire were poised to make a serious commercial breakthrough to match their critical and creative advances, notwithstanding the occasional criticism, from some quarters, for what they regarded as an overuse on the album of keyboards, which to punk recidivists smacked of proggy indulgence and ostentation.

"On this LP, instead of building their by now well-documented bleak/mesmerising atmosphere accidentally through the barest musical proficiency, Wire are in a position to sit back, think a little about what they're playing and calculatedly conjure up an ambience that disturbs, disrupts and distorts," wrote Geoff Barton in a five-star review in *Sounds*. "Through such cryptic titles as 'Another The Letter' and 'Men 2nd', Wire beat critical capacities to a pulp and you have to helplessly succumb." The *NME*'s Monty Smith was less enraptured, noting "the weedy spectre of Syd Barrett" looming large throughout the album and detecting from "the heavily-echoed ooh-aahs halfway through 'Practice Makes Perfect'" something he called "an unhappy attack of the Pink Floyds". Nevertheless, by the end of the review, he did qualify this by concluding that, "At their best, Wire convey controlled derangement better than almost anyone."

For *Record Mirror*'s Bev Briggs, *Chairs Missing* "culminates in Wire not quite reaching their zenith but arriving somewhere in the vicinity" and concluded that "Wire have discovered the NEW direction." *Melody Maker*'s Lynden Barber praised the way Wire "track through a whole range of characters and emotions, moving (for instance) between fear, pain, confusion and jaunty irony". He singled out Bruce Gilbert's guitars and the way they "alternatively hold fire, linger in the background, or swoop down for the kill", and Robert Gotobed's "chillingly clean and taut" drumming, while Graham Lewis and Colin Newman's lyrics were, he wrote, "often (when audible) extraordinarily complex and elliptical".

Producer Mike Thorne offered his own assessment of *Chairs Missing* over two decades after the fact for his website, The Stereo Society. "The perception of the lyrics on the album went up a level, although the vocals are sometimes hard to hear," he wrote. "The punk style of having the voice riding just on top of the supporting cataclysm was still with me, and it wasn't until *154* that arrangement and mixing complemented each other in my production approach. There are several very direct, open statements, such as 'Marooned' and the first overt love song, 'Heartbeat' ('Fragile' on *Pink Flag* counts as the best draft).

"My favourite line," he continued, "is on 'Too Late', a sentence that comes from a planet that I have never visited: 'She pisses icy water on poetic mornings.' Wire lyrics were capable of pretension, but this is the opposite, putting you immediately in a curious emotional space with words that are inexplicable but somehow connect."

It was Wire's very "pretensions" that saw them enthusiastically greeted by European audiences for whom "artiness" and "ambition" were to be admired not condemned; there was a residual mistrust of such qualities in some UK quarters. In Germany, Wire were probably the only British band of their era to impact on the so-called "neue welle" (new wave) of experimental musicians picking up where the "krautrock" generation left off. The Europeans liked Wire, and Wire, in return, liked them.

"We did an awful lot of touring, especially in Germany, and we picked up quite a few interested parties there," recalls Bruce Gilbert. "There was a bit more going on there in terms of culture."

"We liked the atmosphere in Europe," says Graham Lewis. "And it was full of ideas. But it was fun, too, you know. Philosophical, somehow, I think.

"Going to play for the first time in Holland and Germany was incredibly important for us," he adds of Wire's European jaunts. "We all felt a great relief being out of Britain. There were so many things about Europe that we liked, in terms of design, culture, music, books, films, artists, all of those things. It was an exciting period."

Being away from Britain meant being away from punk, which was now being degraded by faux revolutionaries, professional anarchists and a narrow-minded, thuggish sub-punk contingent/movement that would later be known as "Oi!".

"I think," he considers, "that there's a certain British attitude that quite frankly I find objectionable... When Wire went to play Europe in 1978, we all felt such an incredible sense of relief to be away from this thing that was now called punk but which had become an industry of some description, but had lost the whole idea of what it was mean to be about: it should have been about anarchy as far as I was concerned, and that's something you have to preserve on the inside. It doesn't come from the outside. It's not like, 'Hey, anarchy, follow me.' Like sheep, you know? We were more interested in doing what the fuck you want. So we went to Europe and we discovered that our ideas weren't at all strange or weird; nor was it a weird idea that you read books or went to see films or read poetry. These were considered to be quite natural activities. Philosophy is a necessity; it's a tool of life." Lewis is proud that, in a book published a few years back about German punk, Wire were the only non-German band to be included. "I felt very honoured by that. They valued what we did. We were appreciated, and they didn't seem to have any problem with it at all."

Not so the States, at least not at first. Although, as was discussed in the previous chapter, Wire were later embraced wholeheartedly by the American rock underground, where they were categorised alongside the likes of Suicide, Pere Ubu and Devo as conceptual, experimental art-rockers – "bands who create music that has as much to with avant-garde electronic composers as it does three-chord bashing", according to Richard Grabel of *New York Rocker* magazine – their initial live forays there were met with a mixed response. This perhaps befits a band who, as writer Wilson Neate has said, "had been an infamously unsafe bet [live], often performing only unfamiliar material, sometimes in an uncompromising performance-art mode".

Their US trip – a brief two-weekend stint at the legendary CBGBs in New York in summer 1978 – apparently started on a hectic note when "immigration hassles", as the July 20 edition of *The Soho Weekly News* recounted, detained the band. They were kept for so long that, as Bruce Gilbert exaggerated for comic effect in the *NME* a month later, "We got off the plane at about 11 o'clock at night, and we were onstage at half-past 11."

It transpired that a detour to Bangor (in Maine, not Wales or Ireland) and a "traffic jam" over at Kennedy Airport delayed their arrival, and after a lengthy wait for baggage, they were taken straight to the club. "They didn't expect us to play," Lewis told journalist Andy Gill, "but we thought, 'We're here, so we might as well.' We went on with gear we'd never used before, and played at the equivalent of 8 a.m. English time. It was pretty frantic. The next night, Saturday, we played two sets, and the reception was amazing. Incredible."

"They wouldn't let us go," added Gilbert.

Colin Newman has different memories of those CBGBs gigs, recalling today how the band "managed to piss off" the audience due to a typically forward-looking Wire refusing to play much material from *Pink Flag* – "because we weren't terribly interested in that any more" – concentrating instead on their forthcoming second album, *Chairs Missing*.

Back in Blighty, Wire were drawing praise for their live performances, which, as Dave Fudger of *Sounds* noted, was a breakthrough for a band who, he said, some considered to be an arty studio outfit rather than a good-time dance band. "Wire's strength used to lie solely in their music," he wrote, "but now they seem well on the way to shaping the vehicle to animate their art. Don't believe what you read. Find out for yourself."

Ian Birch gained a similar impression after seeing the band in July 1978 at London's Lyceum, writing in *Melody Maker*: "There is still a major gap between the presence Wire transmit on vinyl (just sample their glorious new single 'Dot Dash', for example) and what they project onstage. But the space is getting smaller."

The *NME* reviewer decided Wire were "like a conceptual artist's idea of a modern music band at the mixed-media environment threshold" – quite a prescient remark considering where the band were heading, particularly 1981's *Document And Eyewitness* live album project. Another live review in the *NME* from 1978 was more effusive and unqualified in its praise. "Fending off moans from *NME* colleagues that a band with a singer who spends most of his time onstage standing stone still, staring straight ahead and maybe cocking his head slightly to one side like a crazy android can't be rock or roll, I still happen to rate Wire as by far the most innovative, nonconformist and generally compelling UK unit to have surfaced in recent months," enthused Angus MacKinnon, going on to praise the band's "pulverising motorik" and singling out Robert Gotobed's "supremely flexible" drumming and BC Gilbert's "seemingly limitless supply of unusual chords and tunings".

If there was one thing that united commentators, live or otherwise, with regard to Wire during 1978 and 1979, it was their admiration for 'I Am The Fly', 'Dot Dash' and 'Outdoor Miner', released as singles in, respectively, February and July '78 and January '79. "There was certainly something interesting going on," says Mike Thorne of Wire's under-appreciated melodic gifts and what appeared to be chart success on the horizon. "I remember one very conservative pop-marketing person at EMI saying of 'I Am The Fly' that it wasn't her taste but it was 'really interesting'. I knew then that we were onto something."

'Outdoor Miner' sounded like a particularly good bet as Wire's first serious assault on – or rather, given its sweetly melodious nature, gentle, subversive entry into – the charts. As Bruce Gilbert puts it, "It was so pretty it seemed like an obvious candidate for wider appreciation."

Graham Lewis explained in *NME* that it was a song about an insect. "I was listening to *Wildlife* on Radio Four one morning and somebody asked what makes the lines on a holly leaf? It turns out it's an insect called a Serpentine Miner that lives in the leaves and eats chlorophyll. I just couldn't quite comprehend what the reality of being a Serpentine Miner must be if there is a roof-fall in a leaf. Well... it's a profound thought for a beetle," he said, while Colin Newman, as the one responsible for conveying the "message" to the public, found it a peculiar subject for a pop song. "When I listen to my singing on that I just crease up," he admitted. "I should be singing 'she loves me and I love her' and so on, but what I'm singing about is insects!"

If 'Outdoor Miner' was "pop", it was in that grand tradition of eccentric British pop as purveyed by The Move, Roxy Music, Kevin Ayers and Syd Barrett. Mike Thorne didn't believe the subject matter was a barrier to mass communication. "In our rather hermetic Wire bubble," he wrote in The Stereo Society, "this didn't seem particularly unreasonable at all." He pointed out that this wasn't the first song from Wire with serious commercial potential, identifying 'Fragile' from *Pink Flag* as an early example of Wire's melodic nous.

He also acknowledged the strange position the band found themselves in when the record company asked them to lengthen the track for release as a single – normally the request, for the exigencies of radio-friendliness, is for tracks to be shortened, much to the distress of the artists. In this case, recalled the producer, Wire were "just a little bemused" but not so put out that they didn't acquiesce, adding a chorus, a second verse and, at the label's behest, a piano solo that quickened the pace of the *Chairs Missing* original.

With the edits and changes made, the new single mix of 'Outdoor Miner' was delivered to EMI, who were excited about it and its chart prospects. They were justified in their belief that it was a contender when, soon after its release, sufficient quantities of the record were bought that it reached number 51 in the charts. At this point, the BBC suggested to EMI that, if the single continued to rise up the charts the following week, the band would be invited to appear on *Top Of The Pops*.

Perhaps EMI got carried away at the prospect of their avant-pop charges gaining exposure on the nation's most widely viewed music TV show, because the record company got caught by the British Market Research Bureau (BMRB) indulging in the practice known as chart "hyping" – sending emissaries from the label into "chart return" shops (that is, shops where sales registered on a centrally audited system) and getting them to buy several copies at once and even giving the odd one back to the shop for "free" so that they could sell it again. EMI were by no means the only company guilty of hyping, but they were the ones that got caught, and despite strenuous denials, their punishment was severe: 'Outdoor Miner' was immediately deleted from the charts for that week, which meant that it would struggle to meet the BBC's criterion about moving up the charts.

It was tougher on the band. Had they appeared on *Top Of The Pops*, their career, the whole story of Wire, might have been completely different. Instead of just being fabulous cult heroes, they could have joined the ranks of those bands who meet critical adoration with commercial success. Joy Division, The Cure, Echo & The Bunnymen… Wire could have been one of those.

"Had that *Top Of The Pops* appearance happened, the single would have almost certainly entered the Top 20 and launched a visible 'commercial' career for the group," says Mike Thorne, adding that being "progressive" and "commercial" are not mutually exclusive: he offers as examples Beethoven's *Fifth Symphony* and Dvorak's *New World Symphony*. Was he concerned that the presence of Wire's music in the mainstream would have reduced their impact? "A French philosopher once said, 'Any progressive idea absorbed by the bourgeoisie is neutralised.' Look at Stravinsky's *Rites Of Spring*," says Thorne, who studied music composition with composer Buxton Orr at the Guildhall School of Music and Drama. "Pop, experimental… I don't like labels. I like music to be accessible. I function in pop and classical areas equally." He doesn't accept that Wire's lyrics were too cryptic for mass consumption, citing Magazine (whose debut single, 'Shot By Both Sides', stalled at number 41 after singer Howard Devoto refused to mime on *Top Of The Pops*), Siouxsie & The Banshees and The Cure as purveyors of "difficult" ideas reaching large numbers of people. "There was an audience out there for it." As much as anything, he was disappointed because, as Wire's de facto fifth member and keyboardist, he would have appeared with the band on *Top Of The Pops*. "I'd already planned my outfit," he says, wistfully, and laughs. "We would have worn black. I was pretty disappointed by it; it would have changed everything. It would have put Wire in the Cure/Joy Division realm, absolutely. All you need is a bit of luck sometimes. Wire had bad luck." Did EMI at any stage ask Wire to produce more potential hits like 'Outdoor Miner'? "Absolutely not. They knew it wouldn't go down well with me or the band."

EMI, says Graham Lewis, were guilty of doing "what their fellow corporations were doing" and decided that they would "help it along", but they got caught – "which we were extremely pissed off about". Does he believe that, ultimately, Wire's music, notwithstanding its occasional surface prettiness, was too awkward to cross over? "If you ask Bruce that question, Bruce will say it was the best thing that ever happened because that meant that you could, you know, get on regardless [with being an experimental left-field act]. But I think with what followed *Chairs Missing* on *154,* we proved that we certainly were able to produce a tune, a memorable tune, which people would like as a single.

"You know," he adds, "a lot was said about us producing perfect pop at that time, if I remember rightly. No, the problem was, EMI screwed it up, royally. The week that they got caught, the record had almost gone into the Top 50, and then the next week it sold twice as many copies, but of course because they'd been caught, it was demoted – I think it was another 10 places down or something instead of rising another 20 places. But we were definitely producing the material; it wasn't as if we were trying to avoid writing pop. It has always been part of the mix." He is especially peeved because Wire's *Top Of The Pops* slot was taken by

Donny & Marie Osmond. "We were down to do it, but when all this shit happened, they decided to put them on instead because they were in London. I tell you that didn't go down terribly well. It was a hard one to laugh at." What manner of seditious horseplay did he have in mind for Wire's *Top Of The Pops* performance? "I'm sure it would have been sublime. It would have had to have been sublime."

Robert Gotobed notes that, hit or not, Wire were always "about" the frictional nature of the two opposing halves of the band – the "pop" camp of himself and Newman, and the more experimental team of Lewis and Gilbert. Lewis considers this an absurdly pat and inappropriate observation, pointing towards Gilbert's 'Blessed State' on third album *154* as just one example of the highly melodic sensibility of Wire's "arty ones". Gotobed, however, believes there was an increasingly evident schism. "There's a dichotomy in Wire between, 'Is this an artistic enterprise or is this a commercial enterprise?'" he insists. "And those two sides were always in conflict." Not that either "camp" ever proposed a conscious move either towards or away from pop. "It didn't happen that anyone said, 'We'll do this because it'll be commercial.' If we do something that turns out to be commercial then that's good, but it's never been our intention to do something for the sake of selling. You wouldn't get away with that. We didn't enter into those discussions. Wire are not about style, even though we defined it for other people."

WIRE, like Roxy Music before them, defined style for their generation, and so it made a sort of sense that both groups, comprising art-school graduates, should join forces and perform side by side (well, with Roxy as headliners and Wire as support), which they did on a tour of Europe in early 1979.

With the Eno-less art-rockers now past their inventive prime, however, they were attracting more conservative, mainstream crowds, and so many were left bemused, even bored, by Wire's performances. As for Wire, they were unimpressed by the experience of having to trek across Europe's stadia, travelling between 20 or so cities in as many days, to places where, as Graham Lewis puts it, "nobody gave a fuck what we were playing". They also felt disenchanted with their former heroes.

"Not only was the tour expensive for Wire due to the buy-on fees

etc.," wrote Colin Newman in the sleeve notes to the 2006 reissue of
154, "but it was somewhat dubious in its effectiveness. A pairing of 1979
Wire and 1973 Roxy Music would have been dynamite, but fans of late-
Seventies Ferry's schmaltz were simply not interested in the young Turks
that were Wire.

"Furthermore," he wrote, "Wire themselves could see all the bad
things that fame and success bring [in Roxy Music]. With no one in
the band's circle to counsel them that things didn't have to turn out
that way, they began to descend into the first fits of destructive self-
absorption."

If they were a sign of the disintegration to come, Wire's foreign sorties
with Roxy did at least provide them with a valuable opportunity to
road-test some new material for what would be their third album, *154*,
avoiding as far as possible the dull grind of playing songs from *Chairs
Missing*, which was all of six months old.

This meant that when, in summer '79, they re-entered Advision
Studios with Mike Thorne, Paul Hardiman and Ken Thomas, they were
in a far better position than they had been at the equivalent point with
Pink Flag and *Chairs Missing*. They were ready, primed, a finely tuned
performance unit already used, via the Roxy Music tour, to playing their
new songs to a restless and often intolerant audience.

It was, according to Thorne, "an unusual – and deserved – privilege
and an enormous creative springboard. It was like hearing a new group,
the confidence and strength gained with the songs on the road immediately effective. Since they were delivering so strongly, the foundation of
a track that could then be pulled around and reconstructed was relatively
easy to achieve, so that the overall transmutation could be greater."

Not that the sessions for *154*, the swansong of Wire v 1.0, were as
happy and problem-free as that sounds. In fact, they were quite unpleasant and, despite numerous creative highpoints, Newman, for one, found
them "psychologically draining".

"Some people in the band were frightened of success," he told *The
Independent* in 2006. "That makes moving forward difficult, so *154* had
an element of the last gasp about it. The politics in the band had got so
bad. I was the youngest, who wrote most of the tunes, and I was the
lead singer – a dangerous combination because you're bound to get

bullied. Wire can be brutal. I felt crushed at times. Wire have been play-ing power games for 30 years. They could be an even better band, if not for that."

Thorne remembers, if not fist-fights and smashed consoles, "very intense disagreements that, when they surfaced, led to some, not shout-ing, just stern exchanges" – much "suffering in silence", in the words of 'A Touching Display', a typically dark, brooding track from *154*. Bruce Gilbert likens the mood at Advision at the time to a play by Pinter or Beckett, all bleak lighting, bad moods and, "I'm not staying here for this, I'm going to the pub." "You only remember the traumas, don't you?" says Robert Gotobed, adding that he doesn't "have a recollection of a lot of struggling going on. I think probably by that time we could more enjoy the process of being in the studio, which is how it ought to be. There were more disagreements over ideas rather than over, you know, 'You made a mistake and that's ruined the track for everybody else' sort of arguments. But tension," he concedes, "was just always there. I think it was something that produced our attitude; you couldn't separate it from the group. It was our way of working. It sounds like a cliché, that we did it for our art, but that's why we did it. And then we didn't sell any records! I guess we're just masochists." He ascribes the tension in the Wire camp to them being less a bunch of musicians than an art-based collective. "Maybe musicians band together and go, 'Let's design a hit.' Whereas we sat down together and thought, 'Is it art?' I mean, I'm not allowed to talk about it because I didn't go to art college… I'm just happy to play drums. If I can put my drum ideas into the Wire output, then that's enough for me. I'm not a songwriter, so I didn't have the con-flict of thinking my song's not being used in the way I want it to be. I'm just a manual worker, really."

Graham Lewis does remember *154* being "a very, very difficult record" to make. "Our biggest problem," he maintains, "was that, after *Chairs Missing*, the whole writing process changed, so we had a situation where now there were three of us churning out songs, and material was coming from all sorts of different combinations."

Casting an eye over the *154* credits you can see there are, on Wire's third album, Newman songs, Lewis songs, Gilbert songs, songs by Gilbert and Lewis, songs by Lewis and Newman, even one by Lewis,

Newman and Gilbert and, on the seven-inch single that came free with the album, one title, 'Get Down 1 + 2', written by Gotobed and Newman in conjunction with Colin's old school friend Desmond Simmons.

Thorne believes the album's publishing credits, presenting even less of a united front than on *Chairs Missing*, reflected the process of splintering and dissolution that was well under way. "Many groups start off idealistically sharing credit for the writing, acknowledging that all contribute to the sound and atmosphere even if they don't physically write the music or lyrics. The third Wire album accentuated the jealousies that cause such splits. It may have been that the tension contributed to the music, but it was often very hard work indeed."

Further debates raged about whose songs were going to make the final cut. "Before we even got to *154*, basically, we had at least twice as much material as we needed," says Lewis. "It was a great and terrible problem – deciding which songs were going to stay and which were going to have to go."

In a way, *154* was Wire's version of The Beatles' 'White Album', a series of solo albums within an album made by a group that was becoming increasingly fractured, a division emerging based on aesthetic differences: the pop-minded Newman, Gotobed and Thorne, and the more experimental, abstract, noisenik faction of Lewis and Gilbert. Thorne doesn't believe the analogy can be extended so that he, Newman and Gotobed become the McCartney of the piece, with Lewis and Gilbert as the Lennon, but he does accept that there was good old-fashioned creative tension in the studio, the sort that pushed Jagger and Richards and all the other great rock partnerships to new artistic heights. Did the various projects undertaken in the Eighties by the members after they split for the first time at the end of 1979 confirm what he suspected, that here were four totally different artists struggling to say quite different things? "No," he says, "because I already knew – there was a constructive polarity all along."

Lewis dismisses this view of Wire circa *154* as a band divided into aesthetic camps as too convenient, and feels that such a view overlooks, for example, Gilbert's own melodic sensibility evinced on a track like 'Blessed State' (attention should also be drawn to Lewis' own solo He

Said projects in the Eighties, which have a powerful yet poppy and wistful quality). He ascribes it to laziness on the part of journalists.

"The idea that the band was factionalised wasn't actually true, as you can tell from the contributions of the different members," he says. He does, however, explain that certain members would refuse to play on certain songs on *154*, according to taste, although this wasn't necessarily a problem. "There are certain songs that Bruce, for instance, wouldn't play on, but it wasn't an issue. It was like, 'I don't want to play on that.' 'OK, don't play on it.'

"But I think," he observes of *154* the finished product, "that sonically it's a pretty integrated picture that we produced overall, and you can hear that in the demos for the album; you can hear how great the sense of accord was. We were actually trying to make it work in some democratic form."

For Colin Newman, there was "no longer a common cause". He recalls Mike Thorne suggesting, at the outset, that the band record a series of singles, not an album. He also notes that EMI was becoming increasingly concerned that Wire had yet to make the all-important crossover from critical respect to large-scale public acclaim. But he, too, remembers democracy still being an achievable goal, not dysfunction. "The mood of the band was becoming, by different degrees, more experimental, but it was the different degrees that caused the internal strife. Not everybody played on every track, and 'The 15th' – EMI's choice of single – was turned down for release by a majority of the band for that reason." He describes *154* as a "bad-tempered compromise based more on individual interest causes than total musical merit. In short: a flawed classic."

Thorne has a higher opinion of the album, considering it some of their most accomplished work to date. Nevertheless, the experience was sufficiently draining that he decided he'd had enough and wanted out. "It wasn't pleasant, no. It was tense. The vessel had grown a little small for the five of us.

"Tension," he contends, "can be provocative. But the social wear and tear just wasn't worth it."

"These were fraught sessions," he wrote in an essay for The Stereo Society in 2000. "Perhaps we'd all been living together too long, although the experimental mood on the album was served by the conversational shorthand you develop over a long time, when fewer words are necessary to explain." After a few quick demos to test the water and for the five of them "just to settle in again", he and the band decamped to Advision "where the playing intensity was still often at the very edge of what they could do". The strain of getting a decent performance of, for example, 'Two People In A Room' was reminiscent of the white-knuckle sessions for *Pink Flag*'s '12XU'.

It was the fact that Wire were so exacting and demanding of themselves and each other that arguments flared up. "There's nothing more frustrating than screwing yourself up for the take, hitting the high tension, feeling everything motoring and then making a dumb mistake. The higher the music's intensity, the more a wrong move drives you crazy."

Robert Gotobed's view of *154* is that it "combines a sort of pop sensibility with an improvement in playing ability and us getting comfortable with the studio". It was, he decides, "a crystallizing of a lot of the work that we'd done before".

Despite – or perhaps, perversely, because of – the tension and stress caused by the *154* sessions, it remains Bruce Gilbert's favourite of the first three Wire albums. "It's the most interesting," he says. "I think it was a bit more edgy and stressful, but it certainly seemed to me that we should be pushing it a bit more, stretching the idea of what constitutes a song or a piece of music, and I think there was a bit of tugging and pulling in different directions, which Mike Thorne was very aware of – he tried to satisfy everybody.

"I know Graham and I were very excited," says Gilbert of the *154* sessions and the possibilities that opened up before them for expansion and exploration in the studio. "We were hanging out a bit more and we were very excited by the possibilities of what you could do in a studio when you really experiment. There were times when it was a little frustrating, but it's a confidence thing and maybe partly third-album syndrome. Maybe because we were this ensemble, or because it didn't seem as though the songs were coming as easily or as naturally as they had done previously, where one wasn't even thinking in a self-conscious way about what should be the direction… But obviously after two years, the strain started to show, and people were looking to do their own thing, really, rather than trying to cram it all into Wire." Gilbert's own vision for Wire couldn't be clearer. He was fantasising, he admits, about "Wire being the most experimental band in the world." Others in the band, meanwhile, had other ideas: "Well, other people thought we were basically a pop band."

When did it occur to Gilbert that something had to give? "I think it was obvious from the very beginning of the album that something was going to happen. Colin was already negotiating his first solo album deal with EMI, and Graham and I were cooking up ways of doing something slightly more experimental." He believes Wire could have continued on a more ad-hoc basis, releasing records at greater intervals in between solo ventures. Ultimately, though, he says, "The pressure had to give, basically. We were having too many ideas to fit into the Wire glove."

If the atmosphere at Advision was fraught, it worked in a sense, because the music on *154* was among Wire's most brutal and beautiful to date; cerebral yet with the visceral punch of the hardest rock. On 'Once is Enough' Lewis bashed around the studio full of scrap metal, hammer in hand, creating in the process a prototype for the early Eighties metal-bashing/industrial noise of Test Department and Germany's Einstürzende Neubaten. 'The Other Window' is slower, more menacing, with a voiceover from Lewis that sounds like he's in a dark trance as FX pan across the stereo range and drums trample unsteadily, out of time, with no concern for rhythm or metre. 'A Touching Display' was as dark and forbidding as anything on Joy Divison's *Unknown Pleasures*, released a month or two earlier, with its reference to "thrust and parry". 'Single K.O.' caught the mood of anxiety and simmering resentment perfectly, while 'Two People In A Room' expressed the schismatic nature of the recordings with violent precision.

"It's vicious, isn't it?" agrees Lewis. "It's great, a really, really good song, just like the whole record. It's blitzing. Do you remember the ads for Cadbury's milk chocolate (Dairy Milk), where they had a pint and a half of milk in each bar, and it was supposed to only hold a pint? Well, that's kind of what it felt like when we were making *154*. We tried to pull off the Cadbury's miracle, but there was an awful lot of milk spilt on the floor afterwards in the process." How vicious did it get in the studio? "It got really tough. Mike didn't have an easy time of it. He was thinking about working on a solo record with Colin… There was a lot of shifting about.

"With nearly all the good records that I've been involved in, somewhere along the line there's a change in philosophy during the working process because that's what happens when people work hard. You try to find other ways of doing things, and in that process there is a lot of friction. But the results are things like 'The Other Window', which got transformed in the studio.

"But really, we were just doing what we were trying to do, and we were working damn hard at it. I don't think we were thinking 10 years ahead or anything as daft as that. We weren't that smart. I think everyone just felt like they wanted to survive it, really. We were dealing with this rapid expansion. Everybody started to have ideas about what it might be possible to do, and at the same time we were starting to have problems with the record company. But it [154] is really good, high-quality stuff. There are three or four things on there that could have made great singles."

One of those songs, 'Map Ref. 41°N 93° W', was Wire's most exquisite confection to date and it was, indeed, released as a single, but the lyric about a cartographer, all references to geometry, geography, and longitude and latitude, was hardly the norm for a would-be Top 20 smash. Was there a sense of self-sabotage about the band; that some members were, as Newman suggested, "frightened of success"? Lewis, responsible for the words on 'Map Ref.', is circumspect in his response. "I wrote about cartology instead of writing about something else," he says, then answers the question. "No, not at all. That's what I write about. I write about what I see and what I live through. That's why I wrote the song. It was about the first time I'd ever flown across America, which I found quite astonishing. The second part of the song is about driving through the lowlands of Holland, where you've got another grid system, all canals, so I hitched those two things together. It wasn't sabotage or subversion. I like maps. Maps are good."

Not that EMI dared intervene and make suggestions about musical or lyrical amendments to Wire songs, even though by now they were becoming anxious themselves about the band's future and their failure to produce a hit album or single. They would have got short shrift if they had got involved, though. "We didn't like being messed about," says Lewis. He lays the blame for the disintegration of Wire at this point at the door of the band's management, who he believes "weren't strong enough" to handle them or provide "the protection or the guidance" that they required at this critical juncture in their career. "We could have done with it at the time because we were pretty exhausted. It needed some vision, and we didn't really get that. And because we didn't get it, everyone's relationship with EMI deteriorated."

Wire were, as ever, full of ideas, not just for the music, but for every creative area involved in a record's production and promotion, from advertising to the then-burgeoning video format. But they were stymied at every turn. One brainwave the band had was to advertise *154* on TV, a plan that would have been hugely expensive but one to which a truly supportive label, with faith in their act, might have agreed. Increasingly, Wire were not getting the response they wanted from EMI. "We had meetings with the head of marketing, for instance, and we'd be faced with some guy telling us that, 'No, no, no, no, you can't sell music on TV. We've tried, and it doesn't work.'

"We'd put an awful lot of our lives into what we were doing," he says of the growing feelings of disappointment and disenchantment in Wire. Lewis sensed, as did the others, that it was time to pursue other areas of creative endeavour: solo projects. Plus, they were due another advance from EMI for a fourth album, and their paymasters at the label weren't overkeen on delivering. Wire's next move was obvious. "We decided," says Lewis, "that perhaps it wasn't such a good idea being with EMI any more, and we told them that we'd left." The problem was, nobody at EMI had bothered to inform the band that they wouldn't be renewing their contract, due, according to Lewis, to "deep economic issues within the company". Wire, he recalls, were told that they couldn't just leave the label like that. "They said, 'No, no, you can't do that', and we said, 'Oh yes we can, and we have.' Everybody in the band agreed. We said, 'Look, we've tried this. Perhaps we should do something else."

Thorne was the first to jump ship, resigning during the mixing of the album. He didn't want his resignation to colour the mood or derail the band during recording, so he left it as late as he could in the process. "The writing was on the wall," he says. "I called management and told them I couldn't push it any further but that the album sounded as good as I could possibly make it." He asked manager Mike Collins not to tell the band until the final mix of *154* had been completed. Then he met Bruce Gilbert on the stairs to Advision 2, the mixing adjunct to the recording studio, who had already heard the news. "Bruce said, 'So you've done the deed?'" Did any of the band try to talk him out of leaving? "No."

It was the end of an era for Wire, ironic considering the quality of the album they had just finished. Colin Newman isn't so sure. Looking back at this period a quarter of a century later, he acknowledges that, yes, *154* got amazing reviews in the music press, arguably their most enthusiastic to date, but it just wasn't enough. Or rather, his view of it all has been tainted by what happened at the time, and by what happened next.

"The reviews *154* got at the time would make most bands very pleased," he says. "But I think *154*'s deeply flawed. Some of it's fantastic; some of it's awful and bombastic. Wire made huge mistakes right after it. We drove the bus straight off the cliff. There wasn't a point when we said, 'It's over.' It just fell apart. I think it's a tragedy of contemporary art. I feel disgust at the factors that left Wire, by 1980, nonexistent."

Chapter 6

Witness To The Fact

"We did the honourable thing. We just didn't think we could go on with the situation as it was, so the best thing to do was to stop. But we never said, 'Right, that's it. I never want to see you or work with you again.' It wasn't like that at all. There were still plans that were attempted to be made." – Graham Lewis

WIRE'S third album was, in many ways, the perfect synthesis of *Pink Flag*'s ruthless concision and *Chairs Missing*'s more digressive approach. In a sense, it upped the ante on all counts: its tough moments, such as 'Two People In A Room', were tougher than anything in their repertoire, its explorations at the outer limits of latterday psych-rock went deeper and further (at almost seven minutes, 'A Touching Display' was the longest track on Wire's first three albums), and its sweet moments were sweeter: it featured, in 'Map Ref. 41°N 93°W', their most gorgeous pop creation to date, from that parallel universe where a song about a cartographer (a "cartologist" in the song) can become a giant smash hit.

Although the *154* cover art was slightly different in tone from the sleeves for the first two Wire albums – being, in the words of journalist and long-term Wire supporter Jon Savage, "abstract minimal geo-deco", all straight lines, waves and pastel shades with no information whatsoever (evoking in that respect Peter Saville's masterpieces of minimalist modernism for Manchester's Factory label) – it still forms a piece with its two predecessors.

The first three Wire albums seem like a triptych even if they weren't designed to be considered as such, reminiscent in terms of European avant-garde influence, coherence and ingenuity of David Bowie's 'Berlin trilogy' or the three albums recorded by Talking Heads with Brian Eno in that same late-Seventies time frame. This feeling of a consistent atmosphere and sustained invention was enhanced, obviously, by the fact that it was produced and performed by the same team – the Wire boys as well as Messrs Thorne, Hardiman and Thomas.

Kate Lukas, too, made her third consecutive appearance on a Wire album, playing alto flute, but there were other additional musicians on *154*: at Thorne's behest, Hilly Kristal, owner of legendary New York punk club CBGBs, sang bass vocals on closing track '40 Versions'; classical musician Joan Whiting played cor anglais on the album; while Tim Souster, an old composer friend of Thorne's who had studied and played under Karlheinz Stockhausen, added electric viola.

Along with the brilliant, groundbreaking likes of Joy Division's *Unknown Pleasures*, PiL's *Metal Box*, Talking Heads' *Fear Of Music*, Gang Of Four's *Entertainment!*, The Slits' *Cut* and XTC's *Drums & Wires*, Wire's *154* helped make 1979 the post-punk era's creative high watermark, each band pushing the envelope in terms of sonic ambition and new ideas.

When the album – its title taken from Robert Gotobed's diaries in which he had noted down every Wire gig up to the start of recording, a total of 154 – came out in September 1979, the press were even more effusive in their praise than they were for *Pink Flag* and *Chairs Missing*, reviewers giving no indication that they were aware of the turmoil behind the scenes or that, with Mike Thorne's decision to quit, the Advision dream team was no more.

In June '79, EMI had issued 'A Question of Degree' and 'Former Airline' ("An alluring single from the inscrutable Wire", according to

NME), neither of which tracks would appear on *154*, as a single. The following month Wire embarked on a 13-date UK tour, although, as per usual, there was precious little promotion of the songs on *154* during the concerts, the band instead focusing on brand new material. This is probably why, reviewing their Newport gig of July 4, Hugh Fielder wrote in *Sounds*: "As a promotional tour for their fourth album, Wire's latest series of gigs are a useful affair. There's just one minor snag: they don't actually release their third album until September."*

But if Wire were expecting similarly quizzical or sceptical assessments of *154*, they would have been pleasantly surprised when the write-ups came flooding in. Reviewers were unanimous in hailing *154* a masterpiece of modern music-making.

"*154* beats *Chairs Missing* and a good many art products this year," wrote Jon Savage, on a transfer from *Sounds* to *Melody Maker*. "The album is a musical tour de force," he continued, singling out the "queasy organ quivers" of '40 Versions' and 'On Returning', the itchy guitar on 'Map Ref' and the trickling guitar and blurred voices of 'Once Is Enough'" as examples of Wire's "embarrassment of ideas". Nick Kent in *NME* suggested that *154* was the album that Bowie and Eno set out to make when they worked on *Lodger*, concluding that, "With *154* Wire have delivered a fearsome punch that instantly moves them back into the forefront of rock's new music vanguard. It simply makes 95 percent of the competition look feeble. Don't go for anything less." *Record Mirror's* Chris Westwood commented that the album "balances some of the most naggingly infectious commercial music of the year against lyrics of the most inverted, clipped quality", adding that this contrast was at the heart of Wire's appeal. In their third five-star *Sounds* review on the trot, Hugh Fielder said: "Wire have taken a lot more care during the recording than ever before. They get their five stars for unwavering commitment to their own beliefs... As long as they maintain that commitment then they can have mine, too."

---

* In this regard Wire were again referencing Pink Floyd, although they probably didn't realise it at the time. In the early to mid-Seventies the Floyd made a habit of performing songs live, including the entire *Dark Side Of The Moon* suite, which would not appear on record until at least 12 months later, and occasionally even longer.

Even the Americans loved the album. "Their finest achievement," pronounced *Rolling Stone*'s Kurt Loder, who noted the band's "post-psychedelic sensibility" and compared it to Syd Barrett-era Pink Floyd, deciding that the layered synth sound and what he referred to as Colin Newman's "near-autistic" vocal style brought to mind what Roxy Music's third album would have sounded like had Eno stuck around. "Like the painter Magritte," he furthered, "this band distils a witty, often mordant surrealism from the most achingly commonplace situations." He concluded that there was "more real rock'n'roll invention" on *154* than "most bands are able to come up with in a career".

In all the reviews, however, no one mentioned the free four-track EP that was given away with the first 20,000 copies of *154*. Comprising a series of doodles and exercises in sound – 'Song 1', 'Get Down (Parts 1 and 2)', 'Let's Panic Later' and 'Small Electric Piece' – the idea behind the extra recordings was to approach EMI with the intention of getting them to bankroll a subsidiary label along the lines of Brian Eno's Obscure imprint, enabling each member of the band to have an outlet for their more experimental impulses. Needless to say, it didn't happen. But it did show that, just as Wire were poised to make some sort of commercial breakthrough, there they were, plotting their next move towards the art-rock margins.

"That was interesting," says Graham Lewis of the four-song freebie. "Bruce's 'Small Electric Piece' was very short, simple and sort of naïve. I did a proto-sampling thing called 'Let's Panic Later', which was made with tape-recorded voices – although it's still a song – and was electronic-based. You could see we had ideas and where people wanted to go next – that was already apparent. There were areas that people wanted to investigate."

But there was more to Wire than pursuing intellectual impulses and new directions. It wasn't all austerity and cold menace; there was more to Wire's music than ambient noir with chilling overtones and proto-industrial intimidation. Yes, Wire's music circa *154* could be, as Simon Reynolds wrote in *Rip It Up And Start Again*, "almost oppressively textured", its "glaze of overdubs and guitar treatments" producing what he called "a ceramic opacity, forbidding and impenetrable".

And yet there was emotion and humanity beneath Wire's steely carapace. As arch Wire-o-phile Johnny Marr of The Smiths notes in the foreword to this book, what emerged through the cracks of Wire's songs such as 'Outdoor Miner' and 'Map Ref' and 'Blessed State', like memory flickers of some lost Sixties idyll or shafts of sunlight appearing in a bleak urban futurescape, was a certain mournful quality and wistful, haunted Anglo-pop sensibility that resonated with echoes of everything from the late-Sixties psych-pop of The Move and Pink Floyd to Canterbury Scene acts such as Kevin Ayers and Soft Machine (Newman's voice on 'The 15th' is eerily reminiscent of Robert Wyatt's), to the baroque UK folk-rock stylings of John Renbourn – all the music that Colin Newman and Graham Lewis grew up listening to in the Sixties, basically.

Similarly, in Lewis' doomy, blank voiceover on opening track 'I Should Have Known Better', it would be easy to hear the passionless musings of an automaton, but when you consider the Wire story, their history of friction and the way things fell apart after *154*, lyrics such as "tears in my eyes" (a phrase that also appeared on Joy Division's contemporaneous *Unknown Pleasures*) begin to assume a less vague and gnomic, distanced and detached quality. An emotional essence starts to shine through.

There is also, with *154*, a sense of a culmination, of a story reaching its conclusion, its denouement. In a way, the first three Wire albums could be said to provide a narrative arc: from the confidence and vigour of *Pink Flag*, to mid-period maturity with *Chairs Missing*, to entropy and collapse on *154*. In another way, Wire compressed into three years what The Beatles, The Beach Boys and The Byrds had the whole of the Sixties to evolve in. Certainly on their third album it is tempting to detect elements of autobiography creeping into the writing, notably on a track like 'Two People In A Room', which appears to reflect the rival camps in the band and depicts the atmosphere chez Wire at this point as one of deadly silence and quiet loathing ("Facial movements betray/A private display/Of nervous disorder/And mutual torture").

Graham Lewis is intrigued by the idea of the first three albums telling the story of Wire from 1977 to 1979 but isn't sure how applicable it is. "It's the work that those four people did in that period," he accepts. "It represents what we did and how we lived and where we were and all of those things, absolutely, yeah. But I don't see any entropy on *154*; there's no lack of energy. We did the honourable thing. We thought, 'We can't go on with this situation, so the best thing to do is stop.' But we never said, 'Right, that's it. I never want to see you again or we're never going to work together again.' It wasn't like that at all. There were still plans that were attempted to be made."

According to Lewis, there was even talk of a fourth Wire studio album, whether for EMI or another label, amid guarantees that the four members would ensure a better working atmosphere if they did get that far. "We nearly made another record. We actually had conversations with Mike [Thorne] about doing another one and everybody was going, 'Well, we did promise that we were going to behave a bit better towards each other on the next one.' It got to that stage, but then Colin got an invitation to go and take photographs in India, Bruce and I started doing the Dome stuff, and life started to get in the way. We all became really busy doing other things. It wasn't until Colin came back from India and contacted me that we could start thinking about whether we'd like to do some more. And of course the answer was yes, so the differences between everybody can't have been that great."

Meanwhile, in October 1979 EMI predictably issued 'Map Ref. 41°N 93° W' as a single, which *NME* with equal predictability made Single of the Week ("An exceptional piece of work from initial concept to final execution"). The B-side, 'Go Ahead', was the first Wire track to be put out that had not been produced by Mike Thorne. It was recorded at Magritte Studios in London along with two other brand new tracks: 'Our Swimmer' and 'Midnight Bahnhof Café'.

That same month the band recorded their third John Peel session. Typically for Wire, they chose to use their allotted 15 minutes performing one extended piece of new music that came out of a jam session, 'Crazy About Love', instead of the usual routine for bands in such circumstances, which was – and probably still is – to re-record songs from their current album.

"The problem we've found is that we have an excess of material," Graham Lewis explained to Giovanni Dadomo of *Sounds*, decrying the more standard practice of airing existing material as "a marketing exercise" or "free advertising".

But if observers thought Wire were being bold, belligerent or bloody-minded here, they really hadn't seen, or heard, anything yet.

★

AT the beginning of November 1979 Wire announced that they were going to make initially three (later four) appearances at the 350-capacity Jeannetta Cochrane Theatre in London's Central School of Art (the old alma mater of, among others, Glen Matlock of The Sex Pistols and notorious artist Lucien Freud). They were intending to put on a show called 'People In A Room', on November 9, 10, 11 and 13.

After the constraints, routines and rituals of regular rock performing and touring, this was to make a refreshing change for Wire: four evenings' worth of performances involving each member of the group presenting a 15-minute 'performance art' piece to be followed by Wire the band playing their latest music.

Each evening the audience was met in the foyer by a video camera, which relayed images of themselves to the auditorium. Bruce Gilbert set the surreal tone, taking to the stage and performing a track called 'Tableau' while holding a small trolley and an empty glass. Pushing the trolley about the stage, Gilbert would then come to a standstill, and someone would come out and fill the glass with water. Wire's resident absurdist would proceed to examine the water with a light-pen, before drinking it and pushing the trolley about, repeating these actions for about 15 minutes.

Graham Lewis took his turn during 'A Panamanian Craze?'. The bassist was seen on video screens watching a man and woman – Robert Gotobed and Angela (AC Marias) Conway – as they danced together onstage with a pair of tights on each others' heads and oranges in each foot of the tights. Meanwhile, the video monitors kept pace with Lewis as he darted back and forth between foyer and auditorium to relay the events then going on onstage to manager Mike Collins.

Next up in this Dadaist future cabaret was Colin Newman, who took to the stage to perform 'An Unlikely Occurrence'. This involved 15 guitarists, most of them non-professionals, with five each playing the chords of E, A and D respectively. "Three of the four nights went smoothly," reported Wire aficionado Kevin Eden, "with the sound surging and rolling in waves of chords. However, on one of the nights the power failed and the guitar sounds died. All that could be heard was the sound of jangling strings as the guitarists carried on until the power came back on with an enormous swell of sound."

The first half of this bizarre evening's entertainment concluded with Robert Gotobed's 'The Decorator', the only member of Wire who had never been to art school indulging in some action painting, hurling paint at a huge canvas.

Following a brief interlude, Wire then appeared on stage. Any hopes of a "Greatest Hits" crowd-pleasing set, or even tracks from their latest album, were quickly dashed as the band set about performing the 15-minute improvisational number, 'Crazy About Love', first aired on the John Peel show the month before, as well as other new songs: 'Remove On Improvement', 'The Spare One', 'Lorries', 'Underwater Experiences', 'Ally In Exile', 'Over My Head' and 'Our Swimmer'. Only 'On Returning', 'A Blessed State' and 'Two People In A Room' would have been familiar, being tracks from *154*.

The response to Wire's latest activities in the music press was a mixture of puzzlement and outrage. Dave McCullough, usually the paper's champion of all things experimental and strange, wrote in *Sounds*: "Wire are pretentious, serious, aging, decadent, extravagant, naughty, contagious, zippy, trippy, and *Observer* colour supplement. Wire are Tom Stoppard, Ian McKellen, Melvyn Bragg, they're paid up members of the late 20th Century artistic mediocrity. Oh, we're just steeped in art, dahling! Yes, but you're unforgivably mediocre. The rub? The Jeannetta Cochrane revelation showed that Wire have a space to play onstage and an audience willing to listen. The frightening thing is maybe Wire don't know what to do with that space, and they thus spend their time wallowing in unartistic self-doubt."

Paul Tickell of *Melody Maker* decided that, "Wire's 'People In A Room' tells the usual sorry experimental tale of arty types overestimating the flexibility of rock as a good medium. But what a good idea it must have seemed to the band and their resourceful friends." Rick Joseph in *NME* seemed to be a little more accepting: "Wire may not be everybody's bag of dolly-mixtures, and it would be bad news if their attitude was to become prevalent. They are destined to be misunderstood and unwhistled-along-to. They belong in some twilight zone where the boogie ends and the woogie begins."

And then, silence. Until February 1980, that is, when a terse announcement appeared in the music press accompanied by a suitably sullen-looking photo of the band, which read: "Due to internal and corporate problems currently besetting EMI, there has been a breakdown in communication between the company and Wire. In addition to this, the company's reticence to consolidate future plans and projects has led to Wire taking advantage of the fact that they are no longer under any contractual obligation to EMI." As for EMI, its attitude towards Wire and the band's increasing propensity for the abstract and uncommercial was roughly along the lines, says Mike Thorne, of, "A record company is not an Arts Council."

Ever perverse and reluctant to take the easy route, Wire's next move was not, however, to rein things in, in order to perhaps attract a new record company, but to go further towards the outer limits of acceptability. Instead of using their upcoming London gig at the end of February 1980 as a showcase for prospective labels – there had, apparently, been meetings with Factory, whose boss, Tony Wilson, believed they'd be "better off doing it themselves", according to Bruce Gilbert (the band agreed, especially when they discovered that Factory were thrifty when it came to advances) – they put on a show that had "career suicide" written all over it.

That press release to announce Wire's split from EMI also contained a reference to "Wire rehearsing new material for a London date". That date, at the Electric Ballroom in Camden, on February 29, 1980, took the Jeannetta Cochrane Theatre performance to its illogical extreme.

The first blow to rock-gig orthodoxy came when the band performed from behind a 6 x 12 sheet, which was carried around the stage by two gentlemen by the names of Tom and John. Occasionally, a Master of Ceremonies (actually, manager Mike Collins forced into a role he had no experience of or preparation for) would attempt to inject a note of humour or sarcasm into proceedings, only to be met by hostility from the crowd. Finally, each of the songs, all but three of which would have been unknown to the audience, was accompanied by a ridiculous spectacle. For 'Everything's Going To Be Nice', two men tethered to an inflatable jet were dragged across the stage by Angela Conway. As Newman sang 'We Meet Under Tables' he was dressed in a black knee-length veil. For another number, someone wrestled with a leather coat. During the Captain Beefheart-ishly quirky and jerky 'Eels Sang Lino', delivered by Lewis in something between a bark and a growl, the bassist was accompanied by an illuminated goose. During 'Piano Tuner (Keep Strumming Those Chords)' Newman attacked a gas stove while 'Zegk Hoqp' featured a dozen percussionists wearing newspaper head-dresses as well as musical support from the two members of German proto-electro duo D.A.F. (Deutsch Amerikanische Freundschaft), Gabi Delgado and Robert Görl, who took the song into a previously unforeseen tribal direction. For 'Eastern Standard' a hapless Mike Collins attempted to give a geography lesson while the closing 'And Then…' saw Newman eat two loaves of bread as blank scrolls were unrolled. A fragment of '12XU' was tossed before the hordes with utter disdain for the notion of nostalgia as audience members either walked out in disgust, threw bottles or shouted themselves hoarse.

To make matters worse, Wire's last live performance for five and a half years was recorded incorrectly, the eight-track recorder being set up wrongly, hence the lo-fi, distorted, two-track-only mix that you can hear on the album of the Electric Ballroom debacle, *Document And Eyewitness*, first released by Rough Trade in July 1981, with its rough, shambolic, bootleg quality.

Document And Eyewitness is one of those endurance-test live albums, like The Stooges' *Metallic KO* or The Velvet Underground's *Live At Max's Kansas City*, that you will either love or will have you screaming for the "off" switch. Chris Bohn, in his August 1, 1981 review of the album in *NME*, praised Wire's persistent refusal to do what was expected of them – "and when the unexpected itself became the predictability factor there wasn't really much point in going on," he added. "Where the spectators would have been satisfied with the cosy illusion of a Greatest Hits re-run, Wire demanded that they should participate with their imaginations by playing totally unfamiliar sets. Did that make them arrogant? On the contrary, they were crediting their followers with intelligence to grapple with the unknown." Bohn noted that the Electric Ballroom set captured Wire at their most provocative and extreme, and via a "battery of fringe theatre techniques" succeeded "more in irritating the audience than outraging them". And yet, Bohn decided, despite or because of the wacky antics and aural assaults, the shoddy recording quality and abrasive and barbed nature of song-fragments like 'Eels Sang Lino', Wire "created a vicious tension between audience and performers, which has been caught on this record, making it one of the most compulsive live records in a long time."

The CD version of *Document And Eyewitness*, issued by Mute in 1991, offers a broader impression of Wire after *154* and where they might have gone next. Part one comprises seven tracks, recorded live at the Notre Dame Hall in July 1979, that suggest a fourth Wire album, perhaps with Martin Hannett or Martin Rushent at the controls and released at the height of synthmania in 1980-1, might have proved an interesting compromise between the band's experimental and electronic pop sensibilities. The opening track, 'Go Ahead', is a powerful blast of electronic noise, a series of eerie FX worthy of the BBC *Radiophonic Workshop* whooshing and screeching from speaker to speaker as Colin Newman, like a particularly pissed-off John Lydon, whines about "advertising", "radio play" and "critical acclaim" as the music starts to resemble PiL at their krautrockin' best. 'Ally In Exile' is like 'Louie Louie' as it might have been performed by Cabaret Voltaire. 'Relationship', introduced by Graham Lewis at his most dour, is a *Pink Flag*-ishly brief (1'22") number that ends abruptly when the song runs out of steam as per those tracks on Wire's debut album. 'Underwater Experiences', previewed on the John Peel show the previous October, mixed up proto-goth guitar textures and tribal rhythms, sounding like Bauhaus in a blender with Can. 'Witness To The Fact' sounds like standard-issue fast-paced Wirerock, somehow droney and melodic. 'Two People In A Room' lacks the murderous intensity of the *154* version but is nonetheless great. And 'Our Swimmer', which became the band's last-ever single, recorded in early 1980 but not issued until May 1981, suggests Wire could have had an entryist, subversive-pop afterlife alongside such post-punk mavericks as The Cure, The Associates and the Banshees had they hooked up with a producer like Mike Hedges, who might have teased out the glorious melodic potential of the song and given it his trademark post-psychedelic shimmer.

Part two of the *Document And Eyewitness* CD is a version of 'Heartbeat' from *Chairs Missing*, performed in Montreux when Wire opened for Roxy Music, much to the apparent chagrin of Roxy's audience, who can be heard whistling and moaning throughout the song.

Part three is the Electric Ballroom set, which was opened by D.A.F. (and documented by the duo on their Mute album *Die Kleinen Und Die Bosen*), and is here interspersed with fragments of a taped conversation between Graham Lewis and artist Russell Mills in which they discuss the success or otherwise of the night – to rather smug and self-congratulatory effect, something that Wire always managed to avoid. You can hear Wire goad the audience with their music and sarcasm, never really making it clear whether it's meant or mere art-pranksterism. Part four comprises the band's posthumous single 'Our Swimmer' and the B-side 'Midnight Bahnhof Café' as they were produced for release by the Charisma label – they are fabulous and tantalising glimpses of the Wirepop to come in the mid-to-late-Eighties on Mute and confirm that they could contrive an alluring melody when they felt so inclined.

But maybe they didn't feel inclined. Perhaps they enjoyed not doing what people expected them to do. As Graham Lewis explains, when EMI sent a staff member down to the Jeannetta Cochrane Theatre to find out how many numbers Wire would be playing from their then-current *154*, the response from the band was, he says, "Fairly cagey. I think somebody said, 'Um... four? Three? Five, maybe? We don't know. We'll tell you when we get there.'" Far from seeing the Cochrane and Electric Ballroom concerts as showcases for Wire's extreme noise terror, however, he believes that "many of the songs could have been on *154*", minus the distraction of the performance-art craziness that accompanied them and the band's sheer bloody-minded delivery of the music.

He draws a distinction between the two performances: between the "properly staged production" that was the highly organised Jeannetta Cochrane event, which saw a collaboration with the Central School of Art, their set-designing department and an experimental video-maker, and the far more spontaneous, loose, wild and free-form Electric Ballroom affair where "the attitude was, we wrote the material a week before the performance and basically it was done on a prayer. It was a self-financed and self-governed thing. We were outside of EMI [by this point], we weren't contracted to anybody, so it was put together very, very, very quickly."

He admits that "there was a certain amount of wind-up involved, and we knew it was going to be potential trouble, basically. People seemed to find it weird. Some people laughed, some people hated it – it was a pretty mixed reaction. The punks in the crowd hated [manager] Mike Collins as the MC. He'd seen us spat on and have bottles thrown at us [there is even a track on the *Document And Eyewitness* LP called 'Instrumental (Thrown Bottle)'], but he'd never quite experienced the love and adulation coming from an audience before, so when he came on before this rather unruly punk crowd, they fucking hated him, full stop. His clothes, the way he looked, his manner, the whole thing. It was quite reprehensible of us, really, to make him the MC of our show. They were calling him a fat fucker and abusing him generally. He was a good sport about it, but I think he was fairly shaken by it. He'd had this idea that he was going to be, you know, the friendly happy chappy; he was going to be their friend, and they decided they didn't want him as a friend. It was pretty brutal, although we found it horribly funny. We just wound the audience up. It was good and it was also very depressing at the same time. It's not necessarily what we wanted to achieve.

"It was a multimedia extravaganza, only done for two and six," he furthers. "Even the lighting didn't quite work out. It was done by Simon Miles, who'd just come back from a Ramones tour of Europe. All he had was piss- or green-coloured lights, so you couldn't have any other colours. The whole show was a decision about whether to go from green to piss or from piss to green. As you can imagine, it looked fabulous. And the mood was appropriate, you know? It wasn't a glittering occasion, by any means. Still, it [Wire's 'career'] was ours to break. We thought it was about time. It's good to break your own rules.

"But everybody was rather disappointed after the three nights at the Jeannetta Cochrane shows. We felt that if we'd had another week we could have developed things even further. The audience was nonplussed. The woman who'd become the head of EMI International said that she'd walked out after a while. She hadn't really enjoyed it very much. But she hadn't given it much of a chance. There was quite a range of reactions. The band's performance, musically, was fairly challenging.

"After every show, we met in a pub called the Enterprise round the corner from the theatre, and we noticed that people had been quite stimulated by it." Lewis remembers Brian Eno being in the audience on one of the nights at the Jeannetta Cochrane Theatre and being pleasantly surprised by the impromptu turn of events, when the power failed and the emergency power being switched on created an incredible surge of sound. "Afterwards he [Eno] said, 'Did you plan that?' And then he said, 'Actually, don't tell me.' Things like that are completely unique. You can say it was a mistake, but we didn't freak out, we kept going, so it became part of the composition. We were improvising; we were really pushing what we were doing."

Bruce Gilbert remembers a feeling in the band at the time of the *Document And Eyewitness* concerts that, "We ought to make a statement of some kind, and there was an opportunity and I think we were being encouraged almost to show our wares, and I quite liked the idea of that, but I thought we should show them wares they didn't really want to see; wares that they would rather not buy." He recalls sitting in the pub with Lewis and asking of each other, "What happens in a Wire concert? What would you like to see happen in a Wire concert? What can we do that's completely un-rock 'n' roll and interesting for ourselves?" He doesn't believe the intention at the Jeannetta Cochrane Theatre and Electric Ballroom shows was to sabotage Wire's career or climax the Wire story with something dramatic, good or bad. "I don't think it was deliberate, but as I say, I think we needed to make a statement of some description, to point out that, yes, we've left EMI, but that we weren't going to be anybody's poodle."

Gilbert found the performances "hugely funny. I had lots of fun. The angrier the audience got, the funnier and funnier it became. There was a lot of shouting – the really clever ones shouted out requests. I've been told by a couple of people who were in the audience that it was right on the edge of turning into something very nasty. My favourite bit was the three men tied to an inflatable jet being pulled across the stage by a slightly dressed woman. What was the idea behind that? It was just something I wanted to see." He agrees that the shows were half theatre of the absurd, half Exploding Plastic Inevitable. Would Andy Warhol have been proud? "I think he might have enjoyed it." Was this Wire's equivalent of *Metal Machine Music*, the 1975 Lou Reed triple album regarded today as a giant fuck-you to his fans? "I wouldn't say that. I'm not sure, had we carried on, that we would have carried on doing things as extreme as that, but the tone of the music was something I think would have been worthwhile continuing with. But I don't think we would have turned into performance artists."

Robert Gotobed also remembers a desire in Wire to do something extreme. "It was an extreme example of us following our ideas." He believes it was "quite a destructive expression for the group", adding: "It got a bit silly, less musical and more about performance art." At the time, he says, "I didn't think *Document And Eyewitness* should have been released. I didn't think the recording was good enough." It wasn't, looking back, "a happy time for Wire", nor were they happy performances. "I suppose we were testing the bounds of what we could do in the bubble that we'd created, and maybe that was bursting the bubble and sort of deciding that we should so something else. *Document And Eyewitness* marked the end of that [first] working period. But then we didn't know, when Wire split up at the end of that period, that there would be periods of reforming." Were relations fractious at this point? He believes that "there must have been for it to come to an end. I can't really remember, though. I don't think there were big arguments about what we should do for *Document And Eyewitness*. I guess it was something we'd all agreed to go through, and so we did go through with it, and it wasn't without interest, but as I say: we're not performance artists."

For the drummer, the *D&E* experience was "too chaotic. I like more order than that. I'm not even aware of how long it lasted. But it was chaotic. It's not as if we'd really had practice at putting on something that was more like performance art than playing a gig. But I suppose it had elements about it which probably branched off into what Bruce and Graham wanted to do, on their own [i.e. as Dome]. It wasn't so much mine and Colin's area… So it sort of clarified, you know, the differences of interest."

As for Wire's relationship with EMI, he acknowledges a sense of relief that it had come to an end. "We were relieved because, well, it hadn't become what EMI wanted to be, commercially. And then after the relationship with Mike broke down, we'd lost our connection with EMI. We wanted to move on to something different in some shape or form, even though we didn't know what that was."

Relations in the band at the time, recalls Lewis, were bearable because other projects were looming, taking the individuals' minds off the fact that Wire were going nowhere, fast.

"Colin was about to start making his record [1980 debut solo album *A-Z*, produced by Mike Thorne], we did the single for Charisma ['Our Swimmer'], and everybody started to get a bit busy. We saw each other occasionally, I think. And I know we were talking about perhaps making another record with Mike Thorne as well, but then Colin got an invitation to go to India and so that kind of blew that out of the water. And Bruce and Graham had certainly started work in the studio on what became the Dome things that they did with 4AD, so things came to a natural solution, or rather, dissolution…

"I think we'd been very disappointed with our experience with EMI," admits Gotobed, "so I think the attitude was that it was time to move on in some shape or form. We were feeling bloody-minded rather than suicidal. We never used the word 'career'. But yes, there were elements of *Document And Eyewitness* that were very, very bloody-minded. It seemed to be what was necessary to do. I don't think anyone was thinking consciously about what direction it was taking. But if you go back to *Document And Eyewitness* and listen to the songs from Notre Dame, those recordings were all post-*154*, so it's very apparent that there was more than enough material and direction and strength for there to have been a record after *154*. But I think there was also obviously a need to experiment and to move on somehow."

Chapter 7

Allies In Exile

"It always gets to me: the sheer idiocy of playing a concert with all the rigmarole and the soundchecking... I start feeling that I shouldn't be doing this; that I should be crawling around in mud somewhere screaming or in a studio experimenting, not standing on a stage playing the same thing night after night. I always found the idea of a band quite embarrassing" – Bruce Gilbert

IN 2006, Colin Newman, talking about the last days of Wire Mk 1 and the first few years leading up to the band's reformation in the mid-Eighties, admitted: "I felt very depressed during that period. In the end, everybody just started doing solo records, because somebody would give you an advance for that. I didn't expect there to be a Wire again. We were barely talking to each other."

They might have been barely talking, but they were certainly working, and at a furious rate, even if it was apart, or in factional micro-group spin-offs of the original four-piece. Wire's most recent album, from 2008, was called *Object 47*, so titled after the total number of releases (LPs, singles, compilations, live albums) made in the name of Wire over the years. But if you count all the numerous solo projects and collaborations involving the various members of Wire, starting in 1980 and leading right up to the present, the total would be far in excess of 47. It would seem that being a Wire fan is something of a full-time job; hacking your way through the complex network of pseudonymous projects requires serious time and commitment.

Newman, who has over the years been a musician, a record producer, as well as a record label boss, was already thinking about his next step before the four members of Wire went their separate ways in early 1980, in the fallout after the cataclysmic Jeannetta Cochrane and Electric Ballroom "events"-cum-art happenings. His first solo LP, *A–Z*, was released in 1980 on Beggar's Banquet, much of it having been written during the making of Wire's *154*. The closest any member of Wire has come to creating an accessible follow-up to *154*, *A–Z* was produced by Mike Thorne and featured Newman's old school chum Desmond Simmons on additional guitar and Robert Gotobed on drums.

It was a superb collection and a must-have for Wire devotees, specialising in the sort of melodic post-punk that Wire helped pioneer in the first place. The album veered from the jagged electronica of 'Order For Order', reminiscent of the darker synthpop of Gary Numan or John Foxx, to Banshees-esque moodscapes such as 'Image' and tracks like 'B', which chimed perfectly with the demented disco and fractured funk then being created by brilliant early-Eighties Scottish duo Associates.

Immediately acknowledging *A–Z*'s commercial viability, Newman's US label suggested he tour to break the album, but since he had already had enough of that process with Wire, he declined, although the *A–Z* track 'Alone' would later be heard by millions on the soundtrack to Jonathan Demme's *The Silence Of The Lambs*, in the macabre, menacing scene in which the character Buffalo Bill is seen sewing in a basement. The song was also covered by This Mortal Coil on their *Filigree & Shadow* LP (a track from the demos for *A–Z* but not included on the original vinyl release, 'Not Me', was also covered by This Mortal Coil on their *It'll End In Tears* LP).

Andy Gill's review of *A–Z* in the *NME* in October 1980 praised the album's "layered minimalism, using textual building-blocks of stark simplicity to create edifices of, at times, almost baroque ornamentation." He concluded: "Newman, by refusing to adopt the principles of immediacy and uncertainty with as much rigidity as Bruce Gilbert and Graham Lewis, has managed to make an album in which experiment and accessibility – those strangest and rarest of bedfellows – coexist in peaceful democracy: neither predominates, and the two pull together in harness, rather than cancel each other out."

Newman's second album, the entirely instrumental *provisionally entitled the singing fish*, in which all the tracks were titled for numbered fish, was released on 4AD in 1981. Partly inspired by Lewis and Gilbert's experiments as Dome, this Eno-esque ambient exercise saw Newman and Thorne part company, their relationship foundering because Thorne wanted to make more of Newman's chart potential while Newman himself showed little interest in the commercial success or otherwise of his records.

That said, he did re-adopt a more conventional, group-based, rock approach for his third solo foray, 1982's *Not To* (also 4AD), which, along with original compositions, reworked a number of tracks originally written for Wire. The *NME*'s Richard Cook decided during his review of the album that he missed Wire's "austere subversiveness, their brittle sense of editing, their hybrid of ghoulish chants and Byrdsy chiming". He also surmised, from *Not To*, that, "although they always proclaimed their democracy it now seems clear – given the aimless greyness of the Gilbert and Lewis Dome projects – that Colin Newman was the principal creative force behind Wire; and *Not To* takes up from where *154* left off." Contrasting with earlier positive reviews, he asserted that *A–Z* and *provisionally entitled the singing fish* were "erratic and needlessly fussy affairs that creak under pretensions to alchemy when studio pottering is nearer the mark". *Not To*, on the other hand, saw, as well as Newman's trademark "sarcastic doggerel", a "reversion to melodic strength – the dozen songs, and songs they all are, strike out a course for singalong appeal without apology. Newman isn't distracted by Wire's occasional lip-service to the avant-garde. *Not To* is icicle-cool pop."

Despite such praise, after this Newman became increasingly frustrated with the music business and, after producing The Virgin Prunes' 1982 debut LP *If I Die, I Die...*, he took a grant and disappeared to India for a year to collect sound recordings and generally get his head together.

When asked a few years ago what he learned from his sojourn in India, whether it was a matter of escaping problems back home or seeking spiritual succour, he was evasive to say the least: "Hard question. I personally think that one interpretation of the reincarnation theory is that it is an allegory for life itself. Each phase is like a reincarnation and this is particularly true of my life. I've always had a problem with seeing my own life in non-quantum terms. I suppose what I mean by all this is that it was all relevant at the time, but right now I don't feel much connection with that period of my life."

Even after Wire reformed in the mid-Eighties, Newman continued to make solo records. Having produced the *Raging Souls* LP by the highly regarded Israeli indie-rock band Minimal Compact, he moved to Brussels and, in collaboration with Malka Spigel (founder member of MC and soon his wife), made two more albums: the heavily orchestrated *Commercial Suicide* (1986) and the sequencer- and synthesizer-based *It Seems* (1988). Both Crammed albums featured Spigel.

Throughout this period, both Wire and Newman's own recordings became increasingly computer-oriented. Indeed, it was Newman who would become heavily involved in the utilisation of this new-found electronic expertise in the making of the next-phase Wire albums, after they signed to the home of UK electro-pop, Mute (see Chapter 8).

Newman and Spigel relocated to London in the early-Nineties, founded the Swim ~ label, and put out records by a diverse range of electronic artists including Ronnie & Clyde, Lobe, dol-lop and Pablo's Eye. Energised by the flourishing techno and electronica scenes, he collaborated with Spigel on her *Rosh Ballata* (1993) and under various monikers: Oracle, Immersion, Earth, Oscillating and Intens. In 1996, as Immersion, the pair contributed a sound installation to a group show at the Irish Museum of Modern Art in Dublin. In the late-Nineties, Newman issued *Bastard*, an almost entirely instrumental release with tracks largely built from guitar loops and samples. It was released on Swim ~, and the first pressing of the album came with a free copy of his four-track *Voice* EP.

Meanwhile, since 2004, a team-up with electronic musician Robin Rimbaud a.k.a. Scanner has gone under the name Githead. In addition to working on Spigel's second full-length record, *My Pet Fish*, co-producing

Silo's Instar, mixing (in)credible Austrian musician Fennesz and remixing everyone from underground US electronica artists Bowery Electric to prog overlords Hawkwind and Gentle Giant, Newman returned to performance in 1998-1999, playing gigs in Europe and America with Spigel. Another Immersion album, the abstract, ambient *Low Impact*, followed, and 2000 found Newman and Spigel again playing live as Immersion, this time with more of a multimedia emphasis. Just as Newman had recaptured some of punk's original DIY spirit with Swim ~, in 2001 he continued in the same vein with the launch of PostEverything.com, a web-based store aimed at the distribution of independently released music (until summer 2008, anyway, when the company was dissolved). He has also mixed all new Wire releases since 2000 and today continues to run the Pinkflag label for Wire.

"My records are the ones probably closest to the Wire sound," contends Newman today. "That is, if you go back to my Eighties solo records. Bruce's projects in the Eighties, on the other hand, tended to be more abstract. They were working to a non-pop/rock aesthetic. My solo records were mainly channels for the over-abundance of material I had. There seems to be a bit of a revival of interest in them now, which is interesting."

He explains that *provisionally entitled the singing fish*, on which he played everything, was his attempt to record a real "solo" album, due to his love of Todd Rundgren's 1973 masterpiece of solipsistic studio invention, *A Wizard, A True Star* – although, as he points out, "unfortunately I lacked the means to record myself so I had an engineer". He adds that 4AD label boss Ivo Watts-Russell later told him that, following the advent of samplers and sequencers, *the singing fish* was "a record waiting for the technology to catch up with it".

Of *Commercial Suicide*, Newman says, "The title was ironic. There was a song that had started off sounding like the group Suicide, only more commercial. I was just bored with the rock band format. I've only ever tried to make records I wanted to make. I'm not interested in trying to dress it up in a form more acceptable to any particular market."

He doesn't agree that his solo work saw a shift from guitar-based rock to electronics-based music. "That's an artificial divide," he said in an interview with a webzine in the late-Nineties. "It's just that, at some

Wire join Mute, 1987. (TOM SHEEHAN)

Bruce and Graham share an absurdist, Pythonesque joke, 1988. (PETER ANDERSON)

Bruce onstage during Wire's support slot with
Depeche Mode at the Rose Bowl in Pasadena, 1988.
(URBANIMAGE.TV/ADRIAN BOOT)

Graham Lewis at the Rose Bowl, 1988.
(URBANIMAGE.TV/ADRIAN BOOT)

Wire on stage at Reading festival, August 25, 1990. (PAUL SLATTERY)

Backstage at Reading festival, August 25, 1990. (PAUL SLATTERY)

Wire prepare to read and burn, 2000. (STEFAN DE BATSELIER)

Live at All Tomorrow's Parties, Camber Sands, April 2002. (SIMON CHAPMAN/LIVE)

More Camber Sands action, April 2002. (SIMON CHAPMAN/LIVE)

Wire, live at the Barbican, London, October 25, 2002. (TABATHA FIREMAN/REDFERNS)

Githead, including Colin's wife Malka and Robin Rimbaud, far right. (FRANK LIEVAART)

Githead, live at the Bar Music Hall in Shoreditch, June 17, 2007. (RALF ZEIGERMANN)

And then there were three (l-r): Colin, Graham and Robert, April 2008. (ADAM SCOTT)

Colin Newman, on stage at the Offset festival, Hainault Park, Essex. August 30, 2008. (MIKE BURNELL/REDFERNS)

Remember them this way: the original four, circa *Send*. (MARIUS HANSEN)

point in the mid-to-late-Eighties, interesting rock just ceased to be. The post-punk bands were the last ones who actually tried to be original. Unfortunately, most of them were rubbish…

"I personally don't have a problem with guitars," he continued. "The last year has seen some interesting attempts to reinvent rock from both a dance and a non-dance perspective. The Prodigy are a rock band! The real transition that music has made in the last 10 years is that the narrative song has become increasingly marginalised in cutting-edge material. Who would have imagined 20 years ago that people would be dancing to bare beats with perhaps one synth line? Then again, it's perfectly logical – no one dances to the 'tune' any more. Music has become a lot more abstract, and I like that."

Newman's interest in electronic dance music was piqued, he told the e-interviewer, by such landmark Chicago house, acid house, Detroit techno and UK indie-dance triumphs as 'Oochy Coochy' by Baby Ford; the early releases on the Rhythm King and Warp labels; pioneers of bleepy dance such as LFO; ambient house classics such as The Orb's 'Little Fluffy Clouds' and Vince Clarke of Yazoo's seminal remix of Happy Mondays' 'Hallelujah'; and early Aphex Twin and old-school hip hop. He said that, when it came to the business of composing "songs", his priority was "beats first, nearly always". He added, a touch dramatically, "I don't write songs any more. Haven't you heard? They've all been written."

The idea for Swim ~, he explained, grew from a fascination with early techno and its attendant studio tools. He liked the way a lot of techno was created in home studios in a DIY way. "Malka always had this idea that you could make more interesting and original work in your own space," he said. This was how he got the idea for building his own mini-studio space in his home in South London. "We developed our own studio from the mid-Eighties onward and became increasingly confident about its output. I basically taught myself to be an engineer, mixer, computer operator, etc. For me the revolution of techno was all about how you made the music and under whose terms.

"Swim ~ was a logical progression from having our own studio," he continued. "Like so many things there was a confluence of ideas and other factors. The mid-Eighties scene in Brussels died, both Minimal

Compact and Wire were on hiatus, we wanted to be somewhere else, so we chose London. We deliberately chose a house where we could put a studio. Mute helped us with manufacturing and exports and we found a UK distributor. We sent out a few copies to press and got reviews, good ones, too. A lot of small labels started up not long after us and there was suddenly a context for it all to happen in." He revealed that Swim ~ had some "pretty high-level fans", including Neil Tennant of the Pet Shop Boys (the synthpop duo had even invited one of the label's acts, Lobe, to remix one of their singles). He described the label itself as "an act of curation", adding that, "We also tend to eschew tribalism in music; 'self-niching' is ultimately such a dead-end street. We are very proud of what we have achieved and the quality of the artists we are able to have on the label. I would wholeheartedly recommend that people check out acts like Silo, Symptoms, Lobe, Immersion, etc."

Finally, the webzine interviewer asked Newman which he believed he was most and least talented as: lyricist, guitar player, songwriter or producer?

"It depends on which day," he said, playfully sidestepping the question. "I have a facility with prose text – I occasionally contribute to various papers/magazines – but I am in no way a poet and have very little interest in being one, so I'd say I'm a pretty lousy lyricist. Mind you, I'm also technically a pretty crap guitarist – I can barely play better than I could when I was 17. I wouldn't really regard myself as much of a 'songwriter' any more, at least not in the strumming-an-acoustic-guitar-on-the-toilet way I was in my twenties. I'd say I'm more of a manipulator of information – sometimes sonic – these days. I'm also rather unsure about record production. I don't know what record production is in the third millennium but I can say that I haven't seen the inside of many 'conventional' studios in the last 10 years! So there you go: I'm equally crap at them all."

Bruce Gilbert, meanwhile, considers Robert Gotobed to be a total drummer: "He is drum. He is rhythm. I think Colin is probably the most musical, but I think he viewed music as a form of pop art, and I think it's a similar thing with Graham, really. I just saw everything as part of a sculpture in the end." Gotobed had the most professional musical experience pre-Wire, having sung with a band called The Snakes, which featured future members of The Motors and released a cover of The Flamin' Groovies' 'Teenage Head' in 1976. In 1979, he played drums on one track, 'Rat City', the B-side of a single, 'Punk Rock Star', by a group called The Art Attacks. In the wake of Wire's (temporary) dissolution in 1980, he became the drummer for Frank Tovey, an electronic artist on Mute who performed under the name Fad Gadget. He also played drums on a track from Fad Gadget's 1980 LP, *Incontinent,* called 'Manuel Dexterity'. That same year, he contributed drum parts to 'Rolling Upon My Day' from Dome's debut album as well as Colin Newman's *A–Z.* Over the next few years, he featured on Desmond Simmons' *Alone On Penguin Island* LP (1981), and Newman's *provisionally entitled the singing fish, Not To* and *It Seems.*

After the members of Wire went their separate ways in 1980, Gotobed remained in London for a year, but assumed this signalled the end of his drumming career. He was, he told Mike Thorne's Stereo Society web-site, "quite interested in moving out of London" but was concerned that this would take him away from all the musical contacts that he'd made over the years. But by the end of the year, he began to wonder about life in the country and pursuing a simpler existence. "I just needed a rest and to find a new direction," he said.

He did stop playing or practising for a couple of years, although he continued to pursue an interest in African drumming, even attending a class in Stockwell, which gave him "a new way of looking at drum-ming". With between three and eight people, he would play African dances. "I was looking for new things away from kit drumming," he explained, "which is a more solitary activity." This gave him a new angle on playing rhythms and also got him thinking that "life would be sim-pler without drumming".

He talked to Stereo Society about his formative years, when he "did-n't have any sort of musical basis to draw on in a sort of technique sense". Then, in the early-Eighties, he found a book explaining the rudi-ments of drumming, which he'd had for years but never actually studied. "All proper drummers say rudiments are the essential things you must have. So why not take a look at it and see what it does for me? It was sort of going back to square one, in a way. I also got Ginger Baker's drum-ming video, because he was my original inspiration, to see what he has to say about drumming. I watched that video quite a lot. I was trying to get back to what started me off drumming in the first place. I needed to go back to that original starting point before I could go forward. I'd reached the point of saying to myself, 'I was drumming before Wire and if I go back to that point, I can start again from there.'"

When Wire reformed in 1985 and began making records for Mute, Gotobed found himself increasingly isolated due to the band's increasing use of electronics and drum machines. Eventually, he withdrew completely from the group and did move to the country. "That made me think that everything in Wire was wasted, which sounds sort of drastic but, because I was no longer in the group, I sort of felt it had all been for nothing. That was the reason I stopped drumming. But I haven't reached the point of saying I was drumming before Wire and starting again from there with a sort of basic improving technique and things. I found I was able to build on that, and also being in the country and having space around me meant I could go to my drumming room and not be disturbing anybody else. When I lived in London, I'd never been anywhere I wasn't conscious [of disturbing somebody] – even if people said they didn't mind if you're practising something, I think it is fairly infuriating for people to listen to it. It makes you a bit self-conscious, but if you've got somewhere you can make a noise, then you know it's not annoying anybody. That's quite liberating. So I took practising much more seriously then. I tried to do an hour of playing every day."

When Wire formed, Gotobed felt intimidated because he "thought to be a musician you had to have this magical quality that you were born with. I didn't realise that it was just a matter of hard work and learning how to play. I thought you had to have this special thing that set you aside as a musician." Mike Thorne asked Gotobed about his worry that he's not "a proper musician". Did he believe that most musicians were similarly worried about being found out and that was what kept him on his toes?

"I'm not sure," he replied, adding that the feeling of not being "proper" led back to his starting playing the drums quite late, aged 25. "Obviously, I have no musical background," he said. "And I didn't play an instrument in school. That has always made me feel – although I love drumming – more on the side of non-musicians than musicians because

I didn't know enough about it to qualify. I didn't have any certificates in musicianship. I suppose people who watch Wire think they are musicians. Well, I wouldn't mind them thinking that of me but I know the others would much rather prefer being called non-musicians than artists. They don't like the idea of being described as a musician. But, personally, I always want to feel I am improving what I'm playing. My technique's improving, which means I can be more diverse in what I can offer to the group or to other people who are interested in working with me."

After the split, and increasingly in the Nineties when he left the band, seemingly for good this time, he admitted that he missed playing the drums. "I did miss it, but it didn't drive me crazy. I got through without it. It was time to regroup, I think, that was how I was feeling about it. I needed a starting point. You need some sort of a starting point because the Wire process seemed to me to have broken down completely."

While he was away from Wire, he did utilise his drumming skills in some quite unusual areas. He played the Purcell Room at the South Bank for an evening of American composers, which caused some anxiety because he'd only really ever played with Wire. "The idea of playing with five people whom I had never been on a stage with before definitely gave me sleepless nights, and also the thought that at least two of them were proper musicians," he said. Next, he was invited to play a piece in a John Cage Evening at the Barbican. "I certainly felt very exposed standing on the stage," he recalled. "I wasn't playing drums, I was playing percussion." This involved banging bits of metal and wood.

As for Graham Lewis and Bruce Gilbert, in 1980 they "virtually erupted with full-on experimentalism", as Simon Reynolds put it, issuing either together or apart a series of albums and EPs not just as Dome (briefly the name of their collaborative efforts as well as the label, a subsidiary of Rough Trade, on which they were issued) but as Gilbert/Lewis, P'O (a one-off band comprising drummer Peter Price, clarinettist David Tidball and Gilbert's old girlfriend Angela Conway, alias AC Marias), He Said, He Said Omala, H.A.L.O., Cupol, Ocsid, Hox, 3R4 and Duet Emmo. There was, in addition, a series of art installations and performances in collaboration with artist Russell Mills. Dome's performances took place in art galleries with visual displays that allowed for audience interaction as Gilbert and Lewis performed with tubes made of paper over their heads, thus restricting their vision.

Dome released four albums in the first few years of the Eighties that comprised industrial experiments, noisy works-in-progress and occasional pop epiphanies such as 'Rolling Upon My Day', which confirmed what Graham Lewis pointed out earlier in this book, that a track written by Bruce Gilbert like 'Blessed State' from *154* was no fluke. With their use of found sounds, makeshift improvised instruments and musique concrète techniques, Dome posited Gilbert and Lewis as a sort of surrogate Byrne/Eno, only minus the element of funk-tionality and groove (Eno actually appeared on the first He Said album, *Hail*, in 1986). The partnership's pinnacle was arguably 1982's *MZUI/Waterloo Gallery*, a combination of ambient music and found sound that remains a highlight of Lewis and Gilbert's careers, either with or without Wire. Meanwhile, the *Or So It Seems* album by Duet Emmo (an anagram of Mute Dome) from 1983 saw Gilbert and Lewis team up with Daniel Miller, the boss of the Mute label, for a project that mirrored what Mute major-domos Depeche Mode were up to themselves on their 1983 album of danceable proto-industrial/metal-bashing, *Construction Time Again*.

If Lewis' He Said releases weren't far removed from the widescreen electronic pop of mid-to-late-Eighties Mute-era Wire, Gilbert's solo forays saw him fully indulge his avant-garde and experimental classical tendencies, emphasising his role in Wire as "the artistic wrench in the works" (*Trouser Press* magazine), the one who gave each project a perverse twist. His most famous solo works, *The Shivering Man* (1986), *Music For Fruit* (1991) and most recently *Ordier*, express his self-proclaimed "fascination with the possibilities of sound", the music-artist using everything from minimalist electronic glitch techniques and clangy noisescapes to instrument manipulation in his pursuit of the "right" sounds. The furthest removed of all Wire's members from the pop arena, Gilbert's 1984 collection *This Way* contained his first score for the avant-garde Michael Clark Dance Company and a pair of lengthy minimalist electronic pieces that have been compared to Steve Reich's early-Seventies work. *Insiding* (1991) features two lengthy pieces, ballet scores commissioned by dancer Ashley Page, which unfold and develop intriguingly over their allotted 20 minutes each.

By the mid-Nineties, Gilbert, then 50, was a regular on London's techno club scene, DJing and remixing under the name Beekeeper, most often performing inside a garden shed above the dancefloor for a touch of Wire-like absurdist visual humour. Gilbert has been quoted as saying that being a DJ was just an excuse to "manipulate other people's music" – such projects include remixing 'National Grid' by the group Disinformation, for release on their double CD, *Antiphony*.

The club, started by Paul Smith of the Blast First record label together with a young artist called Russell Haswell, went under the name Disobey. "I was a DJ in quotation marks," says Gilbert. "It was the usual thing – we were down the pub talking about how it would be good to have a truly eclectic club where totally different types of music were played and there were all these different events, all in one night, so you didn't have to go to lots of different clubs. Paul Smith, being a very good organiser and a very resourceful person, made it happen. It was once a month during 1995-6." Gilbert, as predictably unpredictable as ever, knew one thing he didn't want to play on the wheels of steel during his tenure as a "DJ": dance music. "I knew I wasn't going to play beats, so what else could I play? I thought one area that nobody would know much about was musique concrète from the late-Fifties and Sixties, and I liked that because it was quite obscure and it also lent itself to mixing – I would often play two, three, even four things at the same time. It would have been unacceptable to a purist but I thought it was ideal. Could you dance to it? Absolutely not!"

Gilbert got a quizzical reaction at first and the occasional ironic request for him to play something by Madonna, but before long people would approach the DJ booth to enquire what that strange music was that he was playing. Eventually, he got fed up with this line of enquiry and so he started spraying the CDs black so that even he didn't know what he was playing, his rationale being that he "wanted to be as surprised as anybody else".

Graham Lewis would regularly attend Gilbert's club nights. "They were absolutely fucking amazing," he recalls. "It was absolutely one of the best clubs ever. So, so good. It was really, really mixed up. And there was a point where it became really hip as well, because the *Evening Standard* wrote about it, and the paparazzi heard that the likes of Jarvis

Cocker and Brian Eno were going there, and of course Jarvis had at that point made the incredible crossover from being a man of underground taste to becoming a pop star, so suddenly you had this totally bizarre situation where there would be 20 paparazzi taking photographs of people and trying to find somebody famous but not knowing who anybody was in the room! They were all people who were exceedingly important in the electronic music milieu, but who were they? Non-celebrities. So they just started taking photographs of anybody. It was so funny."

Some memorable Disobey nights included the notorious-in-underground-circles occasion when Aphex Twin began mixing on two record decks using two different qualities of sandpaper, with a microphone in an electric food mixer. "That confounded expectations a little," says Lewis, "but it was fucking hilarious. Everybody who came got their own free sandpaper so you could try it out at home." On another occasion, jazz man and arch raconteur George Melly read extracts from the poetry of Kurt Fitze. There were Japanese noise nights, techno nights, even an ex-busker from New York playing a free jazz piece for three-quarters of an hour without taking a breath.

In March 1996, Gilbert released the results of his latest musical experiments, the *Ab Ovo* album and 'Ovo Mix' 12-inch single. His first solo effort not to result from external dance or film commissions, *Ab Ovo* was described by *The Wire* as, "A forceful piece of work which sounds like nothing else around."

Despite the incredible diversity of Colin Newman, Graham Lewis, Bruce Gilbert and Robert Gotobed's non-Wire projects, Gilbert actually considers them to have been/be "similar in many ways". Dome, he says now, was an opportunity for him and Lewis to "use the studio as a laboratory and a place to experiment, although Duet Emmo was a bit different because of Daniel Miller's input – that was electronic music with beats".

Overall, he says of Dome and the other Lewis-Gilbert activities, "We were just following our noses in the studio. Graham and I were experimenting at home and we knew that with the aid of a studio there would be an outpouring of stuff as well as an opportunity to explore some of the ideas or approaches that we'd had for many years." Dome's albums were released on Rough Trade, the label owned by Geoff Travis. Gilbert liked the deal with Travis but believes that, in a perfect world, "There would have been room to do Dome and still do Wire." Nevertheless, he says, he was "very keen" to get going with Dome. "I was very curious to see where it would go." That didn't mean, however, that Dome would become a regular recording and touring unit. "I was starting to have my doubts about this touring thing. It always gets to me: the sheer idiocy of playing a concert with all the rigmarole and the soundchecking... I start feeling that I shouldn't be doing this; that I should be crawling around in mud somewhere screaming or in a studio experimenting, not standing on a stage playing the same thing night after night. I always found the idea of a band quite embarrassing."

Gilbert's favourite experience outside of Wire – his favourite "process" as he puts it – involved working on the Dome and Duet Emmo albums at the then-new Blackwing Studios in London with Depeche Mode, Yazoo, Erasure and Fad Gadget producer-engineer Eric (E.C.) Radcliffe. Dome may have had experimental ideas and methods, but they worked fast and cheap – their first album was recorded in the eight-track studio in 36 hours (or at least, three 12-hour sessions) for about £300, a tiny fraction of the cost of recording the three Wire albums. "He was very sympathetic to our approach and delighted to have his studio used and abused," he says of Mute's in-house studio whiz. "Nothing fazed him at all. He was a willing partner in the experiment. It was a very good period. I'm very keen on doing things quickly, and in the situation we were in, they had to be done quickly – that was part of the process. It was all an experiment, and there was quite a lot of looping going on; sort of 40 foot-long loops and things like that." Gilbert is pleased that, over the years, "a number of people have sampled Dome to death. I'm amazed by how many people are aware of what we did. Still, to this day, people tell me that they got into music or sound after they heard the Dome albums."

Graham Lewis distinguishes between the various Wire members' output by saying, "Robert's a farmer – his mother ran a small farm in Weston – and he plays the drums, that's really easy. He doesn't really do anything outside of that, so he's simple. Really broadly speaking, then you've got Bruce who's done the most experimental work, I would guess. And then you've got Colin who's probably the most traditional in terms of his music. Plus, he's had his label and done some production work and things like that. Over the years, he's accumulated a lot of organisational skills. It's one of his great strengths. He's a real beaver, you know – he works and gets through it."

Lewis doesn't believe that the various Wire offshoots share the same DNA as Wire the band, but he accepts that they represent(ed) different aspects of each of the four characters – with, for example, He Said providing an opportunity for him to explore "the song aspects of things, which I'd been continuing to be interested in". Nor does he necessarily agree that his solo forays were extrapolations on aspects of Wire's work, with, say, Dome as an expansion of the possibilities proposed by the guitar drones on *154*.

"That's like saying that everything relates to everything, which is of course true, but how strictly do you want to interpret that? I'd say that of the noise stuff that Bruce has done over the last few years – well, you can certainly say that noise exists in Wire, but in no shape or form could you say that it was directly related. It's like, if someone does a soundtrack for a film, what it's about is the collaboration with those people. The Wire thing is a combination of those people. That's what makes it sound like Wire, and I think when you come to something else you try to explore with as little baggage as possible. You keep your craft and your technique but try to keep an open mind. If you do an installation in a gallery or make a piece of sculpture, well, I'm sure you could relate it to Wire in some way, but it's not really true, is it? I certainly don't go into things thinking, 'Oh, well, this isn't Wire, so therefore it isn't as good', you know? It's far from that. That's an absolutely ridiculous attitude. One tries to approach everything on its merits.

"I think the DNA is in the creativity," he returns to the original point. "Remember, we do come from an art world. That's not to say that we think any other language is second-rate or anything. It's just that that's where we come from, so that's the way that we approach things. So if you work in a sculptural situation, then you have to be a good sculptor. Being a really good rock musician in that situation just doesn't cut it."

Lewis uses the example of the various members of The Velvet Underground to emphasise his point about rock musicians with an art background exploring other areas without such activities or projects being seen as "offshoots" of one or the other. "John Cale came from a classical and an avant-garde background, and he's brought that intelligence to whatever kind of work that he's done. Obviously he's made a lot of music in the rock world, but at the same time he's made contributions to other things that you certainly wouldn't say were rock and wouldn't have been possible if he hadn't had the background that he did. The same goes for Lou Reed: there are great modern literary concerns in his work, but he has the ability to write a great pop song as well."

He admits that it's been impossible over the years for him to keep pace with all the myriad activities of Wire's members. "There are certain things that people have done that are of interest, and others I have no interest in at all, and I'm sure this exactly applies to them as well. Bruce and I shared a lot of work together because there were lots of things that we had a common interest in – the dance world and gallery work and things like that."

Lewis recalls that the Dome albums were so unlike Wire that Rough Trade's boss, Geoff Travis, was quite taken aback when he first heard them. "He was expecting something a bit more Wire-like," he says. However, far from being disappointed, he proceeded to offer Lewis and Gilbert a deal whereby they had their own bijou label, enabling them to keep 90-or-so per cent of any profits made from any recordings. The pair snapped into action, and then some. "Basically, we started getting busy."

Having captured the various approaches of the Wire players, Lewis proceeds to differentiate between his own projects. "A lot of it has to do with circumstance and collaborations, and the ideas and material you have. I think the He Said thing was very much electronic and sampler-based. That's what I was fascinated with at the time, because that was the newest technology for me, and that's what I wanted to investigate – what it was like to work on something with synthetic rhythms." Does he have favourite works from his solo output? "Not really, but I think the first two Dome records are really very good, since they were the start of a process of trying to work with a studio in a different way, or at least in a way that was not just about using it as a large tape recorder. We actually tried to use the space in a more reflective way; in a way that you'd have used a studio if you were painting or if you were making a sculpture or an installation or something like that." Does he believe that Dome's electronic and sampler-based music, with their use of found sounds and so forth, fed, even if indirectly, into what sound collagists like Art Of Noise and hip-hoppers such as Mantronix later did? "I'm not sure. I think there's a sort of synchronicity as to attitudes towards what can be done... That period when Eno and David Byrne were doing *My Life In The Bush Of Ghosts* [1981] – I think anybody who was, at that time, involved with that kind of contemporary music, that's what everybody was interested in. It was, 'What can you do with this?' The technology was developing, and it was very interesting to see what would come from it."

Did Colin Newman's solo albums and Bruce Gilbert and Graham Lewis' projects reflect the dichotomy in Wire between the former's pop sensibility and the latter's artier tendencies? "I'd say yes and no," says Lewis. "That's been a very convenient way for people to try and make sense of how the group worked over the years. I think the truth of it was that Colin had a bunch of songs and he employed the same template to making his first album [*A-Z*], whereas there were other issues that Bruce and I were wanting to investigate, and that was primarily for the Dome thing. It became Dome, but we'd been talking about trying to do work outside of the studio; other work that was more, shall we say, in the art context, rather than something that was specifically about recording rock songs. Having said that, there are examples where I was still exploring songwriting. But the big mistake is using this convenient distinction, saying Colin has a melodic sensibility and we like noise and that's that. It's too pat, and it's not actually true."

Lewis happily accepts that "Wire is the most popular thing we've ever done", but adds that "other things have spun off and we've been fortunate to have those opportunities". He dislikes the term "side project" – "because I don't see anything 'side' about it. It's different aspects." Two highlights of his extra-Wire career have been the remixes of H.A.L.O. tracks by LFO and the use of one of these remixes on highly rated HBO TV series *Six Feet Under*, in a scene involving a businessman, a masseuse, and a blowjob. "It was such a thrill that something you really thought was so great, eight years later, somebody recognises it. It drops onto someone's desk in an agency in LA who's looking for music for TV or a film, and suddenly – BINGO! – there it is." He reveals that, notwithstanding such successes, making a living operating on the fringes of the music scene for more than 30 years, recording often quite experimental music, has been "bloody difficult", such are the perils of pursuing a career as a freelance musician. "The phrase 'feast or famine' comes to mind," he laughs.

Graham Lewis would be kept busy enough when, following Colin Newman's return to Britain from India in 1984, Wire regrouped for phase two of their career, releasing the *Snakedrill* EP in 1986 and *The Ideal Copy* album in 1987, having signed a deal with Mute. For two members of the group, however, it would not prove to be as miraculous and momentous a Second Coming as they might have wished.

Chapter 8

Marooned

"The most brutal time was making The Ideal Copy. *I just left and came home. There was a kind of jockeying for position. People were working in different ways, with no clear direction. It became very, very depressing. Absolutely awful"* – Colin Newman

DANIEL Miller first met Wire in 1978 through their manager, Mike Collins, when the band played a gig he'd decided to attend at the Factory club in Manchester. Shortly afterwards, they all agreed to go for a drink in London's Covent Garden. Miller, an early proponent of British DIY synthesiser music since his days at Guildford Art School, where he studied film and television from 1968-71, nonetheless saw Wire – essentially a rock band, albeit a highly experimental one – as allies. Both he and the band found rock music frustratingly conservative, and spent the mid-Seventies listening to German "krautrock" outfits such as Can, Faust, Neu! and Kraftwerk. For Miller and Wire, the positive aspects of punk weren't the music so much as the energy and excitement, as well as the do-it-yourself approach and iconoclastic attitude. And for this pioneer of the synthesiser, whose late-Seventies pseudony-

126

mous releases as The Normal – on the label he'd just set up, Mute – had a dramatic impact on the burgeoning synthpop scene, Wire's increasing use of the instrument from *Chairs Missing* onwards meant that, for him, they could just as easily be placed alongside his favourite proto-electro terrorists Throbbing Gristle and Cabaret Voltaire as they could any of the post-punk guitar bands. It was inevitable that Miller and Wire would become friends and, later, work colleagues.

"I liked all three of their EMI albums," says Miller today. "Even though they were a guitar band, and I was completely electronic, they were very much on the same wavelength."

Miller had been sufficiently enamoured of Wire's first three albums to pay attention to their next moves, and duly went to catch the band's performances at the Jeannetta Cochrane Theatre and the Electric Ballroom in 1979 and 1980 that wound up on the *Document And Eyewitness* record. Like everyone else present at the concerts, he was taken aback by Wire's latest direction – or rather, by what would turn out to be the swansong(s) of Wire v 1.0.

"To be honest, I thought they were disappointing," he says of the performances. "I wanted to see Wire. There were good moments, but I thought the best part was the video camera outside [the Jeannetta Cochrane Theatre] and the screen inside, with people looking at the camera and being able to see their projection on the screen. It was fun, if a little embarrassing. And Colin's thing ['An Unlikely Occurrence', featuring 15 non-professional guitarists playing the chords of E, A and D respectively – see Chapter 6] was good. It was an adventurous experiment, which was great, and it partly worked, but it partly didn't."

By this point, Miller had got to know Wire well (especially Graham Lewis and Bruce Gilbert, but also Robert Gotobed, who began drumming with Mute act Frank Tovey a.k.a. Fad Gadget after Wire split up) and they were able to freely share ideas. Did he consider them a pop group with experimental ideas and tendencies, or an experimental group who just happened to operate in the "pop" arena?

"They were an experimental pop group," decides Miller. "Their pop songs were pretty experimental. They're pop, and they're experimental, which are the same things in my mind. That's why they're great – I love both, and they've always managed to do both at the same time really well, even though they require different approaches, sonically." Are they destined to be viewed as the Velvet Underground of post-punk – that is, well regarded by the cognoscenti but without the mainstream success they deserved? "Well, they were almost on *Top Of The Pops* with 'Outdoor Miner', which is one of the all-time great pop tracks." Miller believes Wire made life difficult for themselves by doing things like refusing to play their current material live. "They bucked the trend. If I remember rightly, people were more usually talking about them as the Pink Floyd of post-punk, and I can see why – even if I don't necessarily agree – especially around *154*. Maybe they decided that that's what they were going to be." How does he believe they shape up in comparison to those other giants of electronic, experimental pop, Depeche Mode and Joy Division/New Order?

"Well, I love New Order and Joy Division – I can't speak for Depeche because I'm too close to them – but I prefer Wire to both of them; I think they're brilliant. They were always poppier than Joy Division, and I liked that. I listen to Wire more now than I do Joy Division or New Order. New Order did a similar thing to Wire; so did Depeche – all those groups appeal to me; they're totally original bands, and that appeals to me more than anything else. They all stand head and shoulders above most other bands, and they all come from the same place, in a way. They're not rock bands: Wire weren't a rock band. And none of them are particularly good musicians, but they all had good ideas and understood pop music and how to work in that form." Miller believes Wire were quietly influential in the development of electronic pop, not just because of their work together, but also via their solo projects and various collaborations.

One of those quietly influential Wire offshoots was Duet Emmo, a one-off collaboration between Daniel Miller, Graham Lewis and Bruce Gilbert that spawned an album and a single, both titled *Or So it Seems*, and released in 1983. Duet Emmo was an anagram of Mute and Dome, the former Daniel Miller's record label, the latter the name of Gilbert and Lewis' first post-Wire foray. All three had been using the same South London studio, Blackwing, and the same engineer, Eric Radcliffe, and an initial project had been mooted as far back as 1980, but the success of Mute acts Depeche Mode and Yazoo meant that Miller was too busy to get involved until the end of 1982.

"It was really good fun," recalls Miller of the Duet Emmo project. "It was weird because it didn't take long to do but it was done over a long period of time. We started it around the same time that Depeche Mode got started, then it got mad for a while and we couldn't finish it for ages, then we finally did finish it, and it was great. Eric Radcliffe was a superb engineer: he was prepared to experiment."

Duet Emmo was by no means the last collaboration between Wire and Daniel Miller. In fact, it was just the beginning of their relationship with the Mute boss and his record label, one that would last five years, longer than their arrangement with EMI.

Phase two of Wire began in 1985, when all four members were back in Britain – Colin Newman had returned from his year-long sojourn in India, suffering from hepatitis and living in Manchester. According to Lewis, Newman phoned him, "With a mind," he says, "to perhaps having a songwriting partnership. Then I saw Bruce, and I said, 'Mr. Newman's reappeared'. Colin was going to come down one weekend and have a conversation about it. So Bruce, Colin and I went to my local pub and we said, 'Let's start from scratch and see what we can do, and if Rob wants to be in, fine, we'll do it as Wire, and if Rob doesn't want to do it, then we're going to call it WIR.' That's where that came from. It was like Year Zero again: we booked a rehearsal place and we gave ourselves three days. The first two days were pretty crap, actually, and then on the third day I'd been messing around, using delays with the bass for quite a long time, and something just clicked. And out of nowhere we had 'Drill' and 'A Serious Of Snakes'. We were like, 'This is pretty damn good.'"

Next, there came an invitation to perform live for the first time since 1980's Electric Ballroom show. Only, this being Wire, it wasn't a regular gig. Lewis and Bruce Gilbert had been approached by a friend to "do something" in one of the galleries at the Museum of Modern Art in Oxford. "And it seemed to fascinate everybody," says Gilbert, who has fond memories of the night. "It was fun. People travelled a long way to see it."

Lewis remembers that the newly reformed Wire simply needed enough material to last half an hour, no more, no less, with the proviso that they would play "only new stuff; nothing old." Wire duly played for

30 minutes. The applause, according to Lewis and Gilbert, lasted 45 minutes. "Some of the audience had tears in their eyes," says Gilbert. "No
one thought it would happen again." "It was quite strange," says Lewis,
"but we didn't have anything else to play, and we weren't playing
encores, although I actually did do an encore, an a cappella version of a
song called 'Up To The Sun', because that was the only thing we had. We
didn't realise how difficult we were making our lives, by not playing anything old, but that's never stopped us before."

Following the success of the Oxford show, the next logical step, recalls
Gilbert, was to begin recording again as Wire. This would be the first
time they had done so since the sessions for the 'Our
Swimmer'/'Midnight Bahnhof Cafe' double-A-side single, which they
recorded for the Charisma label in early 1980 (although according to
Graham Lewis there had been a meeting circa 1982 at Centre Point in
London between the band and Mike Thorne about the prospect of a
fourth Wire album with Thorne at the controls. Recalls Lewis, "Mike
was going, 'I'm sure we can get finance from somebody, however you
want to do it.' And then Colin went off to India for a year, so that fell
apart").

And so the four agreed to start rehearsals and build a second body of
work for this second phase of Wire activity. The decision was made to
recommence recording in summer 1986. The consensus was that they
would perform and record in a "stripped-down, basic way", according to
Gilbert, based on repetition and noise. The band jokingly referred to this
as the "beat combo" approach, in which they would utilise a funkless but
powerfully compelling rhythm they nicknamed "dugga" – it's no coincidence that the first song they wrote together after five years apart was
titled 'Drill', because that's what it sounded like.

"'Drill' was the key song, definitely," says Gilbert. "Psychologically and
technically. It describes the way we were stripping things down to the
bare minimum. It was a key piece in terms of how the band were going
to function together, and how the pieces of the jigsaw fit. We were all
reading from the same hymn sheet, basically, and because of the nature
of it, it required everybody to be rhythmically in tune with each other.

"I'm not sure if the term 'dugga' had been coined yet; it might have
been in the rehearsal rooms. Graham might have said, 'That "dugga" bit'

or, 'You start your "dugga" now'. It might have been a way of describing things in the studio."

Down at the Strong Room, the studio in East London where the 1986 sessions took place, Eric Radcliffe engineered and Daniel Miller produced (although at one point Brian Eno was apparently mooted as producer). "We had a good relationship with Daniel and there had been some talk about our work coming out on Mute, so it all seemed quite natural," says Gilbert. "Plus, Daniel was familiar with the new and interesting ways of recording, so he seemed the obvious choice."

Four tracks were recorded at the Strong Room – 'A Serious Of Snakes', 'Drill', 'Advantage In Height' and 'Up To The Sun' – for an EP that would later acquire the title 'Snakedrill'. The music on the 'Snakedrill' EP foreshadowed the extensive use by Wire of electronic instrumentation on the six albums they would record for Mute (the tracks are now included as bonuses on the CD version of their debut Mute album, 1987's *The Ideal Copy*), which did cause some problems for certain band members. In fact, the reunion, according to Wire-ologist Wilson Neate, was far from harmonious, "as Wire struggled to find a new group sound under the burden of critical expectation carried over from their first period".

Daniel Miller was delighted to have Wire as part of the Mute roster (having issued albums by Dome and Bruce Gilbert in a solo capacity) alongside the eclectic likes of Depeche Mode, Yazoo, Erasure, Einstürzende Neubaten, Nick Cave & The Bad Seeds and Diamanda Galas. Having Wire on-board created a bit of a buzz at Mute HQ, he says. "God, yeah, to the extent that anyone worries about things like that. But it was great, partly because they're a great band, and partly because they didn't compete in anyone else's space. They're not like Depeche or Nick Cave & The Bad Seeds or whoever else. No one was threatened by them." Miller acknowledges that Wire, coming from the art world as they did, were always going to be different to work with from anyone else. "Well, they were and they weren't. I recognised where they came from, but they were particular characters with their own complexities. We spoke a similar language. We understood what each other was talking about."

Miller admits to feeling "scared shitless" when the band approached him to produce the 'Snakedrill' EP, even though he had Mute producer Gareth Jones on hand to help (and Andre Giere as assistant engineer). "It was quite difficult," says Miller, "because in the interim [i.e. during Wire's hiatus] Graham, Bruce and Colin had got more into electronic music and were using drum machines to create mechanical rhythms, and they found going back into the conventional band format quite difficult. So the 'Snakedrill' sessions weren't super-smooth, or at least the process wasn't. For whatever reasons, they'd stopped working together [in 1980] and then they got back together and Colin was sceptical of me and I knew the others well, so that was a problem, but we got over that quickly.

"They've always had differences of opinion and that's part of their make-up," he adds. "None of their recording sessions were easy. There were always issues to overcome. The personalities in the band are quite strong-willed and very opinionated, but that can be great; that's why they're so great. I'd rather be with a band like that than one that says 'yes' to everything.

"It all worked spectacularly well on the track 'Drill', though, which is one of the best things we [Mute] ever put out. They wanted to programme the drums on it, but Robert wasn't very into that." Gilbert, by contrast, remembers Gotobed "enjoying himself" during the 'Snakedrill' sessions. "He'd been doing some session work and enjoyed drumming on a regular basis, and something like 'Drill' was tailor-made for him. Fast, medium or slow, he enjoys the physical effort. For Robert, drumming is almost a martial art."

Lewis, however, believes the introduction of a sequencer programme into the recording scheme of things during the 'Snakedrill' sessions signalled a shift towards the electronic from which there was no way back, with its attendant repercussions for Gotobed. "Once Gareth [Jones] took delivery of this early Steinberg sequencing programme, that was it, really. Once that was introduced, everybody understood that that was the way ahead, basically, and I guess as far as Robert was concerned, that was the beginning of the end."

The main thing that the creatively ostracised drummer remembers of this period was that "computers became this massive force in recording and in music-making, and that was the beginning of the end for live drums for Wire. I suppose computers are still a massive force in recording, but drums have been allowed back because they're acknowledged as having something to contribute themselves, whereas I think when computers first became an influence, the idea was, well, 'We don't need drums now. The computer does all that and it's more accurate.' Because of that new direction for Wire, I was made to feel less and less happy."

The problem was, Lewis, Gilbert and Newman had grown accustomed to using electronic equipment, and saw no good reason not to continue doing so. "In the period before coming to make 'Snakedrill' and *The Ideal Copy*," explains Lewis, "the work that I'd been doing was extremely involved with using whatever limited computer-power one had, and sequencing electronics, so to me it just seemed to be absolutely the most natural place to be, and I'm sure that was the case for Bruce as well – we'd been using machines [as Dome, etc] for generating rhythms for a long time. Accuracy was something we found extremely interesting because it has a very different effect on the music. Robert's problem, basically, was that he had no intention of learning anything about it, which effectively meant that he excluded himself. But that was his decision, and that decision tended to put the onus on us. I can tell you that considerable amounts of time were spent discussing this with him. And he refused, basically. Everybody else understood that something new had happened, that there had been a change in technology, and you had to learn something about it, otherwise you weren't going to move on." Far from being coldly isolated, then, Lewis maintains that every effort was made to involve Gotobed in the new studio processes. "Absolutely, and trying to accommodate his attitude took up considerable amounts of time, and I think in lots of ways held back what might have been a very creative process."

Nevertheless, Lewis remembers there being "a pretty good feeling" in the studio for the newly reconvened Wire, the atmosphere lighter than at Advision, and at least for now Gotobed was still in the fold, laying down drum patterns that could then be replicated by machines "for accuracy". Songs were written differently this time as well – constructed in the rehearsal studio, where sounds were added and rhythms and textures built upon, rather than someone arriving with a fully-formed tune. One exception was 'Advantage In Height', for which Lewis penned the words and Newman came up with the melody. The band, says Lewis, had "great faith" in the new material, especially 'Drill' and 'A Serious Of Snakes', and they were enjoying their new working relationship with Gareth Jones and Daniel Miller. "It was like we were on a mission again. We had an idea about what we wanted to do, and although we had plenty of heavy baggage to carry, we knew we weren't going to play anything old – all the things that make life easier. But that's what we decided to do."

Musically, the four new tracks that made up the 'Snakedrill' EP were quite different from Wire's first three albums, although the way they were put together, from live performances, recalled the band's working methods circa *Pink Flag*. 'A Serious Of Snakes' was a comparatively melodic opener, even if it was less of a song and more of a linear "groove", with a blend of guitar strumming and picking from Messrs Gilbert and Newman. "The real secret of Wire's new sound," wrote Wilson Neate, "lay in what was omitted rather than what was added. Gone are the grating low-fi noises and crashes which haunted *Chairs Missing* and *154*. Gone, too, are the cymbals, which Gotobed discarded as irrelevant." 'Drill' was a strange kind of pneumatic dance invocation based around a single chord – far removed from the luscious musicality of 'Map Reference' and 'Outdoor Miner', although here the delight lay in the sonic layers and textures rather than any melodic twists and turns. 'Advantage In Height' was slightly more song-like, while Graham Lewis' a cappella 'Up To The Sun' was like a one-man Gregorian chant.

Lyrically, 'Snakedrill' was similarly varied, Wire utilising several techniques. 'A Serious Of Snakes', given that it was the pop song of the piece, exuded a strange kind of arcane menace, featuring some idiosyncratic terms of abuse such as "you pea-brained earwig" and "you tulip", the latter, according to Wilson Neate, carrying connotations of stupidity and folly in medieval iconography. 'Drill', meanwhile, comprised little more than the title, Lewis and Gilbert blankly chorusing the word as though it was some sort of quasi-religious mantra.

Give or take some misgivings from Robert Gotobed about the technology used to achieve the machine sounds and rhythms on the 'Snakedrill' EP, Wire's return to the fray had, on a creative level at least, so far been successful.

★

IT was when the band, producer-engineer Gareth Jones and assistant engineer Andre Giere decamped to Berlin's Hansa studios by the Wall to record fourth album *The Ideal Copy*, their first since 1979's *154*, that the problems began. Bruce Gilbert wasn't overly aware of too much internal friction, although he was conscious of Colin Newman becoming increasingly uncomfortable with the way things were going in the studio. On the whole, though, for Gilbert it was simply a matter of collecting together the various pieces of music that the band had been working on after the 'Snakedrill' EP and "presenting it to the world as a substantial object".

"I thought the sessions were really good," says the guitarist. "We were wandering into areas and textures that we hadn't wandered into before. It was slightly fraught because Colin was increasingly unhappy with the situation: he felt that he didn't have enough control over the production after his burgeoning production career and I think his impression was that the music we were recording was a bit rough and perhaps not commercial enough. But working with Gareth was great; we got on very well with him. He was very different from Mike [Thorne], but they were both meticulous in their own ways."

Gilbert believes the sessions for *The Ideal Copy* recalled those for *Chairs Missing* in that the band were, stylistically speaking, "careering all over the shop", as well as those for *154* – "only a spikier, stranger version". Overall, for the guitarist, recording in Berlin reminded him of the very early days of Wire. "I enjoyed it because we were approaching the excitement of the very early years, feeling our way and experimenting. Everything was up for grabs in terms of textures and approaches. We were concentrating on finding sounds for the guitars and creating atmospheres and Gareth was always very careful to preserve the ideas while they were fresh." He credits Newman with "coming up with some quite catchy numbers" for *The Ideal Copy* and appreciates the four-way songwriting credits on the album sleeve. "I thought it was the correct thing to do, because we were all pulling on the same rope. And much of the music was created in the studio, so it felt fair." Does he have any favourite songs on the album? "The abiding memory I have is of recording 'Feed Me', which Graham wrote mostly. I was doing this guitar overdub in Hansa and we had the feeling that it should feature an out-of-control guitar gesture, all feedback and sound, so we set up this situation where we had as many amplifiers as possible, all turned up to the max, and fed the guitar into them. There was nowhere to stand in this huge studio. We had to build a camp in the corner where we could take shelter, where the guitar wouldn't feed back. The feeling was of edgy chaos, and I rather enjoyed that. It felt very physical."

Gilbert also enjoyed being in Berlin, although he "ventured out", as he puts it, less frequently than Graham Lewis. "We did use some little bar a couple of streets away – there were bars opening every week in Berlin, tiny little places, all with strange themes – the Allies were pouring money in to keep it going so there were lots of bars opening up weekly. Nobody was from Berlin, though; instead, there were all these young people from all over Germany. There was a lot going on."

Gilbert may have been unaware of the difficulties being faced by the band, some of whose members were then going through some quite extreme changes in their personal lives, including Newman, whose first marriage was at an end and second, to Malka Spigel, had just begun, and Lewis, who had himself just ended a nine-year relationship and whose life, as he puts it, "was basically up in the air". Add to that what Lewis refers to as "a clash of ideas as to how it was that you went about making a record" and you've got a volatile atmosphere in camp Wire. "As you can imagine," says Lewis, "through the experiments or the work that everybody had been undertaking [since the split], of course various and varying ideas had come up as to how you went about making a record."

With regard to the division of labour, songwriting-wise, this time round, Lewis describes it as "an awful lot more mixed up". He cites the way Dome worked, their process often involving simply turning up at the studio with nothing written, "and not feeling insecure about that; in fact, we invited it to some degree". He believes this was "a new way of working" for Newman. "He felt quite uncomfortable about it, in some ways, and that's unfortunate. But it happens to everybody. At that time we were experimenting with that, and we were pushing it further and further. 'Ambitious', for instance, was very much a lyrical hybrid that we made in the studio with Daniel. Colin was hardly there on that one. 'Madman's Honey' I wrote the text for and Colin wrote the music. For 'Ahead', I came up with the riff and wrote the words, and then we completely rewrote them and restructured them. Bruce and I came up with 'Point Of Collapse' in the studio. 'Feed Me', Colin wrote and I came up with the tune. He felt uncomfortable with it, so I ended up singing it. 'Over Theirs' was a combined thing. 'Still Shows' was the result of me saying, 'I think we're still short of a number', and I had a text, and Colin had an acoustic guitar and the next morning he turned up and said, 'It goes like this.' And we went, 'That's great.'"

Newman concurs with Lewis' assessment of the taxing nature of the reunion when asked what it was like to be working again with Gilbert, Lewis and Gotobed in the mid-Eighties. "It was often difficult," he admits. He felt particularly alienated and on edge being the youngest in the band, as well as the one "who wrote most of the tunes." Plus, he says, in a damning assessment of this period in Wire 20 years later, in the mid-Noughties, after the final departure of Bruce Gilbert, "I was the lead singer – and that's a dangerous combination because you're bound to get bullied. Wire can be brutal. I felt crushed at times. Wire have been playing power games for 30 years. They could be an even better band, if not for that. I'm not that guarded. But it's the way people have rubbed up against each other. Without Bruce, the power play has changed: the trio is inherently more stable than the four-piece, where people always pair off. With three, if one feels left out it collapses to a line. We're all keenly aware of that and it gives a positive dynamic. There's no point in falling out."

Even more than the sessions for *154*, which themselves were quite tense and strained, Newman found recording *The Ideal Copy* hard going. "Making *154* was pretty brutal, but the most brutal time was *The Ideal Copy*. It was absolutely horrible; the hardest record we ever made." At one point during recording, Newman apparently upped and left, returning to his new marital home, then in Brussels. "What made it hard was this kind of jockeying for position. We were all people who worked in different ways, only with no real clear direction. It became very, very depressing. It was absolutely awful. I just left and came home. I said, 'I can't take this any more.' I was persuaded to continue to work with the band because it was Daniel Miller's money. I couldn't fault that argument. We'd never been on an indie label and Mute had invested quite heavily, and I'd known Daniel since he was a bloke in a mac who'd come to all the post-punk gigs in the late-Seventies, so I thought, 'OK, we'll figure it out.'"

By the next album, 1988's *A Bell Is A Cup... Until It Is Struck*, he maintains the atmosphere had improved dramatically. "We lightened up," he says. Ironically, *The Ideal Copy* sounds anything but fractious and fraught. Released in April 1987, the album – titled, according to Graham Lewis, after a dream Bruce Gilbert had about the ideal copy being DNA (it was also about other "social organisms" with acronyms such as the IRA, CIA and FBI) – sounds like a polished piece of high-quality mid-'80s electro-pop, which offers the impression that everything was smooth and harmonious within Wire. The first three tracks – 'Point Of Collapse', 'Ahead' (issued as a single in March '87) and 'Madman's Honey' – were supremely melodic, anthemic techno-pop, with driving rhythms, attractive textures and surging choruses.

'Ambitious' and 'Cheeking Tongues' were no less infectious. 'Over Theirs' was slower, with a subtly insistent, insinuating beat. And even though 'Feed Me' and 'Still Shows' weren't obviously catchy, there was something in, respectively, Newman and Lewis' vocal delivery that drew the listener in. Wilson Neate has detected in Wire's fourth album "a sense of nervousness, from the edgy minor chords of 'Point Of Collapse' to the twitching textures of 'Still Shows' and the suitably schizophrenic atmosphere of the 'cold war' song 'Over Theirs'. Despite this, the record remains accessible." Accessible, and designed for acclaim. "Wire are pure luxury," wrote Simon Reynolds in his *Melody Maker* review, in which he reflected on Wire's love of pure sound and mistrust of meaning. "Here are a bunch of superior sound technicians with an immaculate grasp of the sculptural and architectural possibilities of rock, who nonetheless refuse to deploy these gifts to any particular end. Wire despise the uses people subject music to, detest the currency of rock discourse; driven by the desire to avoid being reduced to a synopsis, they create a vivid, blank and quite inconsequential beauty. The aim: to dazzle, rather than enlighten; build edifices, rather than edify.

"Along with Verlaine's Television," continued Reynolds, "Wire were one of the first instances of rock as abstract art, as an energy dislocated from any precise function or venue. Don't approach Wire looking to come away with something beyond a faint afterglow of bliss. Don't even expect to be involved; Wire music is like something that aches in the distance, something to gawp at; crenellations, cataracts, constellations, cumulus... remote splendour." He noted the similarity between 'Ahead' and New Order's 'Temptation', but that was more than made up for by 'Feed Me', which he described as looming "like the predatory tread of a giant, echoing through some vast cavern", and by 'Madman's Honey', which "pours over the ear like a cascade of nectar, shimmers like a squadron of dragonflies, is spun from the most nightingale luscious harmonies since 'Outdoor Miner'."

So with such an exquisite collection of electronic pop, not to mention one of the few artistically successful comebacks in rock history, under their belts, what was the problem for Newman during the *Ideal Copy* sessions? "I have a particular dynamic relationship to the recording process," he explains. "As time went on, through the Seventies, I became increasingly involved in the process of how the records were made; I became very interested in the assemblage, to the point where I started making and producing my own records, and then producing other people. It was a very different approach from the one used by Graham and Bruce. They had their own creative approach but it was not necessarily the best way to make a Wire record. Then I started to have my own studio circa *The Ideal Copy*, which is when I first met [wife] Malka, a modern musician in her own right. Then I began to make music in my own space, so I became increasingly critical of all other production methods. I was much more hands-on. I needed to know how everything worked, technically, to engage in that process."

This, reveals Newman, is why he also found it difficult working with Mike Thorne towards the end of Wire's time on EMI, as he found himself wanting to become increasingly involved in the recording process. "He was from the George Martin school of production: he was all about the atmosphere and making the circumstances right for the performances, practising lots and then playing it in the studio while the engineer captures it all." This, he says, can be a good, even exciting, approach, "especially for an ideas-based band like Wire", but for someone with Newman's knowledge of the studio and facility with the console, it can quickly pall and become boring – "Hence," he says, "all that tension and interest in working with machines."

When asked who or what it was that he imagines so disturbed Newman during the recording of *The Ideal Copy*, and about his feeling that he was being "bullied" – an odd assertion given that, to all intents and purposes, he and Graham Lewis were in charge – Lewis says, "That's kind of weird, isn't it? I think it's got to be Bruce, then, hasn't it, really? I don't know. Colin's always had this thing about being the youngest in the group, even though he's only about nine months younger than me! I think he mustn't have had a good time at school – that's what I've always thought."

Lewis also points to the problems everyone was experiencing outside of Wire, while being away from home in Berlin, where they were staying in small apartments within the Hansa building complex. This undoubtedly exacerbated the situation. "It was very difficult, changing the process [i.e. using the new technology], and not getting on terribly well. For Bruce and I, well, our lives weren't very happy at all, but having said that, I felt pretty good in Berlin. I was a bit nomadic at that point, and I had a great space to work in because I was also making huge collages, doing a lot of Xerox work. Photocopying had arrived and it became a very bad habit of mine. I was trying to develop things all the time and, you know, we were making *The Ideal Copy*, so... While we were making the album, I was told by the people at Hansa that I could use Studio 2, so I'd be busy making huge collage pictures using photocopying, which was great. And Bruce and I were modifying our apartments – Bruce was into lighting and shadows, really beautiful stuff, very modern. And I'd started developing mine, in a lighting direction, but I don't like nylon sheets, so they got me some new ones." Newman was less excited by the spaces and opportunities provided by the band's temporary new home. "Colin was not so long married and thinking of building a nest and stuff like that, so for him it was not the ideal place to be, whereas I felt really quite comfortable and excited by it."

Wire were in Berlin for a total of about six weeks. The band did a lot of work, but according to Lewis they also lost "an awful lot of work, a couple of reels of really interesting things", including a remix of a track from *The Ideal Copy* that was going to be used to score a modern dance. He also remembers scrapping a lot of music made in the first few weeks as the band got to grips with the new technology.

To what extent was Daniel Miller involved in recording at this time? "Let's see," says Lewis. "'Snakedrill' – very involved; he and Gareth worked very much as a team on the recording and the mixing of it. For *The Ideal Copy*, Daniel came out to see how things were going, and things were going... well, they could have been going better, put it that way. He had given us the go-ahead to take on the new approach because he was convinced that it was the right thing to do. And when he did come to the studio, he was a great help. We were having a tough time, but he was there for support. He was there for the making of 'Ambitious', for example – he provided the bass-synth part if I remember rightly. Things like that he was very, very involved with."

With Miller's track record of critical acclaim being matched by chart success with groups like Depeche Mode, Yazoo and Erasure, did Wire sense much pressure from him to create a hit record? "I don't know," says Lewis. "The thing that's great about Daniel is that he always wants things to be successful. And 'successful' you can take on many levels, which was why Mute thrived. Gareth always used to call it Daniel's Gallery, and he's got a lot of room in it for a lot of different people because he has truly catholic taste. That's one of the reasons we all got along famously, because he loves pop, he loves blues, he loves weird, he loves avant-garde, he loves electronic, he loves hardcore. He likes 'good', basically, like we all do." Lewis recalls Miller's catchphrase during the recording of *The Ideal Copy* being "every one's a classic". "It was useful in that it helped dissipate the tension, and it was also kind of amusing," he says.

Later, during the recording of next album *A Bell Is A Cup...*, Miller came up with another catchphrase: Think Pop. Were Wire put under any pressure by Miller to be a pop group?

"I encouraged the pop side because I thought that was their great strength as a band," says the label boss. "There were a lot of experimental bands at the time but Wire were different in their pop or song structures; that was their strength – their experiments in conventional song structure. Stuff like Dome and Bruce Gilbert solo were really good and I'm really proud of what they did, but that was Wire's strength. But they're grown-ups and they had to make their own decisions in the end.

"I liked them but maybe they lost some of the focus on their strengths," he adds. "'Drill' was great, all the different versions of it, and I thought *The Ideal Copy* was brilliant, but after that initial period they started to peter out a bit. They obviously realised that, too, which is why they stopped again [after 1991's *The First Letter*]. There were definitely differences between their [Mute] albums – there were massive changes in the way they worked from the first album to the last, changes in the sonic processes. That's why the tension kept on growing. I might have nudged them in a certain direction, but more as an A&R man than as a producer. I didn't exactly push them in any one direction, but I did try to help them get the best out of what they'd already got. Sometimes bands do need a little focus or someone with a fresh ear to help them, but not, like I say, as a producer."

Does Miller believe the tension in Wire, apart from the differences in the way they approached the recording process, was the result of a Lennon/McCartney-style split, with a "pop" camp and an "experimental" camp? "Maybe," he laughs. "Then again, they often used to write alone, in private, so... And don't forget that He Said [one of Graham Lewis' projects] were quite poppy, and then Colin got into minimal techno..." Was the intention, with the temporary move to Berlin, to capture some of the spirit of David Bowie and Brian Eno's work there in the late-Seventies? "Not really. We were doing a lot of work in Berlin with Depeche Mode and Nick Cave, and Gareth lived there. It was a moment in time when, pragmatically, you could get a much better studio there than in London and have a good time. The studio we had there was great, and much cheaper than London, and it was also a nice place to work. But we weren't really going for a Bowie-Eno vibe. The band may have thought of that but really it was more like, 'Let's go to Berlin and have a drink afterwards.'" Did they go on many benders there? "Oh, yeah," he says." One New Year's Eve, [after] we worked right through Christmas, we went out for a very long night with Graham Lewis; a very long night indeed. It was good fun. But it wasn't all a big party thing; they worked hard. They were hard-working guys."

Much of that hard work didn't – couldn't – involve Robert Gotobed. "That," says the drummer, "was the first album we made where more time was spent on the computer than doing anything else in the studio. I couldn't tell you much about the process, but it took hours to get the sound you wanted on the computer. I mean, Gareth was programming things into the computer rather than recording us playing as a group. I think that was the first time that Wire played without me; the computer was playing the drums, and they were playing along with the computer, so that didn't make me feel very good at all."

Despite receiving praise for his drumming throughout Wire's existence, Gotobed felt increasingly isolated. Did he have to argue the case with the others for the inclusion of more conventional drum parts? "Well, I only have to point you to WIR," he says of the new name for Wire coined following his departure in the late Eighties, with the attendant loss, by this highly conceptual four-man group, of their name's fourth letter. "WIR was the new group, and it didn't last very long, but as far as everybody else was concerned, this was the new world of Wire." And it all began on *The Ideal Copy*? "Yes. The use of a computer became so important that, well, I think it came down to the option I was given between being a programmer and not doing Wire. It may be pig-headed, but I am a drummer and not a programmer, so there was nothing for me to do as far as I could see."

According to Colin Newman, *The Ideal Copy* was the hardest Wire record to make. Does Gotobed remember it like that? "Well, it wasn't a lot of fun, although for me, for different reasons. I remember having a conversation with Gareth about why I didn't like computers, but he couldn't really understand. As far as he was concerned, it was like, 'This is all new, and new is better; Wire does new things, this is how everybody wants it to be, so what's the problem?' He couldn't see that drumming has a value for me. I don't know whether he was putting across a group or record company policy. But I just started to feel a bit, you know, 'Why am I here?' Now I suppose if I had thought programming was better than drumming, then everything would have been all right, but I'm afraid I didn't fit into this new format."

While the others were busy with the programming, Gotobed was either hanging around the studio or going for long walks around Berlin. "Gareth did make an effort to include me, in finding me things to do in the studio, which is a bit absurd – I think I arranged some samples or something – but for me, it just stopped being a group. I was at odds with what everybody else was doing and what they were talking about. I didn't feel like it was Wire. I know we were supposed to have come back on a new basis, but this just wasn't anything that I could recognise, and I didn't feel like I played a part in it. What I do, its value had gone.

"Gareth would record individual instruments – I remember recording some hi-hat – and parts like that would be put together with the other drum sounds on the computer, and that would be the drum track. That was his idea of putting on drums – they were put together artificially; it was all computer timing." Graham Lewis has said that *The Ideal Copy* was tough to make because the players' personal lives were in a state of flux, but according to Gotobed "the flux in Wire was more of a problem for me than the flux outside." Did he start to think of finding work outside of Wire? "Yes, I suppose I did think, 'If this isn't going to work I ought to think of doing something else.' I'm trying to remember what I did do. I had ideas about drumming elsewhere, but Wire had been such an intense period of work... People have said to me, 'You could have joined another group,' but that's the last thing I wanted at the time. I didn't want anything to do with groups. It just seemed like it had been a hell of a lot of work that hadn't really gotten anywhere, for me. It had come to a full stop, and Wire no longer existed – WIR was the new group, and I wasn't a part of it."

Chapter 9

So And Slow It Grows

"I felt that Mute was the perfect place for Wire to be, but Daniel [Miller] wasn't making money out of us. I started to feel uneasy and guilty about that. I can't remember if I discussed it with the others, but it was becoming obvious to me that our sales weren't justifying the faith that Daniel had in us" – Bruce Gilbert

*T*HE *Ideal Copy* may have been, by all accounts, a difficult album to make – "a very weird record, psychologically, to make", in the words of Graham Lewis, who attests that "everyone's lives were pretty fucked-up at the time, apart from Colin [Newman], who was pretty happy but homesick" – but it was a triumph of often quite commercial electronic pop. With its shiny surfaces and driving momentum, it could have capitalised on Wire's already strong reputation among the alt rock community in the US and gained traction from the increasing popularity stateside of the band's British synthpop peers, Depeche Mode, New Order and Pet Shop Boys.

Actually, Wire did spend some time in the States in the late-Eighties, and it did indeed look at one point as though they might make some sort of breakthrough there. They even satisfied their conceptual art-prankster side – and those among their American fan base still clamouring to hear their early material – during one US tour by inviting rock journalist Jim Derogatis' Wire tribute band, the Ex Lion Tamers, to open for them, so that they could perform *Pink Flag* in its entirety as a warm-up for Wire themselves, who, as ever, were determined to play a new-songs-only set. At one gig in New York, as soon as Derogatis and co came onstage, some members of the crowd, presuming the Ex Lion Tamers to be Wire themselves, were apparently heard wondering how it was that the decade-old band looked so young. There was even a live review in *NME*, recalls Lewis, which opined that "Wire's material was not as strong as the opening act's"! Both comments were taken in good humour by Wire. "There were loads of jokes going around," says Lewis, "and loads of games started to develop around this whole question as to who and what was Wire, what wasn't Wire, what was *Pink Flag*, and so on. There was a whole identify shift, but it was great fun. We all had a great time on that tour."

Less enjoyable an American experience was Wire's introduction to the joys of the US chat-show circuit when, following the release of *The Ideal Copy*, they were invited to appear on *The Suzanne Somers Show*, a coast-to-coast affair with a huge audience hosted by the titular ex-star of the US version of sitcom *Man About The House*, the actress having taken over the role of the show's presenter from comedienne Joan Rivers. As Lewis remembers it, it was Wire's appearance on the programme that effectively ruined their chances of breaking the States. "You can see it on YouTube," he says. "It's great. We actually managed to destroy our career in America in one night." "It was all rather strange," agrees Bruce Gilbert, who recalls being picked up at the airport in LA in a limo. "It all seemed rather unreal and Hollywood-ish." Somers, decides Lewis, was "attractive, in a bimbo-ish way". But that wasn't the problem. No, the problem was her rudeness; that plus the show's staff's intractability and Wire's refusal to, as per usual, play the game. "First of all, she didn't come and introduce herself to us; she came to say hello to Mel Brooks, who was [in the dressing room] next door, and we thought that was extremely rude." As for the show itself, it was "complete pantomime". Lewis saw it as the show's staff "really trying to screw us up". During negotiations between the programme and the band's US record company, it was decided that, of the two numbers Wire were invited to perform, it would be prudent for one of them to be the single 'Ahead', as well as the band's own choice, 'Drill'.

The first point of contention was the length of the songs – they would need to cut and edit their version of 'Ahead' before showtime, ditto 'Drill', whose length kept changing because of its improvisatory nature – and the second was the backdrop and drum riser, neither of which Wire wanted (too conventionally rock'n'roll, presumably). "They kept asking how long the songs would be," says Gilbert. "We said, 'We start it ['Drill'] and it [the length] depends on how well we're feeling or how well or badly it's going.'" Concurs Lewis, "The thing about 'Drill' is that nobody ever knows what's going to happen. It's got its own life. So anyway, we played it, and the guys started saying, 'Please will you repeat that?' And we go, 'Yeah, yeah, no problem.' Well, we play it again, and upstairs [in the control room] they're like [polite but testy American voice], 'That sounded completely different. How can that be, sir?' And I said, 'Because we don't know what's going to happen.' So this situation developed and there was a rescheduling of the show and we were told we could only play one song now. So we said, 'We're going to play 'Drill'.' And then it all started going very weird. Our sound guy told us they were trying to fuck us up, putting delay and reverb on things, trying to make it sound more commercial."

"And the other problem," says Gilbert, picking up the thread, "was that the sound people kept interfering with Rob's drum kit and he was getting very, very annoyed. He had to tell them, 'DO NOT TOUCH MY DRUMS!' There was an atmosphere of dismay among certain representatives..."

"It was ramping up," says Lewis, "and they were getting really fucking freaked out. We were on their shit-list, you know? We'd had the whole business: the make-up, photographs taken, the production assistant..."

As soon as they finished their performance of 'Drill', Wire were approached by a flustered Somers to say "hello" and meet the members of "Wire – one of the biggest bands in the world". First, she attempted a quip, saying that she was "trying to sing along [with 'Drill'] but couldn't catch the words." Then, a poker-faced Newman handed her over to an equally dour and unresponsive Gilbert, who proceeded to introduce "Mr Graham Lewis" as "our anthropological expert" and Robert Gotobed as "our agricultural consultant". As for Colin Newman, Gilbert joked that "they'd only just met", which made the presenter even more confused and anxious. Stuck for something to say, she asked Gilbert how they got the name of the band, to which he replied, "We take these things very seriously and we wanted a name that didn't mean anything, so we chose Wire." Then she turned round, only to discover that, over on the other side of the stage, she was being filmed by Lewis, who had brought his video camera along with him. "Am I on video?" she laughed nervously. "You're sort of a far-out group, aren't you?" To which Gilbert replied, "I doubt it." Somers announced that there would be a break, and the show's resident band immediately began playing T Rex's 'Get It On', at which point Lewis asked Somers to dance. Her off-air reply? "Fuck you." Two weeks later, she was fired. "Stupid woman," says Lewis.

Asked how their debut US television appearance affected their chances of making it in the States, the bassist says, "It really fucked things up for us there." Gilbert acknowledges that it could have proved pivotal, had they been "nice clean-cut boys playing a nice little tune". Still, after the show, Wire drove downtown for a gig with the Ex Lion Tamers and, according to Lewis, "the whole place erupted", having caught Wire on TV.

"Was it fun?" Gotobed ponders the question for a moment. "I don't think, for me, that was a fun period. I don't really look back on it and think I was enjoying that. There used to be a lot of tension around over different things. The tension seemed to go with the job at the time, which didn't really improve relations between us. I don't know what was going on. It couldn't even really be explained. 'Ego clashes' is what people in groups talk about, isn't it? It's when people start hating each other."

Wire came even closer to reaching a popular audience, in the United States at least, with an ill-advised spot opening for Mute label-mates Depeche Mode in front of tens of thousands of teens at the Pasadena Rose Bowl in June 1988. It coincided with another near-miss with the fabulously contagious single 'Eardrum Buzz', which occasioned an infamous in-studio appearance on MTV's *120 Minutes* and came accompanied by a wacky made-for-MTV video featuring cameos from Howard Devoto of Magazine, Bernard Sumner of New Order, Vince Clarke of Erasure, John Peel and many more.

"It was bizarre, completely unreal," says Gilbert of their Depeche support slot in the enormodome that was the Rose Bowl. "The audience were 500 yards away and still taking their seats for the main event while we played. There were some British fans there who were encouraging [towards Wire] in the front row, but some were shouting 'fuck off!' – maybe to get Wire angry and show the Americans what we were about, which is diffidence and menace."

Lewis' memory of the day is that it was "a bit unnerving", mainly because it was a daytime slot. "Playing in daylight doesn't always add up. It doesn't bother me now so much, but at the time I found it quite odd. Also, the Rose Bowl holds 80,000 people, and when we played, there must have been 50 there. It was very bizarre. I remember looking out into the crowd and seeing [UK rock writer and long-time Wire aficionado] Jon Savage, with Daniel [Miller] sitting 20 or 30 rows back, and thinking, 'That's weird.'"

Even weirder was that Wire played the Rose Bowl in the afternoon, and at midnight on the same day they played "this strange lodge place" in MacArthur Park – "and MacArthur Park," reminds Lewis, "is an infamous drug area" – to a sold-out crowd of 1,000. And then the following night they appeared at LA's Peppermint Lounge, where the capacity is under 200. "It was quite an extraordinary 36 hours," says Lewis. "It was like, telescopic, only in the wrong direction." Which performance did he prefer out of the three? "Well, they were all different. I think probably the one in the middle was the one I liked the most. But the Peppermint Lounge one was really weird, to go from this very distant experience to a situation where the dressing room is right at the back of the club. You had to walk through the audience to get to the very, very small stage. And I remember walking through and someone touched me on the head, and it just freaked me out. I don't know why. It was very bizarre to have somebody touch you. As you can imagine, one was pretty fragile having played three shows in 36 hours, after having been on the road for three weeks already." Did he have a word with the punter in question? "I said, 'Don't do that again.' And I meant it."

OVER the next three years, Wire recorded five more albums for Mute. In May 1988, they released the follow-up to *The Ideal Copy*, titled *A Bell Is A Cup… Until It Is Struck*. It was, like its predecessor, produced by Gareth Jones and engineered by David Heilmann at Preussen Tonstudio in Berlin, where, explains Bruce Gilbert, the band "all had separate accommodation in various people's flats on loan to us, in different parts of the city". There was very little socialising going on this time. "After each session we might go to the local restaurant and afterwards for a few drinks, but then we'd go our separate ways." And yet Wire's fifth album was a fine record, and an even more commercially potent, streamlined collection of left-field electronic pop songs than *The Ideal Copy*.

It was, says Graham Lewis, an easier record to make than *Ideal Copy*. "We made a conscious decision that it was going to be, because *The Ideal Copy* was so hard to make. Everyone decided that it had to be easier. And we had the material. I still reckon Gareth could have done a better mix – I think it's a bit lightweight myself, but the material's really good."

Bruce Gilbert observes that the band were starting to use more techniques during recording, which he admits "caused some problems". He wasn't too enamoured of the sonic details and textural overlay – what he calls "the plinky-plonky bits all over the album, which I soon got bored with, all the xylophone sounds. But it was interesting, I suppose." He notes, too, the "atmosphere of menace" that pervades the album, which possibly accounts for the lack of interest from radio programmers. He puts that atmosphere down to a "natural predilection" in Wire "for the eerie and gloomy". Overall, Gilbert prefers *The Ideal Copy* these days to *A Bell Is A Cup…* "I was getting bored with not playing in the studio. Songs were being assembled and reassembled by computer." Did Colin Newman still feel, as he did during the recording of *The Ideal Copy*, as though he was being bullied by the sixth formers in the band? "I don't really remember it being like that. Maybe that's his way of describing his not having enough control." As Gilbert sees it, the dynamic had changed within the band because of Newman's "growing expertise on computers". And in fact, if anyone was feeling left out, it would have been everyone but Newman. "Things were being taken out of one's hands; it was becoming a matter of choosing noises and textures rather than playing them." In this new set-up, it was Newman who was more than anyone, and more than ever, the one at the helm. "It did feel like that sometimes. Because of the major use of computers there would be lots of hanging round, waiting for them to be processed, or waiting for the editing. It all became very distant. Was there aggro in the studio? More like ennui and the dissipation of energy." Did the Mute recordings feel increasingly like academic exercises? "No. We were on a roll with all the technological developments."

What was the mood like in the band at this time? According to Gilbert, it was "relatively happy". They introduced a new method to rehearsals and songwriting "which was exciting", in which they all (except Robert Gotobed) jammed on guitar-synthesisers, or MIDI guitars – which meant that the notes played would feed directly into a computer. The drawback was that the end result was "rather sterile when translated back into a normal studio sound. Nuances were lost."

They may have lacked the edge and scratchy post-punk appeal of their EMI work, but creamily produced confections such as 'Silk Skin Paws', 'The Finest Drops', 'The Queen Of Ur And The King Of Um', 'Free Falling Divisions', 'It's A Boy' and the single 'Kidney Bingos' were among Wire's finest recordings to date. In fact, *A Bell Is A Cup...* was described by *Trouser Press Record Guide* as "Wire's most ruminative album... It will twirl your lobes". Allmusic went further, hailing it, "Arguably Wire's best album and certainly its most accessible. *A Bell Is a Cup... Until It Is Struck* is a work of modern rock genius." The online magazine praised Wire's fifth studio release for its "peculiar pop songs full of stream-of-consciousness lyrics", citing as an example of the latter the chorus of 'Kidney Bingos' ("Money spine paper lung/Kidney bingos organ fun"), a surreal litany of non-sequiturs virtually crooned by Colin Newman as though it were a regular pop love song. Coming in for praise, too, were the wonderful textured melodies, the overdubbed layers of guitars, treated and phased until they ebbed and flowed around the songs, propelled by Bruce Gilbert's throbbing bass and Robert Gotobed's gently insistent, techo-lite rhythms.

The words weren't quite as accessible as the melodies, although fortunately Wire's chief lyricist, Graham Lewis, is on hand to help. He explains that 'The Queen Of Ur And The King Of Um' paints a portrait of Thatcher's Britain, a place where there is "no society", just a populace comprising barely literate squabbling drunks and proto-chavs. 'It's A Boy' he likens to "a perverted TS Eliot". 'Kidney Bingos' was Bruce Gilbert's idea about a future where "people would play scratch cards or bingo to get organs on the national health". 'A Public Place', with its "private hedge pissers in anxious alleys", he describes as "horrible".

In his review of *A Bell Is A Cup...* Michael Azerrad of *Rolling Stone* joked that "you need a special decoder ring (not included) to understand the lyrics, but maybe they were designed to be misunderstood". Does Lewis believe Wire's cryptic lyrics ('Point Of Collapse' from *The Ideal Copy* was, he says, "total Pinter") speak only to a cultured, elite minority who "get it"? "There's nothing elite about them," he replies. "That's nonsense." He considers some of his lyrics to be allegories and at all times relishes the myriad meanings they offer the listener. "I like ambiguity. I think it's really good when people have their own reading – or misreading, as the case may be." He doesn't believe there is a "right" or "wrong" way to view a Wire song. "I certainly hope not. I don't think that could be. I've read some good things. I read an article by a guy that was his analysis, from a political point of view, of our Eighties period. I thought it was really good. Colin hated it, but then, Colin's not really that interested in politics. But I thought it was really good because he picked up on a hell of a lot of the references that I deliberately put in there. And they are there, but that's not the point of the work. It's not folk music. It's not The Clash." Are his words a form of journalism, transcribing the events of the moment and turning them into images for the music, or poetry? "It's all of those things. I don't know about poetry, though. Isn't that an elite activity? I've used epigrams, and a lot of anagrams. 'Eels Sang Lino' [from *Document And Eyewitness*], for example, is Los Angeles." Lewis uses many techniques, as much to entertain himself as anyone else. "It's like, can you make a good text out of 'the Moon in June'? So then the challenge becomes to put into the lyric every month of the year. There's even a song on *Document And Eyewitness* featuring every letter of the alphabet – it's like that idea about someone being such a great singer they could sing the telephone book." Are all these ways of avoiding saying the obvious? "No, they're all ways of saying what's specific. It's writing songs about things that exist. In a sense it's the materials you use. That's what I think is important: the way you embed your language and your metaphors into your culture, and the way you understand your culture." There is often an atmosphere of dread and sense of impending doom in Wire's songs, even on their Mute recordings, when much of their music was so easy on the ear. "Well, we were in Berlin in 1988," he says, "where many people believed something apocalyptic was going to happen. I tell you one thing for certain is that nobody expected it [the fall of the Berlin Wall] to happen in the relatively violence-free way it did. But yes, I guess it is foreboding – there's movement on the border or in the hills, you know?"

Gilbert agrees that the lyrical themes were broader on *A Bell Is A Cup...*, being a series of responses to global events and geopolitical change. "The themes may have got more universal, larger, as a consequence of what was going on in the world. Some things were written in Berlin, and that gave the songs a certain perspective. There was a certain aura about the place; things were happening. It could have gone either way. There was a lot of excitement. It was literally on the edge."

How do Lewis' lyrics, dense with images as they are, compare with, say, Ian Curtis'? Was he more autobiographical? "No," answers Lewis, "he was more about reading books, I always thought; more about libraries." Then again, he describes 'So And Slow It Grows' from 1991's *The First Letter* as "like Beckett", only Beckett set to a gorgeous pop tune.

Have any of his songs been seriously misconstrued? He cites as an example of this 'Champs' from *Pink Flag*, which most assumed from the references to "speed" to be about amphetamines when actually it was about "the need for speed" of racing drivers, particularly the late Formula One driver Ronnie Peterson, who died in a first-lap collision at the Italian Grand Prix. Lewis watched Peterson's British rival, James Hunt, reacting to his death on TV and thought, "I'm going to write about this."

Still, for all the arcane references and esoteric subject matter, the disturbing front cover, a pale wash of off-colour browny-purple featuring a starkly cut-out horse's head and a filing cabinet, and the hard-togauge title (a Zen reference, courtesy Gilbert, to the way certain objects can be transformed by their use), *A Bell Is A Cup...* was probably as approachable an album as Wire were ever going to make. In fact, Daniel Miller's catchphrase as the band recorded it in Berlin was "Think Pop".

"We were all saying that," recalls Gilbert. "It became an ironic mantra." "Yeah, 'Think Pop'," echoes Lewis. "That was his instruction for *A Bell Is A Cup...* because we'd always ask Daniel for a gnomic quote, after 'Every One's A Classic' for *The Ideal Copy*. He [Miller] came over [to Berlin] and hung out for a bit. What I always really liked about Daniel is he has a tremendously wide taste in music. It's one of the reasons we signed to Mute. Basically, all Daniel cares about is, 'Is it any good?' He's not genre-obsessed. And he likes a good tune as much as he does a great piece of experimentation. Throughout that period, Daniel tried to help as much as he possibly could by saying, 'Just one hit, one hit would be great, one hit would be so good for all of you'. But it's not like he was putting any pressure on anybody. He was just saying that it could make life so much easier for all of us. And so consequently Daniel was always there, always very interested, because he's always loved the pop side of what we've done, as much as he has the rest of it. That [Wire's innate pop nous] really appealed to him because he's the same as us – well, Colin and I, at least – in the sense that he came up listening to Sixties music and he's got a real ear and a thing about pop music. Does it still exist? So he was always getting involved when it came to choosing singles. That's when you really saw the incredible class that Daniel has for shaping things and being able to hear what something will sound like on the radio."

'Kidney Bingos' was deemed to be the best bet from *A Bell Is A Cup...* to secure the all-important daytime radio play when it was issued as a single two months ahead of the album, in March 1988. Sadly, it didn't quite happen. "Well, Daniel's not a man to make ridiculous claims," says Lewis. "He knows that, somewhere along the line, you need a stroke of luck to get a hit record. It's not just about how good the song is. But it was the same all the way from 'Ahead', which everyone thought was going to be big, and it did do very well in the States, or relatively well anyway. And 'Kidney Bingos' got on the air. We had the whole shebang:

videos were made, teeth were gnashed, money was spent, and faith was had, but also, unfortunately, disappointment was endured."

BUT not so much disappointment that they gave up trying: indeed, within a year of the release of *A Bell Is A Cup...*, Wire had issued another studio album, *It's Beginning To And Back Again* (also known as *IBTABA*).

Well, it was a sort of studio album. Wire's sixth long-player mainly comprised reinterpretations of live performances of material from *A Bell Is A Cup...* (plus 'Over Theirs' from *The Ideal Copy*). The recordings were based on performances cut in Chicago, Portugal and London and subsequently reconstructed in a studio in Brussels (so that Colin Newman could be near his wife and newborn son) and remixed by Wire (with assistance from Paul Kendall and John Fryer), often to the point where they were unrecognisable from the original versions (something that would also be true of their next album-but-one, 1991's *The Drill*).

Although it was difficult to discern the point of the exercise – it was half a remix collection and half a collection of new songs – there is no denying the quality of the material on *IBTABA*, much of it sounding like a dream collision of their "dugga" rhythm and some of their most gorgeous melodies to date. Apart from containing the single 'Eardrum Buzz', which in May 1989 became the band's most successful single in their history, charting at number two on the *Billboard* Modern Rock Tracks chart and number 68 in the UK (as well as a second, 12-inch version, which turned up the almost facetiously chirpy, brassy brightness), *IBTABA* also featured 'German Shepherds', 'Illuminated', 'The Offer' and 'In Vivo'. The latter tracks were apparently recorded in a few days at the behest of Daniel Miller, who once again was, ever so gently, trying to tease a hit single out of Wire. And although a Top 20 chart entry remained elusive, it wasn't for want of trying: 'Eardrum Buzz', 'The Offer' and 'In Vivo', particularly, were gorgeously pretty pop songs that sounded like The Byrds chiming and harmonising their way through the New Order catalogue.

"That was OK," says Bruce Gilbert of *IBTABA*. "As a concept I'm not sure whether it was without its faults but it was an interesting way of doing things, piecing together performances we'd already played, in a studio in Brussels that was still being built. They were live recordings, which seemed an attractive prospect; it was also interesting to see how live recordings can change and mutate. We wanted to capture that in the studio, by playing live and recording in a traditional way."

"Oh God, that was quite hard, actually, as well," says Graham Lewis, offering the by-now predictable assessment of a Wire recording session. "We said, 'OK, we'll do it in Brussels to accommodate Colin' – who had a new child and was doing some other work with a French rock star – so we turn up to work in this studio where they'd just laid the concrete floor in the live room. So, yeah, it was quite taxing, plus the apartment we were living in was crap. I wouldn't say that we didn't have fun – that's compulsory – but one certainly had to dig into one's reserves to stay in Brussels and have a good time. It's not my favourite city, I have to say, and at this point it had changed considerably. But we thought the process [of reconstructing live performances] was interesting. We thought it was worth investigating, to see what might happen. It definitely counts as one of our studio albums."

Gilbert reveals that 'Eardrum Buzz', like 'Kidney Bingos' before it, was originally intended to be far harder and louder. "'Kidney Bingos' was the hit that should have been, possibly. But I always heard that song in my head as a brutal heavy metal track – somehow it just became a pop song! I heard the chords and the edges, but it got softened by the sounds people were using, so it became rather jolly, which worked in the end because the subject matter was not likeable but it had a jaunty, poppy feel to it, and that contradiction can be very attractive. I probably would have wanted 'Eardrum Buzz' to be brutal heavy metal, too..."

Behind the scenes, meanwhile, says Gilbert, there was a sense of anxiety among certain members of the band and their record company that Wire were failing consistently to deliver the hit record they so richly deserved. "Things started to get a bit uneasy," he says. "Me personally, I felt that Mute was the perfect place for Wire to be, but Daniel wasn't making money out of us even though we were still getting advances from them. I started to feel uneasy and guilty about that. I can't remember if I discussed it with the others, and Daniel certainly never said anything – there were no meetings with flow charts – but it was becoming obvious to me that our sales weren't justifying the faith that Daniel had in us. Not that everybody gave up, though – we were still thinking along the right lines all the way up to 'So And Slow It Grows' [another should-have-been hit, from 1991's *The First Letter*]."

There were several signs that they were thinking along the right lines on their next album, 1990's *Manscape*. It was produced by David Allen, a producer, engineer and mixer known for his work with synthpop and goth-rock bands like The Cure, The Sisters of Mercy, Depeche Mode, The Associates and The Human League (and not to be confused with Dave Allen of Gang Of Four/Shriekback, or Daevid Allen of Seventies prog band Gong) and recorded and mixed at Seventies bubblegum pop haven RAK Studios.

Manscape, its striking cover image of a phallic monument in the centre of a public place courtesy of designers Neville Brody and Jon Wozencroft, saw Wire exploring more deeply than ever the possibilities of electronic music production and computer technology, informed as they were by the dance/house/techno explosion of the late-Eighties, hence all the sequenced riffs and machine rhythms (although Wire's relationship to said movement was given an ambiguous twist by the reference to "the third-rate butcher's dance-hall mix", during the opening track, 'Life In The Manscape'). In fact, bass and drums were mostly sequenced both within and outside the studio: the band's 1990 UK and European tour saw them performing live for the first time without Robert Gotobed, and as per usual playing mostly new material from the LP plus a few older songs reworked to fit the new electronic mode.

If the music on *Manscape* was irrefutably modern, the lyrics tackled perennial themes: 'The Morning Bell' concerned the British public school system, while 'Small Black Reptile' took potshots at our political systems and culture of greed. 'Life In The Manscape' and 'Stampede' were contemporary meditations, however: the former adressed the role of the press and free speech in the new Europe of the former eastern bloc, while the latter captured the mood of disorientation following the collapse of the East German regime in 1989. 'Sixth Sense' was a humorous sideswipe at those who use personal columns for nefarious ends ("Edible hunter seeks credible victim/Sincerely rich seeks sceptical poor"...). *Manscape* ended with Wire's longest track since 'Crazy About Love', the 14-minute-long anti-Thatcherite anthem 'You Hung Your Lights In The Trees/A Craftman's Touch', sung with doomy detachment by Graham Lewis as the skittering beats, accidentally anticipating UK garage and grime, skimmed across the surface of the minor-chord melody.

Manscape has been described as both "edgy, brainy dance music" and "a nadir in the Wire corpus", the general view being that the "electronification" of Wire's studio process led to overproduction and had a sterilising effect on the music. Colin Newman describes it as a "really good record", albeit one that was "badly recorded and really badly mixed". Bruce Gilbert concurs, adding that "the feelings of unease in the band were reflected in some ways in the music, with sterility increasingly a feature. We did lots of sequencing." To make matters worse, he "didn't really like the [first] studio in London where we recorded it; there was something a bit odd about it". Did the band visit many of London's techno and house clubs at the time? "Obviously one had exposure to it [dance music], but really Colin and Graham were more interested in the dance world and that sort of approach. I wasn't consciously picking up on that stuff."

Graham Lewis describes the *Manscape* sessions as "chaotic". "It was a long process. It's going to sound as if we're obsessive about technology, but it is there, and if it's there you tend to use it." The intention was to use the technology, not be used by it – and to involve Gotobed in the process. "There was a development with the technology where it was possible for you to record while it was 'playing back', which we thought could be a very good way to provide some spontaneity in the composition and perhaps make Robert feel a little bit more involved." And yet, as Newman, Gilbert and Lewis got "'teched up" and "got their heads down to learn about what to do", Gotobed "sat in the corner, looking a bit miserable". Lewis, for his part, remembers a feeling of excitement about the "cybernetic possibilities" of it all as the band decamped to Mickie Most's RAK studios for the final part of recording.

Unfortunately, just as they did, David Allen's personal life, recalls Lewis, "went into the most spectacular free fall", as the producer's brother began experiencing marriage problems and his father, from whom he'd been estranged for many years, suddenly died, following which his (father's) house was broken into and robbed and his wife unexpectedly fell pregnant. "He [Allen] became exceedingly depressed. It was very, very intense, and obviously very disruptive, which sounds like a cruel thing to say but isn't meant to. But it wasn't conducive, shall we say. Plus, we all had our own tensions and individual problems that come with life, so it was a pretty difficult set of sessions, really, not helped by the fact that Colin and I were both not living in England by this point [Lewis had moved to Sweden in 1988], so we were both away from home. It made for a mighty weird situation. I think if we had been luckier, it could have ended up being extremely good, but in the end Dave understandably didn't have the concentration to pull it together. And I think he found it rather difficult working with us because he'd been used to working with people like Robert Smith from The Cure, where it was, basically, what Mr. Smith wants to do is what the group does, you know? And then he's faced with us, where you have three people with ideas of their own.

"It wasn't so much fractious as, 'Oh God, what do we do now?' It was very difficult. There were a couple of moments when Dave, to his credit, went, 'I fully understand if you want to get somebody else in.' But such was the complexity of the process, we just kept thinking, 'How on earth can we drag somebody into the middle of this huge technological train set or whatever the fuck you want to call it?' But there are glimmers on *Manscape* of how great it could have been, I think."

As Lewis said, there were now three people in Wire with ideas of their own – because it was during the *Manscape* sessions that fourth man Robert Gotobed's reluctance to become involved in the new studio processes reached its inevitable conclusion. Despite having to all intents and purposes provided the beats for the Mute albums – even if they were later processed and programmed beyond all recognition – he was getting bored in the studio and being made to feel terminally isolated. And so he left, just like that.

"Because of Robert not programming, as he would have said, it was 'a redundant situation'. I'd have said, well, I'm now free to go and be a tourist or whatever else. But he seemed to feel he was redundant. But that's because he wasn't part of the process. There was no formal announcement," adds Gilbert. "He just said, 'I'm off!'"

"I suppose it was a downwards gradient from when we first reformed for the 'Snakedrill' EP," says Gotobed. "I thought that was meant to be Wire getting back together, but I don't think it was. I think that was the beginning of WIR. So it came to the crunch, and I decided to go."

Chapter 10

... And Back Again

"I have a big problem with the comeback idea. It's just bollocks. Wire are not making a comeback. We're not on any nostalgia trip" – Colin Newman

FOLLOWING Robert Gotobed's departure, Wire released two albums as WIR (or Wir). The loss of their fourth letter, first mooted at the start of their stint on Mute when they weren't sure whether Gotobed would want to be involved, was an acknowledgement by our arch-conceptualist heroes of the drummer's absence. In the wake of these two releases, Wire would take a second hiatus that made their first layoff seem like a blip in time.

The first of these albums, *The Drill*, came out in 1991 although it was actually recorded before *Manscape*, when Gotobed was still in the band – he left during rehearsals for a 1990 UK tour, a week before the dates were due to start, which meant the band had to go out as a three-piece with pre-programmed bass and drums; "not," notes Graham Lewis drily, "terribly good form".

As a consequence, *The Drill* – produced at Mute's Worldwide Studios in London by Wire in conjunction with Paul Kendall – does feature some Gotobed rhythms, even if they're more programmed than played. Contrary to the more widely held version of events that he virtually faded from view as the Mute recording sessions went on, according to Colin Newman Gotobed did, in fact, do a substantial amount of live drumming on *The Ideal Copy* and *A Bell Is A Cup...*, he did some drum programming on *Manscape*, and even a little for *The Drill*, before leaving.

"He didn't like it but he can do it," says Newman, who explains that in the Eighties he developed a system – a hybrid of a live drum kit and sequencing – "that he [Gotobed] sort of liked but didn't. We wanted to work with sequencing and Rob wanted to be the rhythmic spine of the band, which he was live but it wasn't possible [in the studio] with Eighties technology – to attach sequencing to live drumming. It was too complex for our brains to work out."

Originally designed as a means of trying out the new computer technology to be employed on *Manscape*, *The Drill*, comprising eight versions, including one by Gareth Jones, of their "dugga" apotheosis 'Drill' (plus a ninth version recorded live), was more than a remix album. It was Bruce Gilbert's idea: to take a theme and extemporise around it – "like Bach", says Newman, drolly. "It's Wire's *Canon Of Fugue In D Major*." A series of doodles and experiments within the genre that would later become known as "electronica", and featuring lyrics that elaborate on those of the original song, *The Drill* ranges from slow, fluid numbers such as the gently pulsating 'What's Your Desire?', to more frenetic tracks such as '(A Chicago) Drill (Live)' that chime perfectly with the then-current "industrial" rock of bands like Nine Inch Nails and Ministry. Indeed, Gilbert today wishes the whole album, which he considers "a bit soft and pretty", had explored more fully this industrial direction. Then there is the jerky, tricksy 'Jumping Mint', which anticipates such future micro-genres as drill'n'bass and glitch techno, the latter a form of dance music comprising the clicks, cuts, static and hiss you get on CDs as they degrade. Elsewhere, the chattering, clattering 'Arriving/Staying/Going?' chops and dices the linear flow of the original with psychotic finesse, 'Did You Dugga?' sounds like a cartoon version of house music, while 'In Every City?' offers a hybrid of 'Drill' and '12XU' from *Pink Flag*. Overlooked at the time of its release as an idiosyncratic venture too far, the album probably sits more comfortably alongside 21st-century

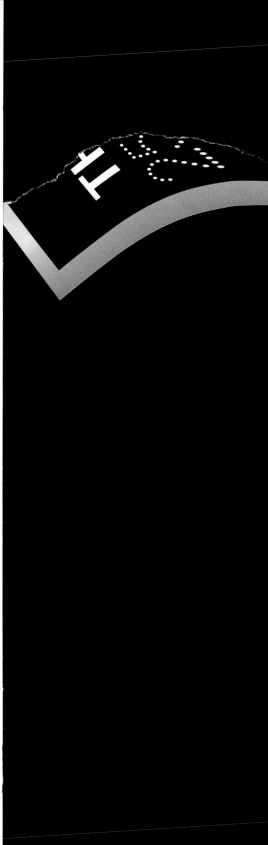

electronica (there is even an album of 'Drill' cover versions by other artists called *Dugga Dugga Dugga!*) and was described recently as possessing "an extraordinary thematic clarity and stylistic coherence, rather like Kraftwerk's *Computer World*."

The next Wire release – or rather, the first Wir release – was *The First Letter*, recorded at Swanyard Studios in London, released by Mute in October 1991 and again produced by the band and Paul Kendall. It is one of only two releases credited to Wir (the other being a hard-to-procure limited-edition two song EP called 'I Saw You/Vien') and was as close to a straight techno record as the band had yet come; it wasn't that far removed from an early-Nineties techno outfit like The Shamen (whereas, says Newman, the intention on, say, *It's Beginning To And Back Again* tracks such as 'In Vivo' was to create highly commercial dance-pop on a par with Madonna).

Almost completely machine-made, *The First Letter* saw the remaining three members looping and programming to their hearts' content, in a process with which they had all become quite comfortable. For the most part, it is an improved version of *Manscape,* a superbly executed, computer-assisted retooling of Wire that incorporated both dense experimental fare and slick potential hit singles.

Lewis – who remembers being among 2,000 black kids in a house club in Chicago in the late-Eighties, an experience he found "absolutely joyous" – acknowledges the symbiotic relationship between British bands and American dance music during this period: the Detroit techno and Chicago house pioneers then exerting an influence on UK techno had been influenced by UK electronic music/synthpop from the early-Eighties before changing the course of dance music themselves.

Among the highlights of this often-overlooked collection, given an A-grade by the self-styled "dean of US rock critics", Robert Christgau, were the circular groove of the early-New Order-esque paean to the *Financial Times* Stock Exchange, 'Footsi-Footsi', and the grinding 'Take It (For Greedy)' on which Wir sampled their own back catalogue, including 'Strange' from *Pink Flag*. 'Take It' was, explains Newman, meant to be harder and faster – "like ZZ Top" – and, with its Wire samples, was designed as a riposte to their detractors who felt they'd lost their innovative touch.

As with all their other Mute albums, *The First Letter* also contained at least one should-have-been sure-fire chart entry in 'So And Slow It Grows'. Featuring a lugubrious, doomy baritone vocal from Lewis that dovetailed nicely with the haunting electro melody, 'So And Slow...' came in original and remixed form, the latter courtesy of feted Belgian dance producer Pascal Gabriel. It remains about the only track on the album that Newman can bear to listen to today, so unhappy was he with the final mix and overall sound.

"[The idea behind] 'Take It' was great – we were sampling Wire before anyone else did! But it should have been the ultimate two fucking fingers to everything," he says. "The idea for it is like what we developed during the *Send* [2003] period, all grinding guitars and thumping beat – that's how it should have been. But I didn't feel it was my place to say, 'It should sound like this', and I wasn't living in the country at the time...The 'So And Slow' remix by Pascal Gabriel was great, though. He totally 'got it' musically, but the rest of the album was needlessly avant-garde. Skill with sound is one thing, but mixing is also about arrangement and making a piece of music work. It's not about how to impress listeners with cool sounds."

Gilbert doesn't recall the reaction to *The First Letter* over at Mute HQ, but feels it was "probably a good thing" that 'So And Slow...' didn't become the big hit single that everyone at the record company, and Daniel Miller in particular, had been waiting for for so long. Did the band somehow sabotage their success? "Well, it [success] probably worried me more than it did the others," he says. "Because I wasn't sure about it – it's hard enough for a project to survive without success; with success it [Wire] would probably have exploded more rapidly. Being a subversive presence in the charts was a fun idea, but I always believed it would have changed the situation and subversion would have quickly turned into subjugation."

How different would life in Wire have been had they had that elusive hit single?

"Obviously there would have been a higher quality of drugs and bigger swimming pools," jokes Graham Lewis, before taking the opportunity to muse on the subject of success. "What was it that Dieter Meier [of Swiss pop techno-crats Yello] said? He said, 'The great artist catches the golden bullet of success and turns it into shit.' Well, I don't know if we've even come anywhere close to being fatally wounded, so it's very hard to say. It's very easy to look down your nose at other people's behaviour when you see success happen to them, and I have seen it happen to people. You can see success kill people because they don't know what to do with it. It's not something that anybody is prepared for, or is able really to deal with: the amount of pressure, the amount of work, the amount of attention is horrible, you know? I think Jack Nicholson said, 'Success is another career, but there's no training.'"

Were there periods in Wire's career when he saw major success looming?

"No. At the end of that first period [on EMI] where we produced those three incredibly good pieces of work and I thought we ticked all the boxes, I was very pissed off. I was very pissed off with EMI among other people that it didn't, you know, happen. It didn't happen. That was the point. And then it [success] becomes an impossibility. But then, who knows – maybe we would have just turned into a bunch of wankers.

"So instead, what happens is you continue to try and be serious about your work, and try not to be too serious about yourself; you try to preserve your sense of humour, to survive and be flexible. And you end up with a different kind of fulfilment, a different kind of success, because it gives you the opportunity to do so many other things."

Lewis and the other members were given that opportunity after *The First Letter* because, although they didn't realise it at the time, it would be the last Wire album for 12 years. It was also the last album by The Band Briefly Known As Wir, and yet another of their records that didn't perform as well as it was expected to, a situation not helped by the fact that, around this time, their second manager, Brian Grant, suddenly became very ill and was out of action.

"I think you always go into making a record thinking it could be the last one, because that's the only way that you can sensibly approach it," says Lewis, "particularly with Wire – that's always been the case. So no, nobody knew really. If things had turned out differently, who knows what might have happened, but yet again [we were victims of] a combination of circumstances... Brian Grant, who was managing us then, became really ill, on top of everything else."

165

"It all just disintegrated," says Newman, who admits that, in hindsight, he "never really felt comfortable as a three-piece", at least not in that configuration. "It was," he adds, "the wrong three people."

Following the release of *The First Letter*, in a calculated bid by Mute and the band's management to seriously up their profile, there was talk of Wir going on tour in the States as support to Vince Clarke and Andy Bell of Mute electro-poppers Erasure. Not everyone in the band, however, was keen.

"Look," says Newman, "they [Erasure] are nice people, I've met them both and they're very likeable but it just wasn't Wire. It felt like, 'So it's come to this?' I absolutely hate their music. I had this conversation on the phone from [my home in] Brussels with Bruce and I said it was the wrong thing to do, even though they [Mute] were going to put money into it and it would mean big exposure for Wire. But my feeling was that Erasure fans just weren't going to like Wire: 'Wire are peculiar, they'll not like us.' Maybe I was wrong, but Bruce said, 'I don't want to go either; I think it's a bad idea.' So I called our manager and said we should do something else and he told me he'd put a lot of time and energy into it. He said, 'Call me when you've decided [to do it], but until then, goodbye.' Graham was disappointed because he really wanted to do it, but Bruce and I didn't so it [Wir/Wire] sort of fizzled out. I had no reason to be in London so it just dissolved."

This also marked the dissolution of Wire's relationship with Mute. As Daniel Miller tersely puts it when asked how the band came to an end: "They just decided to stop working with each other. They called it a day."

Surveying their period with the label, Newman judges *Manscape* the most reviled Wire album. "Bruce's quote was the best: 'You'd have thought someone would have listened to it before putting it out.' If it had been remixed it would have been a way better record. In a way that's the start of me feeling I needed to be more hands-on with the production, because we were moving more into machine production and records being produced by equipment we could own. With *The Ideal Copy*, I didn't like the way the production was going and I felt we could do better." Newman explains that, apart from the single version of 'In Vivo' [from *IBTABA*], he didn't do any "hands-on production" until *The*

First Letter – "and even that was given to someone else to mix, although I felt I could have done a better job." So which is his favourite of all the band's Mute albums? "*A Bell Is A Cup...* I'd eventually go for. I'm not sure about the loud snare drums and Eighties effects, but there are really good songs on there like 'Kidney Bingos' and 'Silk Skin Paws'."

Lewis' favourite, meanwhile, remains *The Ideal Copy*. "I think it's charged with something quite unique," he says. "I know it was not an easy process for anybody, and there was quite a bit of blood spilt. That's a bit of an exaggeration, but psychically, there was... But I think it's rather good. *A Bell Is A Cup...* I was never fond of the mix of it although it's got some great songs and I think it's a good record, but I prefer *The Ideal Copy*. I enjoyed lots of *The Drill* as well – it's got some really good tracks and it's unlike anything else we've ever done."

Does he see the Mute albums as being "of a piece", like the EMI albums?

"I suppose so, although they were made over a far more extended period, and we were continually trying to find processes that we thought were suitable for the work and we were trying to make work. But, what with all the new technology, which was changing all the time, the advances we made actually made the work quite difficult."

Asked whether there is an essential difference between Wire's late-Seventies output and their Eighties/Nineties records, he says, "Of course there is. Because you're absorbing, reflecting, dissecting, or whatever you want to call it, the culture that you're living in. You move on and try to produce something contemporary and relevant. In the Eighties we weren't trying to go back to the Seventies or emulate *154*. That was done, finished. You've got to push on and do what you think is right. It was our new Year Zero." Lewis isn't sure whether all of Wire's records, played back to back, provide some sort of narrative arc, or whether they tell the story of Wire. But there is a sense of consistency and coherence to the body of work. He draws a comparison with artist Francis Bacon. "You see Bacon's early work and his later work, and it looks the same, but it's not the same at all. But it still looks like Francis Bacon. And I think that's a very important thing in terms of how you identify the work: the content changes and the style and the abilities and the skills change, but still, superficially, it has the same form. Even our newest records like *Send* and *Object 47*, even though they don't sound the same as *Pink Flag* or any of the records in the middle, you can identify who it is."

There was one final stand of Wir/Wire v.2.0 and that occurred when, in 1992, Newman and his wife, Malka, moved to London. "I thought, 'Maybe I'll do something with Bruce', so we recorded 'I Saw You/Vien', then we did a one-off performance in Vienna and a show at the Clapham Grand," says Newman. "And that, basically, was the end of Wir."

THERE would be no new Wire product for another decade, and the band spent the majority of the Nineties apart, exploring other avenues: Colin Newman's solo forays and record label Swim ~; Bruce Gilbert's ballet music commissions and Disobey club nights; Graham Lewis' projects as H.A.L.O. and He Said; and Robert Gotobed's dual career as a farmer and occasional drummer-for-hire. They rarely communicated with each other during the first half of the Nineties, and certainly there was no talk of another reunion.

Until 1996, that is, when the decision was made to reconvene for Gilbert's 50th birthday. No one is quite sure how it happened, but the consensus seems to be that their (and Gilbert's) new manager, Paul Smith, was behind it. "He was determined to have a celebration of some description," says Gilbert. "We were friendly with the events manager at the South Bank and so we stripped out one of the arches and created this raw space. He said, 'What do you want to do?' And I said, 'I suppose for a laugh it would be funny if Wire played 'Drill'. And that's how that occurred. We did 'Drill' because it was the only song we could remember without rehearsal. It was good fun."

Lewis remembers the performance being on MTV. Newman doesn't recall the "fun" part. "It was a bit rubbish," he says, "and it left a bad taste. Our relationship [with Smith] is still suffering – there are legal matters ongoing. Before he'd even started managing us, he basically asked us if we wanted to play. Now, if you ask a bunch of British blokes if they'll help get a car started, of course they're going to say yes. But it was suddenly being sold as 'Wire's last ever gig'. I said, 'You've got no fucking right to say that – who knows if we're ever going to play again?' Then he started managing Bruce and in the end got deeply involved with the band and it all ended very badly. We should have known from how it started off."

Gilbert's birthday party wasn't the last Wire gig ever, but it was the last for four years: in 2000, all four members reconvened once again for a Living Legends show at London's Royal Festival Hall, at the invitation of curator David Sefton, a fan of the band from back when he used to see them play at famous Liverpool punk hang-out Eric's. Lewis remembers preparing for the prestigious event with "two weeks of rehearsals trying to learn how to play the bloody numbers, having not played guitar for 10 years or something." He found it hard-going; they all did. "I think," he says, "everybody was very happy to survive that one."

"It was weird to be a legend, really," says Newman. "But it was a way in which the band could come back together from having no reason to be together. It [the show] was probably all right. I'm not sure about those big, publicly funded events. I think Wire are best seen in a sweaty club where you can barely see the stage."

The Living Legends show also provided, says Newman, "an entry point to start a discussion about what else Wire could do". So they did an American tour during which they realised they needed some new material. After recording some gigs back in Britain, in London's Garage venue, at the end of 2000, Newman wondered whether the rough and ready but fast and furious sound could be captured and "turned into a piece of production".

It was this "completely moronic" inferno of sound that offered the seeds of Wire's approach in the 21st century – the concept for which Newman describes as "what Fatboy Slim would be like if he was doing pub rock, like dance music and punk at the same time." Lewis concurs with this when he says of their first recorded work of the new century, "It was made with guitars, but was informed by the 12 years of work with electronic music that Colin, Bruce and I had all been individually pursuing in different countries."

In January 2001, Wire issued, on their newly formed *Pink Flag* label, the '12 Times You' seven-inch in a transparent bag adorned with a sticker, a stripped-down affair designed to keep costs down but which, even after 2,000 copies sold, made the band no money at all, although it has subsequently become the most sought-after artefact in the label's catalogue. "I could easily sell it for $100 or more," says Newman.

From this single came the idea for the material that would appear on the 'Read & Burn' EPs throughout 2002, which was, says Newman, to ally "slow chords and fast beats with shouting – an interesting formula". And this was the genesis of 2003's *Send*, the band's first LP release as a four-piece since 1990's *Manscape*. A quasi-compilation comprising seven songs from the two low-key 'Read & Burn' EPs the group released on the *Pink Flag* label, plus four new tracks, *Send* was a fierce, fearsome blast of rhythm and noise from a band who refused to go on the comeback trail armed with a bunch of hits for nostalgic old age punksioners.

As Allmusic wrote, "They tore through [the music] with a vigorous energy that teetered on the brink of violence. Thick walls of clamour are constructed on each song. Dynamic, taut, feisty, and clever as ever, *Send* is this group's fourth-best album." Meanwhile, website Pitchfork Media praised its "fury, malevolence, and crushing immediacy... The guttural bile-spitting, robo-hypnotic snare simplicity, and guitars as head-rattlingly violent as a boxing match between a power sander and a jackhammer – it's all as sharp as ever."

Send was produced by Newman in a studio in the basement of his home in South London. He knew how it should sound, but it was hearing the mixes of 'Read & Burn – 01' that convinced collaborator Lewis that Wire's guitarist should be at the helm. "He said to me, 'You're the best producer that Wire has ever had." I was genuinely excited that I'd got that out of the material."

Using techniques acquired from building dance tracks in the Nineties and a lot of new digital technology, Newman "learnt how to make a record and brought that to Wire". One of the first things he did, sonically, was to place Robert Gotobed's drums right up front in the mix. "That set the tone for the way things proceeded from there. After 15 years of hearing dance music I realised – have the drums loud! It was kind of a revelation and put the band in a different light. We weren't just about guitars and voices. Rob is one of the distinctive elements of Wire with his powerful, minimalist rhythms. He deserves to take centre stage."

The way *Send* was put together was, explains Newman, partly the result of Gilbert visiting his home once or twice a week, "To play riffs, basically." At this point, with Lewis in Sweden, there was very little bass. "He [Lewis] wasn't that involved," says Newman, who compares and contrasts his two bandmates: "Bruce is very stimulating to work with but then he might go off in one direction, whereas Graham is easier to understand and more fun to work with."

Lewis recalls that "everything was constructed in such a way that it was very, very hard, and very, very fast. We certainly didn't want to expose ourselves to the possibility of critics turning around and saying we were a bunch of lazy, old dozy bastards, playing everything at half-speed. Everything was armour-plated. We were damn certain we were going to make a record that was not going to be accused of being soft or weak. I think its greatest achievement is that it completely refuses indifference; it's not a record you can be indifferent to. It's a very sonic piece of work. It's not about songs, although there is text. It's like reportage, or advertising copy. The words seem to be incredibly fucking mad about something, which you can't quite work out, which gives it its uneasy quality. It's very, very aggressive."

Both Newman and Lewis agree about the sheer hard attack of *Send*. "*Send* is a laser beam, brutal, monophonic; an incredibly claustrophobic and furious piece of work, although I'm not quite sure what it's furious about," says Newman, while Lewis likens it to "John Lee Hooker dragged up to date and plugged in to the mains".

In many ways, *Send* was Wire's most successful album since *154*. Strange, then, that Bruce Gilbert should choose this moment to leave the band.

OR perhaps not that strange: according to Colin Newman, along with behind-the-scenes reasons involving manager Paul Smith that remain sub judice, it was *Send's* very success that drove Gilbert — who in 2005 sent the other three a brief, three-line email by way of explanation and as his formal "goodbye" — away for good. And it was, he contends, Gilbert who derailed Wire the first time round, poised as they were to become as big as New Order and The Cure at the start of the Eighties.

"Bruce is absolutely petrified of success, you have to understand that," he says. "That's how I understand it. He drove the bus off the cliff after *154*! It was him. He's the oldest, he was the gang leader; Rob looked up to him and Graham was in his pocket. Suddenly, after *154*, it was, 'We don't want to do this and we don't want to do that.' We'd just made our best-received album and there was no tour, just three and a half gigs. And then, nothing. It was pathetic. In hindsight, that's how it looks. And the only way I can rationalise it is: fear of success. Because if we'd kept going into the early-Eighties we would have been *the* band. We'd have been right there at the birth of MTV. It's tragic in a way. But hey, that's life. There's no point in being bitter."

Gilbert's departure after *Send* – Wire's best-received album since *154* and the perfect launch pad for a third phase of success – represented, says Newman, a second suicidal gesture.

Lewis puts a positive spin on Wire's internal strife, agreeing that, in a way, their very fractiousness has kept them going over the years. They're not there, he says, because they have to be, but because they want to be, a crucial distinction, one that separates those mythical so-called Last Gangs In Town who actually reform for financial reasons, and those frictional alliances like Wire who are drawn together, often against their better judgments, for compelling artistic reasons. "I think that's true. One of my favourite John Lennon quotes is the one where he said The Beatles weren't a gang and The Rolling Stones were. And it was obviously a very unique point of our group: that it was the same four people all the way through and one of the strengths of the group is that we did have three people who wrote in the group, in different combinations at different times. But we were never a gang; that's not what we were trying to achieve or the way we went about what we did.

"When we decide to do something, it's not because we're mates and we've fallen out or anything like that. It's usually because there are good reasons to do new things. That tends to focus you when you come to the work. And it is work, you know?"

It's work that comes with a new set of procedures – and attendant problems – each time. "Well, the nature of doing things that are new and different, or not repeating what you've done before, tends to make things that way," furthers Lewis. "Because you're not just repeating something; you're trying to create something new, and usually with fairly strict budgets and under time constraints. So things do tend not to be that easy, and yes, I'm sure we could have made life easier for ourselves as well, or we could have been easier on each other, but that's not the way it was."

One of the difficulties experienced by Colin Newman over the years was a constant feeling of being bullied, as the youngest member of the band, even though he has been, since day one, along with Lewis the de facto leader and creative force behind Wire.

"Well, I'm the youngest and it's totally my point of view but I always felt it was problematic for an older guy [Gilbert] if someone young has a lot of ideas and knows how to make them work." Ironically, Newman and Gilbert had a good, productive working relationship right up to the end. "I became quite close to Bruce during *Send* and then we drifted apart suddenly. I don't know how that works. But, without wanting to sound arrogant – put it in quotes – my 'prodigious talent' can be threatening to some people. I can be very fast at working out ideas and combinations. Sometimes I surprise myself. It's magical, and I don't know how it works. There are short cuts in the brain that make things effective. If I'm trusted by the people I work with, I am very inclusive: it's not all about me and I do like collaboration. If you work with someone you sleep with – as I do with Malka – you have to learn to be a collaborator otherwise you're just an arsehole.

"And," he concludes, "I never got to that point with Bruce. We became close but we never collaborated on equal terms."

For legal reasons, Newman can't go into the details of Gilbert's departure; suffice to say it's "a horrible, horrible story". He's not certain if "Bruce himself would have left: maybe it was how he wanted to go out; he's got his own agenda and world view and he just doesn't regard Wire as the most important thing he's ever done. But it wasn't malicious. It was just: 'That's it, I'm off.'"

For Lewis, what was "far worse" were the circumstances surrounding the departure of manager Paul Smith, who in his opinion was "far more problematic" and "a destructive presence". He found it odd returning to record the follow-up to *Send* in January 2007 without Gilbert. "It was rather strange that Bruce wasn't there," he admits, although he also recognises that, really, Wire were just back to the core Lewis-Newman writing partnership they'd always had, "so it wasn't like it was something we'd never done before. It was awkward to begin with, and to say I was sad that he left doesn't really cover it, really. But basically, he resigned and said he didn't want to discuss it, and I still haven't had a satisfactory explanation for why he wanted to do it. But you just continue, and after that it's not a problem him not being there."

Talking about the difference between Wire with and without Gilbert, Newman says, "I don't want to slag off the person not in the room. Everyone has their own psychological problems, and perhaps Bruce had more demons than anyone else; he can be quite self-destructive. But we're none of us angels, we all can be annoying, including me, but you have to start from the standpoint of, 'Is the thing worth doing?' After Bruce and the manager left, we sat down and we asked, 'Why should we do Wire?' And the answer was, 'Because it's worth doing.'

"Why should someone dictate the terms if they say, 'I'm taking my ball home.' You can always go to the shop and buy another one! I don't think Bruce believed we would do it without him. But he's always had a problem with public performance and being seen as a member of a rock band; he doesn't like seeing himself as that person. Bruce is an Artist, not an artiste. Now, I know Wire has high-art credibility and can be accepted within the fine art world as a very interesting art object, but that still doesn't take away from the fact that we're a rock band. You can't just Get Away With It if people have paid money to see something great. There are a whole set of attitudes that you need to have in a rock band, however conceptual or however much you say Wire is an art object. Of course Wire is an art object but it's also a rock band. It would cease to be interesting if it was one or the other."

When Newman, Lewis and Gotobed, flushed with the success of *Send*, decided to get back together to record their 11th studio album – and 47th piece of product – they called it *Object 47*, just as they titled *154* after the number of gigs they had played up to that point. Immediately, the drummer benefited from the new dynamic, giving him a new lease of life and inner confidence.

"The fact that Bruce wasn't there made Rob look at what he was doing, and it became incredibly easy for him to get involved in the methods of production and the working of the machines," says Newman. "In fact, when Bruce left, we all realised that, if we wanted to have this, we were going to have to work at it, to fight Wire's corner. And that's been incredibly important. For the first time ever, there is stuff we're talking about that we've never talked about before: we've never discussed how to go about things; they either just happened or someone took a decision and we all had to live with it. Now we talk about it and figure out the best way to do it. We have a strategy. That's never happened, and it makes it genuinely interesting."

Object 47 was recorded, says Newman, "in a room with the classic rock band set-up of guitar, bass, drums and vocals". It was released in July 2008, five years after *Send*, long enough for the press to label it another comeback. But Newman was ready for that one. He told this writer at the time: "I have a big problem with the comeback idea. It's just bollocks. Wire are not making a comeback. We're not on any nostalgia trip."

Object 47, accompanied by more live dates than the band had undertaken for over two decades, including a blistering performance at London's Scala that saw the audience drag Wire back onstage for encore after encore and simply refuse to leave the auditorium, was another triumphant release from Wire Mk 3. The antithesis of *Send* and its dense, compressed sound that eschewed nuance and variation, *Object 47* evinced a broader, more colourful canvas and a more pronounced melodic sensibility, the combination of stop-start buzzsaw guitar rhythms with Newman's bright, tuneful vocals proving highly contagious.

"*Send* is very specific," the singer told the author in summer '08, comparing and contrasting their two Pink Flag LP releases. "It's black and white. It's brutal. This time, we wanted to do something a little bit more classic. The whole time we were talking about it, it was like, 'It's got to be in Technicolor, widescreen, like a European art movie, you know?' It had to have that breadth, to reflect that sort of large space.

"My job as a producer was to give it that sort of size, even though it was being made in a personal studio, one that's not very fancy. But it had to have that sense of ambition. It had to sound as good as anything from a more expensive studio. I'm not into lo-fi; I'm not into doing something that sounds a bit apologetic and a bit like it was recorded in your home studio. This has got to compete at the highest possible level."

The response to the album around the world was, in Newman's words, "life-affirming".

"Wire are the only group from the class of '77 who have constantly broken new ground," wrote Mike Barnes in *The Observer*, a typically effusive review that matched the deliriously positive appraisals of Wire's live shows across Europe and America throughout 2008. "*Object 47* is short, to the point, and boasts some of Wire's most vital music."

"Graham described *Send* as a guided missile, and it was quite dark, but *Object 47* is way more joyful," says Newman, who is already contemplating Wire's next move. "We've discovered pop again."

He laughs.

"That's good for Wire," he says. "And it's good for pop as well."

Acknowledgements

Even though this is an unauthorised book Paul Lester would like to thank for their consistent and continued cooperation during its writing producer Mike Thorne, Mute label boss Daniel Miller, and particularly the four members of Wire – Bruce Gilbert, Colin Newman, Graham Lewis and Robert Gotobed – who gave a series of candid and forthright interviews throughout 2008 and early 2009, even during Christmas! The book simply would not have been so thorough and illuminating without their input, and he is immensely grateful to them all. And a special thanks to Johnny Marr, who was originally intended to be a fleeting 'talking head' in the book, but who proved such a huge Wire fan, and so insightful and articulate on the subject, that his interview with the author in late 2008 just cried out to be used as the foreword. Final mention must also go to book editor Chris Charlesworth of Omnibus Press, who consistently failed to get angry during the writing of the book, even though each chapter was consistently late.

Discography

Wire's discography is complex, but this is, as far as the author is aware, a reasonably comprehensive and hopefully accurate list given the astonishing number of offshoots, collaborations and side projects undertaken by the four members of the group over the years.

See www.thestereosociety.com for further information.

WIRE

Studio albums

Pink Flag (Harvest/EMI, 1977)
Chairs Missing (Harvest/EMI, 1978)
154 (Harvest/EMI, 1979)
The Ideal Copy (Mute, 1987)
A Bell Is A Cup... Until It Is Struck (Mute, 1988)
It's Beginning To And Back Again (Mute, 1989)
Manscape (Mute, 1990)
The Drill (Mute, 1991)
Send (Pink Flag, 2003)
Object 47 (Pink Flag, 2008)

Singles and EPs

Mannequin / 12XU / Feeling Called Love (Harvest/EMI, November 1977)

I Am The Fly / Ex-Lion Tamer (Harvest/EMI, February 1978)

Dot Dash / Options R (Harvest/EMI, June 1978)

Outdoor Miner / Practice Makes Perfect (Harvest/EMI, January 1979)

A Question Of Degree / Former Airline (Harvest/EMI, June 1979)

Map Reference 41°N 93°W / Go Ahead (Harvest/EMI, October 1979)

Our Swimmer / Midnight Bahnhof Cafe (Charisma, May 1981)

Crazy About Love / Second Length (Our Swimmer) / Catapult 30 (Rough Trade, March 1983)

Snakedrill (Mute, November 1986)

Ahead / Feed Me (live) (Mute, March 1987)

Kidney Bingos / Pieta (Mute, March 1988)

Silk Skin Paws / German Shepherds (Mute, June 1988)

Eardrum Buzz / The Offer (Mute, April 1989)

In Vivo / Illuminated (Mute, July 1989)

Life In The Manscape / Gravity Worship (Mute, May 1990)

Twelve Times You (Pink Flag, January 2001)

Read & Burn – 01 (Pink Flag, June 2002)

Read & Burn – 02 (Pink Flag, October 2002)

Read & Burn – 03 (Pink Flag, November 2007)

Compilations & live albums

Document And Eyewitness (Harvest/EMI, 1981)

And Here It Is... Again... (Sneaky Pete, 1984)

Play Pop (Pink, 1985)

In The Pink (Live) (Dojo, 1986)

The Peel Sessions (EP) (Strange Fruit, 1987)

On Returning (1977-1979) (EMI, 1989)

Double Peel Sessions (Strange Fruit, 1990)

154 Pink Chairs (Antler-Subway, 1992)

1985-1990 The A List (Mute, 1993)

Behind The Curtain (EMI, 1995)
Turns And Strokes (WMO, 1996)
Coatings (WMO, 1997)
On The Box: 1979 (Pink Flag, 2004)
The Scottish Play: 2004 (Pink Flag, 2005)
Live At The Roxy, London (1977) / Live At CBGB Theatre, New York
(1978) (Pink Flag, 2006)

WIR

Albums

The First Letter (Mute, 1991)

Singles

So And Slow It Grows / Nice From Here (Mute, April 1991)
The First Last Number (Hafler Trio remix)/ The Last Last Number
(Hafler Trio remix) (Touch, November 1995)
Vien: The First Letter, Sexy And Rich (Janet) (Touch, September 1997)

COLIN NEWMAN

A–Z (Beggars Banquet, 1980)
provisionally entitled the singing fish (4AD, 1981)
Not To (4AD, 1982)
Commercial Suicide (Crammed, 1986)
It Seems (Crammed, 1988)
Bastard (Swim ~, 1997)

GRAHAM LEWIS

He Said
Hail! (Mute, 1986)
Take Care (Mute, 1989)

H.A.L.O
Immanent (MNW Zone, 1995)

Collaborations

He Said Omala (with Mattias Tegner and Andreas Karperyd)
Catch Supposes (Origin, 1997)
Matching Crosses (Origin, 1998)

Ocsid (with Carl Michael Von Hausswolff and Jean-Louis Huhta)
In Between (Origin, 1999)

Hox (with Andreas Karperyd)
It-Ness (Origin, 1999)

BRUCE GILBERT

This Way (Mute, 1984)
The Shivering Man (Mute, 1987)
Insiding (Mute, 1991)
Music For Fruit (Mute, 1991)
Ab Ovo (Mute, 1996)
In Esse (Mute, 1997)

Collaborations

A.C. Marias
Just Talk / No Talk (Mute, 1986)
Time Was / Some Thing (Mute, 1988)
One Of Our Girls (Has Gone Missing) (Mute, 1989)

Gilbert / Hampson / Kendall
Orr (Parallel Series, 1986)

Bruce Gilbert / Ron West
Frequency Variation (Sähkö, 1998)

DOME (Graham Lewis / Bruce Gilbert)

Dome (Rough Trade, 1980)
3R4 (4AD, 1980)

Dome 2 (Rough Trade, 1980)
Dome 3 (Rough Trade, 1981)
MZUI/Waterloo Gallery (Cherry Red, 1982)
Will You Speak This Word (Nor. Union, 1983)
8 Time (4AD, 1988)
Dome 1.2 (Mute/Grey Area, 1992)
Dome 3.4 (Mute/Grey Area, 1992)

LEWIS AND GILBERT

Pacific/Specific (WMO, 1995)

CUPOL (Graham Lewis and Bruce Gilbert)

Like This For Ages/Kluba Cupol (4AD, 1980)

DUET EMMO (Graham Lewis / Bruce Gilbert / Daniel Miller)

Or So It Seems (Mute, 1983)

P'O (Graham Lewis and Bruce Gilbert with AC Marias)

Whilst Climbing Thieves Vie For Attention (Court, 1983)

ROBERT GOTOBED

The Snakes
Teenage Head / Lights Out (Dynamite, 1976) (vocals)

The Art Attacks
Punk Rock Stars / Rat City (Fresh, 1979)

Fad Gadget
Incontinent (Mute, 1980)

Dome
Dome (Dome, 1980)

Colin Newman
A-Z (Beggars Banquet, 1980)
provisionally entitled the singing fish (4AD, 1981)
Not To (4AD, 1982)
It Seems (Crammed, 1988)

Desmond Simmons
Alone On Penguin Island (Dome, 1981)